Advance Praise for *In Defence of the Ordinary*

'This book neither ascends nor descends into the ordinary. Instead, it accesses and exceeds the everyday. Dev Nath Pathak scrabbles and scrambles the personal as the public, the routine as the transgressive, the affective as the constant, the image as the immanent, the vernacular as the cosmopolitan, the word as the world and vice-versa. A haunting work intimating spectral challenges—across the ruins we inhabit.'

—Saurabh Dube,
Noted Historian and Anthropologist; Professor at El Colegio de México and Fellow at Institut für die Wissenschaften vom Menschen, Wien/Vienna, Austria

'Taking clues from personal experiences, folklore, classical epics, literature and cinema and of course academic discourses, the author of these essays delves into a range of emotions with the objective to awaken the dormant potential of emancipation every day rather than waiting for an occasional charisma induced by a holy book or a secular gimmick. The book encompasses everyday situations and "ordinary" (hence universal) experiences of life, including the ultimate and inevitable one—death, and tries to take the reader along on this journey of reflection. The result is a delightfully composed prose with interesting insights.'

—Purushottam Agrawal,
Renowned Cultural and Literary Critic and Author; Former Professor at Jawaharlal Nehru University, India

'What is a book? It is assumed to have certain universally shared features such as structured thoughts, formalised expression while respecting the rules of consistency and coherence. By their very nature, these features undermine the authenticity of ordinary human experiences and do injustice to their fluidity and richness. How then should a book be defined and written? This fascinating book provides one answer and exemplifies it through practice. It is full of insights and will repay close study.'

—Bhikhu Parekh,
Eminent Philosopher and Member of the House of Lords of the UK

'*In Defence of the Ordinary* is a book that will appeal to a wide range of readers. It covers a wide range of subjects, all of which touch upon author's life and experiences as a teacher, scholar, husband, father and son(-in-law). He brings his experience as a sociologist and his work on folklore to the text in a way that is lively and interesting.'

—Roma Chatterji,
Seasoned Anthropologist of Folk Art and Professor at the Department of Sociology, University of Delhi, India

'A splendid work of art, *In Defence of Ordinary* returns drama, pleasure and awakening to everyday life. It takes us on an ambitious but quiet journey, through poetry, politics, philosophy, religion, livelihoods and everyday encounters between selves, others, gods and things, in the tradition of cultural critics like Ashis Nandy and Umberto Eco. It risks academic protocols and disciplinary boundaries, and with great courage cuts through the division between thought and life that plagues modern academia. The book is one of a kind.'

—Prathama Banerjee,
Noted Historian and Political Theorist; Professor at Centre for the Study of Developing Societies (CSDS), India

'In this fascinating collection of essays, Dev Nath Pathak explores a wide range of questions related to ordinariness. A *flâneur* of our everyday spheres of life, he excavates the multiple layers of social, political and artistic thinking and experimentation of the Indian society with an unparalleled lightness of prose worthy of a *Baltasar Gracián* and Georg Lichtenberg.'

—Ramin Jahanbegloo,
Philosopher, Professor, Vice Dean and Executive Director at Mahatma Gandhi Centre for Peace Studies, O.P. Jindal Global University, India

'This book is a reflective and joyous celebration of the ordinary. Drawing on diverse examples of everyday life, from dealing with babies to more weighty issues around love, the book builds an engaging web of thoughts about things which are ordinary but in their very ordinariness hide deep social truths. Using examples from commonly enjoyed music, stories and films, Pathak brings a lightness to his critical eye while reminding us how much of the ordinary has been forgotten in academic pursuits.'

—Sundar Sarukkai,
Renowned Philosopher and Thinker in Contemporary India

'From cosmic continuities to the unanticipated and incessant interruption of everyday life, the "ordinary" is both a shifting terrain of inquisitiveness, inclination and an anchor in the volatility of human relations with the earth. Dev Nath Pathak speaks to us from the middle of these things, unafraid of muddying the waters with reflections that intertwine his inordinate knowledge of Indian philosophy, cinema and storytelling with improvised ruminations on everything—fatherly play, compassionate lust, youthful disagreements, friendship, journeying and fandom. Throughout, there is the pursuit of the sensuousness of teaching, of what it means to convey and impart in an implicit critique of how corporate education has become, how easy it is to defy authority and how sharing and equanimity can be demonstrated in multiple encounters not needing a classroom. There is a resounding surfeit of liveliness in all of these "parables", a sense of really being alive as something accessible to everyone no matter how difficult their situation or how commodified and performance-oriented living has become.'

—AbdouMaliq Simone,
Seasoned Urbanist and Professor of Sociology at Goldsmiths College, University of London, UK

In Defence of the Ordinary

In Defence of the Ordinary

Everyday Awakenings

Dev Nath Pathak

BLOOMSBURY
NEW DELHI • LONDON • OXFORD • NEW YORK • SYDNEY

BLOOMSBURY INDIA
Bloomsbury Publishing India Pvt. Ltd
Second Floor, LSC Building No. 4, DDA Complex, Pocket C – 6 & 7,
Vasant Kunj, New Delhi, 110070

BLOOMSBURY, BLOOMSBURY ACADEMIC INDIA and the Diana logo
are trademarks of Bloomsbury Publishing Plc

First published in India 2021
This export edition published 2021

Copyright © Dev Nath Pathak, 2021
Illustrations © Sajal Roy

Dev Nath Pathak has asserted his right under the Indian Copyright Act to be
identified as the Author of this work

Bloomsbury Academic
An imprint of Bloomsbury Publishing Plc

All rights reserved. No part of this publication may be reproduced or transmitted in
any form or by any means, electronic or mechanical, including photocopying,
recording or any information storage or retrieval system, without the prior
permission in writing from the publishers

This book is solely the responsibility of the author and the publisher has had no
role in the creation of the content and does not have responsibility for anything
defamatory or libellous or objectionable

Bloomsbury Publishing Plc does not have any control over, or responsibility for,
any third-party websites referred to or in this book. All internet addresses given in
this book were correct at the time of going to press. The author and publisher regret
any inconvenience caused if addresses have changed or sites have ceased to exist, but
can accept no responsibility for any such changes

ISBN: HB: 978-93-90358-17-5; eBook: 978-93-90358-25-0
2 4 6 8 10 9 7 5 3 1

Typeset in Manipal Technologies Limited
Printed and bound in India by Replika Press Pvt. Ltd.

Bloomsbury Publishing Plc makes every effort to ensure that the papers used in the
manufacture of our books are natural, recyclable products made from wood grown in
well-managed forests. Our manufacturing processes conform to the environmental
regulations of the country of origin.

To find out more about our authors and books visit www.bloomsbury.com and sign
up for our newsletters

To Sir
(Avijit Pathak)
With Love

For,
a teacher can seldom retire
from the life of a student!

Contents

Preface: Off and On Stage   xiii

Embryonic Intrigues: On Something and Nothing
1. A Defence of the Ordinary, or Wishful Thinking   3
2. Seeing, Ordinarily, the Seen and Unseen   18

When There Was Nothing
3. Lullaby, Tales and Play in the Kindergarten   31
4. Anger, Love and Intersections: A Scheme of Ordinary Emotions   40
5. Lotus, Mud and Fear of a Sex Beast   51
6. Jokes, Abuse, Friends, Enemies and Something Called In-laws   59
7. Defiance, Rebellion and Protest: From Embryo to Artificial Intelligence   70

There Was Something
8. Flirtatious, Lustful and Committed: An Ordinary Romance   83
9. Match, Friendship and Marriage: Looking for Romance   91
10. The Teacher, the Taught and Traditions: A Dream Lost   102
11. I Am Nothing, Just a Teacher: A Dream Found   111
12. Not the Owls of Minerva: Teachers in Higher Education!   121
13. Mundane Divinity, Rigid Religiosity and Everything Trivial   131
14. Ordinary Gandhi in the Time of Extraordinary Gau-Raksha   139

Cacophony of Celebration?
15. Awry October, Fury of Festivity and Destruction of Virtues   149
16. No Ram in the Rant   157
17. Blissful and Blasé: Tourism versus Pilgrimage   163
18. Models without Roles!   174
19. Our Ordinary Amitabh Bachchan: Politics, Prejudice and Pride   180
20. Gandhi, Nehru and the Politics of Extraordinary Names   186

21	Vernacular Cannibalism: When a Big Language Monster Eats Up Smaller Ones	194
22	Spectacles of Success and Failure	204

Thou Shall Be There, Nonetheless

23	Ordinary Art and the Quest for Distorted Icons	215
24	Lost and Found, Friends and Enemies, Buried in Ordinary Trousseau	224
25	Living and Dying, Medicine and Songs, and Folk Philosophy	231

Index	243
About the Author	249

Preface

Off and On Stage

Why should I write? Or why should anyone write? To some prolific writers, these may appear to be rhetorical questions. Some others may still try to answer. In fact, there is an elaborate industry promoting creative-writing courses that answer the question in one manner. Indeed, there could be many answers, recounting the utilitarian benefits of the mathematics of success and failure in life and career or romantic ideas about the fulfilment of desire and connection with the world at large. The global pandemic has triggered an opportunity to rethink our basics. I need to write since it is the only way I can find a release from the repressive mechanism that is at once imminent and immanent. It is a cultural practice of therapeutic value for the author and for the readers and critics in case they are interested in such experiences as release! This book is an enactment of that release, to begin with, of the author, followed by the use of various pronouns across the essays such as I, you, we and us. The idea of release is central to this book. Precisely, it is a release from one realm of the ordinary to another. We can understand the significance of release if we allow ourselves to pay attention to one of my favourite satirist Sufis, Mulla Nasruddin. I recount two parables to justify the authorial liberty jarringly felt across this book:

> Seated backwards atop his rushing donkey, holding its tail, once Mulla Nasruddin was hurriedly passing by a market. Someone from the crowd called out for Mulla, to which he instantly replied, 'Not now, can't you see I am busy? I am looking for my donkey!'

The meaning is in the ridicule in which the parable invites us to join. For over a decade or so, I felt I was like Mulla, riding my donkey, seated backwards, and looking for it with undue haste and, of course, waste. I needed to turn inwards and set my position right; else, my donkey would take me on a tour while I'd nurse all these misplaced notions.

There is, however, no guarantee that riding the donkey seated on it facing forward will ensure good judgement. But one should, at least, try something different. Fine, then. I shall write something different, I thought. Then every time I wrote, I recalled Mulla in a different situation, as in the following:

> Lately, Mulla Nasruddin has been complaining that he had to eat the same food every day. Someone said, 'Why don't you ask your wife to cook something else?' Mulla said that he was unmarried. 'Oh! Then who cooks for you?' Mulla replied, 'I do it myself.'

For all my pathos, in which my friends, colleagues, kith and kin, peers and such people have been active participants, I am the only one who can be held culpable. I did not muster enough courage to find my point of departure. I could not say, like elsewhere a magnanimous scholar named Herbert Read[1] exclaimed, 'To hell with culture!'

An anti-human pandemic, that has intrigued epidemiologists, masters of medicine and state machineries, ought to be doing something to my settled intellectual issues. It must unsettle everything that is taken for granted in my profession and practice, vocation and vacation, reason and relations, and intellect and emotions. This book comes as a concrete and, perhaps, a baby step towards dismantling my settled mind. This is to tell all my peers that this is a polemic against myself. The accusatory tone in these essays targets me, the lament is about my fall and any pontification is to protect my vulnerability. Also, I grittily agreed to delete details that may be offensive in a time of social vulnerability, at times leaving a skeleton of a chapter without flesh and arteries. The objective is to persuasively communicate rather than nourish any ever-ready-to-get-offended minds. One may sufficiently feel the effects of 'sanitising' in the book.

Writing the preface of a book could be a coveted experience for an author. Additionally, it is a liberating one, since it allows the author to do something unusual. Usually, authors compromise and make the preface sound as disciplined, correct and sophisticated as the rest of the book. I usually rejoice in heretic speech acts while writing a preface. Some of my friends and colleagues may pop up to say that this author is a heretic even in his lived life, let alone lived experience or the account that this book offers. Such is the matrix of good and evil that we do not see logic when we stereotype an action. The judgement of superego often reveals my true, sinful self—sinful and heretic because revealing one's craft, motive, purpose and becoming-unbecoming is usually deemed deviant in formal academic writing. To my mind, however, it is imperative in a preface to reveal the positions, perspectives and prejudices of the author. Emotional truthfulness is not welcome in formal academic deliberations, yet it is important to disclose the emotions underpinning the book. The hard (scientific) facts are not central, but the fabulous (fables-based) facts are. The book, if at all, locates scientific rationality in emotional reasoning. Be that as it may, I persist with the idea of coming out naked and letting everyone have a laugh, if they must! The author of the book invites ridicule and sarcasm in response. Academic writing would be boring to write and read if there is no sense of humour, even at the price of a superior ego or an alter ego or a Freud's superego. Let there be bashing in the banter.

A candid confession could be a useful point of departure. This book on and about the ordinary does not satisfy academic expectations, ambitions and loyalty to known standards. If that is at the top of your considerations when you pick up this book, you have to be kind to yourself. The book, as it is, is the outcome of a personal problem with experiences. Everything that has perturbed or pleased this author in a decade, in the 2000s to be precise, has gone into the making of the book. That means a wide gamut of issues encountered in the academic profession, the vocation of teaching and learning, family life, relationships with kith and kin and colleagues and high-decibel matters that newspapers present to us as burning topics. In this scheme, one tends to see the relationship between personal problems and public troubles. It gets clearer why I hate some colleagues; it is because I see them in the light of the national and international discourses in which I locate my authorial self as well as that of many people around me. This manifests in the book as short deliberations, with abundant jump-cuts in time and space, through innumerable instances, parables and anecdotes dipped in nostalgia and selective aversion. Also, the references at the end of the book are an afterthought, since originally the essays were thought of without a systematic perusal of references. Hence, there are plenty of evident omissions.

In short, this book comprises a collection of essays with serious sarcasm, poetic polemics and suggestive propositions on a wide range of aspects related to ordinariness. The first and foremost analysand, the subject of scrutiny, is the self of the author. There is little hesitation in operationalising the author's subjectivity and rendering experiences from the book of life into the subject of conversation in this book. Therefore, when one analyses oneself, you can very well imagine a rattled mind blabbering and an unnerved body giving way to ramblings. In speech acts, this manifests in the tone and temper, adulation and accusation, and theatrics of the opening and ending of each essay. Some serious deliberations on violence, victimhood, servility and subjecthood have informed us about such an outcome. The book in its various chapters retains the rawness of ramblings so that anyone trying to relate with equally raw energy does not hit a dead end of sophisticated articulations. And why not? After all, many of our personal problems—we may again recall a basic lesson in social sciences—are related to public issues, political regimes and sociocultural structures. If it helps, one can recall the rich discursive terrain available to us due to prodigal feminist philosophers, sociologists and theorists. Many of them helped us to see the central role of experience without the loss of location, situation and lived everyday life.[2] Without any name-dropping, we can simply recall that even though the feminist thinkers were keen to develop a science of women's experience, they considered it duly appropriate to call it a successor science, another science, a science in which nobody speaks from nowhere.

The chapters in this book invite individuals in contemporary India to rethink ways of seeing, understanding, enacting, emoting and relating. Although it was planned and penned before the coronavirus cast its spell on our sensitivity and sociability, these chapters were revisited during the lockdown in India in the light of the intellectually stimulating comments received from the publisher. The anonymous reviewer made some valid points about the centrality of personal preferences and jump-cuts in the treatment of the book. Such a determinant criterion, vis-à-vis personal preferences of cultural materials, could be delimiting.

This book undertook precisely this as a challenge and tried to effect the delimiting personal approach into an enabling one. There is no denial of the importance of systematic analyses, theoretical approaches and narrowed focus on select issues, as our training in universities instil these almost as sacred values. Instead, this book marshals a bewildering abundance of facts and fables to make a point or an argument without compromising on the potential relational value. What is the point if the book offers an argument that only generates intellectual effect and no emotional affect? Unabashedly, therefore, the discourse in this book seeks to tickle, trick and touch. The idea is to let anyone interested have a variety of smells, sounds, sights and shocks through the words, sentences and syntax.

The reviewer and the publisher may be genuinely concerned about the nature of the book. But then, the lockdown dawned, and so did various orchestrations that either made us all follow every instruction unquestioningly or step out, think, sense with the total sensorium and ask a few fundamental questions.[3] To frame some of these questions, why do we become something that is the choice of others? Be it in social life or academics, should we not ensure that our ordinary selves are released rather than repressed? Why surrender our authorial agency to the seduction of norms, standards, quality and rigour? And is it any less rigorous to be oneself in deeds, words, lectures and writings? A realisation begins to unfold. In the act of reasoning, any author's or reader's 'I' cannot be entirely enslaved by the significant or general 'we'. This goes against the points raised in the debate in Michel Foucault's 'What Is an Author', which was a rebuttal of Roland Barthes's 'The Death of the Author'.[4] Barthes declared the death of the author to allow focal centrality to the readers and the text. Foucault, on the other hand, deemed the author, text and readers encapsulated in discourses. Here, in this book, neither is the author fully dead nor is he fully enslaved by the discourses. However, both Barthes and Foucault could aid a reader to see the author wriggling and slithering with a wounded body, resorting to the most easily accessible discourses based on personal, lived experiences. The latter is like a straw for the drowning body to stay afloat, almost as though anything is fair in love and war.

As an author, the most fundamental question that enabled me to persist with this book is: Why should we expect each book to fulfil the same criteria that we have imbibed through our training in higher education?[5] In other words, I was curious why each book should abide by the norms, standards, expectations and aspirations within given paradigms. Is it always necessary to fetch materials to quench the egoistic hunger of academic peers? Contrary to the familiar, tried-and-tested methods, there could be authorial risk-taking, wondering and wandering, frolicking and meaningfully meandering to try out a less popular format. After all, intellectual reasoning solicits all kinds of unheard experimentation. During the lockdown, when the pandemic was an absolute source of social paranoia, one could sense the old epidemic of academia and intelligentsia in innumerable webinars that almost outnumbered the cases of Covid-19. The intellectual insensitivity of scholars to the idea of ordinariness surfaced far more violently. In the way of seeing the woeful instances of migrant workers, subservience to the instructions coming from the leadership and circulation of wishful thinking as medical propositions on WhatsApp messages and social media platforms, we were able to see the failure of our reasoning. It was obvious that those who control and sustain discourses await the macabre transformation of the ordinary into the exceptional, the quasi-extraordinary. Ordinariness and its layers, currents and countercurrents, do not seem to make good cases for studies unless the seeker of knowledge is sure of employing some extraordinary intellectual apparatus. In this wake, the author of this book received more confidence to stick to the broad contours of conversation available in this book.

Stitched together in a hopefully seamless flow, the book posits some provocative ideas, inviting us to disturb set norms, value orientation and predominant practices. In an interrogative nutshell, it asks: Why do we not value ordinariness? How does our pursuit of extraordinariness mislead us into mindless mishaps, repressive rigmaroles and cognitive cul-de-sacs? Without a return to the ordinary core inherent in every human, there is no way to achieve the key objective of human existence, unless one helplessly relapses to age-old metaphysics. The human existence is central to modern as well as para-modern theories, philosophies, metaphysical ruminations and mythologies. Whether we are mere biological accidents in the master narrative of evolutionary biology or masters of our existence is a perpetual dilemma in those various discursive terrains. With someone like Sartre,[6] one may bring it down to a simpler formulation: shall we be identified with our essence (inherent in us) or with our existence (entailing processes and experiences contingent upon the forces from outside)? If allowed, we enter a realm of fascinating debate, recounting positions, perspectives, profundity and banality. But this book will not get lost in that usual activity pertaining to the scholar's habitus, so to say. Instead, it dwells on simplicity, at times jarring and irritating for anyone in love with complexity.

The objective is to awaken the dormant potential of emancipation every day rather than waiting for an occasional charisma induced by a holy book or a secular gimmick. We came across many such acrobatics during the lockdown when our social sense was heavily dominated by and restricted to the virtual, à la social media-based social existence. The rank and file of stars, celebrities, political leadership and anybody and everybody of major or minor significance jubilantly exhibited their privileged performances during the lockdown. With singing and dancing, cooking and eating, doing yoga and acrobatic exercises, and reading and writing, some of us tried to console ourselves and pretended to impress upon others that we can cope happily. One can add the other activities we did in response to the evocative instructions coming from our leadership. Be it joining the chant of 'go-corona-go' or banging on pots and pans or lighting lamps, all such known and various lesser-known activities only revealed how uncertain we had become about ourselves. The spectacular and the banal joined hands, but we were still running away from our ordinariness. We wanted to cope with the crisis, considering it a sporadic event, rather than make a reasoned return to our ordinary selves. We performed domestic chores, spent time with children and enjoyed conjugal conversations. Was it all by way of coping rather than really making a thought-out decision to live with our ordinariness? It began to show that we were fine with online education, in school as well as in universities. That we are still asserting our drive away from ordinariness in the way we longed to consume services was revealing. That we hankered for one spectacle after another was a telling tale. Our ability to sit back silently and rejoice in solitude with family is still repressed. Hence, the series of ramblings with reason that this book holds out seem valid.

Everyday awakening, rather than a spectacular interjection by a heroic god, goddess or god-man/woman, is the need of the hour. Underpinning this book is *prabuddh*, a word in Hindi that underlines an awakening in which knowing is an effortlessly ordinary activity, and sharing is only yet another ordinary attribute of humans. This is significantly different from the enlightenment sold by garden-variety gurus these days or the one Enlightenment in modern European history. Rather than 'waiting for Godot', the book invites us to imagine the emergence of an imminent cultural revolution of an ordinary nature. This could be a far more effective means for releasing the bewildered prisoners of spectacles, excellence and extraordinariness. In sum, we all ought to arrive at the ordinariness—the spine, breath, vision, emotions—in short, chassis, an existential core. Only then can one take a flight across the vast sky, with awakening from within, knowing the unknown and unearthing the buried significance. The book retrieves the idea of humanism lost in the grandeur of purposes, perfection and planning.

Divided into five tuneful sections, creating a lilt for the whole of the book, the chapters display lightness of prose and presentation with nuanced layers of ordinariness. One can fathom a sinister design, a mischievous logic underpinning the division of the sections and clubbing of the chapters. The way the book is structured is no less dramatic than the polyphonic drama of the ordinary. The sync between life and book is bound to happen. Both the book and life are as meandering as a monk's wandering, akin to *Ghumakkadi*, literally meaning wanderlust. A thinker in modern India named Rahul Sankrityayan employed *Ghumakkadpan*, an idea which he used to mean more than simple wanderlust, as an epistemology, a premise and a proposition, all at once in most of the books Sankrityayan penned. He never shied away from accepting it, at times implicitly and at other times very explicitly. So, we could get for our posterity a trail of being ordinary as an author, wanderer, seeker and a relational creature.

The chapters are liberated from academic restrictions about the permissible sources of information, manner of systematic analyses and the imperative of a convincing scholarship—so much so that it all appears to be a part of light banter with a sincere objective. The whole book is in a way an academic's conversation with the self and the rest of the world at broadly three levels—personhood (emotions and relations), vocation (education and ideology) and culture (religiosity, spirituality and return to personhood). The chapters speak through popular cultural-poetic texts to offer critical insights. Besides, each chapter unfolds in the mode of experiential narratives, suggesting to any reader that the speaker in first person could be represented by any pronoun that we learnt in grammar. Frequently switching from one pronoun to another, so as to curate the dramatics of conversation, the chapters suggest that the narrated experience could belong to any reader. We, you, I, they—all seem to join in as the first person with due grammatical hazard. There is a modestly implemented politics of pronouns in the experiential narratives in this book.

Even though each chapter deals with the issue of ordinariness and the chances of awakenings in everyday situations, the chapters invariably allude to the cultural-political constraints in contemporary India. Regimes of repression, allegedly and arguably, are the most sinister challenge to the necessary release from one stage of ordinariness to another. The dynamics of ordinariness are at the mercy of the powers that be. Hence, the book elucidates instances of ordinary struggles against such regimes of repression. The mode of conversation enables the book to be accessible, to an optimal extent, for both experts and lay readers. All it presupposes is a modest openness from any potential reader.

I am thankful to the anonymous reviewer of the manuscript. It was a fairly critical review that expected the book to follow the familiar norms of writing an academic-referenced work. The expectation that this book, like any other, shall give a clear discursive trajectory of the approaches to the issue of ordinariness is well placed, but that was not what the author deemed fit in this manuscript. It is not due to authorial stubbornness or any imagined high position. Instead, it is due to the temperament in which the whole book is thought out. It is not planned to cater to the need of academic peers; hence, it has minimalist notes, citations or bibliography, more as an afterthought than as a means of communication. The book also tries to shy away from exhibiting any other such techno-academic genius. Is there no way we can speak and think through simple stories, poetry, prose, personal accounts and anecdotes? Yet, while we do all this, can we be sufficiently intellectual, scholarly or academic? The question needs more detailed deliberation on some other occasion. It suffices to say, here is the first offering in the direction of the question, if not as an answer to the same.

At last, I must acknowledge a few of those who expressed interest in reflecting on this manuscript and standing by its nature, scope and content. My friendship with some of them became a victim of this time, the pandemic paranoia and lockdown logic. I do not blame them. They must be hard-pressed and, hence, they took offence where none was meant. I thank Sasanka Perera and Anoli Perera for taking note of any merit in this kind of book. They were, however, of the same opinion as my students, Joyashree Sharma and Anakshi Pal. Interestingly, Chandra Sekhar from Bloomsbury, who was always keen to carry this manuscript forward and took a personal interest in reading it, held the same idea, that is, this book is still not suitable for the label of non-academic work. I must admit that I tumbled from some imagined high ground when I heard this. My self-congratulatory sense of radically leaving the burden of academic virtues behind turned out to be half-baked. They all saw an intellectual challenge in these essays that the author holds out for any reader. All the readers may not be at equal ease. Like the anonymous reviewer of this book who was commissioned by the publisher, Sasanka Perera was reminded of Roland Barthes's *Mythologies* or Umberto Eco's essays by the manuscript. This was even more disastrous. Honestly, there was no such aspiration, even remotely. Since I have admired Barthes's writing from an early age in the university, I know the difference between Barthes's systematic analysis and the celebration of chaos and incoherence in this book. Umberto Eco's ruminations were nicely cooked and served. I happen to be a terrible cook, except for basics such as rice and lentils. Since I know I am a bad cook, I tend to decorate my meagre lentils a little too carefully. But that does not mean that I can declare my cooked basics as the best of the cuisine.

That heresy is not my cup of tea. I sincerely believe that Perera and the anonymous reviewer did not mean it. This book is indeed not available for comparison, and you would understand what it means when you critically note the errors or reflexive modesty abounding in the chapters. As an author, however, I do not have much problem with self-conscious errors in mine as well as others' works. Errors by design, with clarity of motive and planted on purpose are indeed a prerequisite in the discourse in this book. The meaning of a deliberation on ordinariness is intricately tied to human but reasonable errors. So, one of the most dominant errors in this book is to borrow a formulation from Milan Kundera, an unbearable lightness of being!

I must acknowledge the significance of some very irritating friends with whom I have mostly long-distance talking relationships, irrespective of the pandemic. They annoy me and, hence, they are useful. Many of them are colleagues. So, for the reasons of my safety, I must not acknowledge them with proper nouns. But the friends who would not mind being named as the agents of annoyance are Jhunna, Pankaj and Rajan, among others. Prabhjyot can kill me with her bizarre comments, and she did deliver such comments while listening to the many chapters of this book. My former doctoral student Ratan Kumar Roy is a dangerous fellow who speaks English with such a heavy Bengali accent that I decided to speak with him in very sanskritised Hindi. He never shies away from giving his one-liner: 'so you are turning spiritual with these essays!' Sadan Jha is usually not irritating, but, at times, his reticence about whatever I write can drive me nuts. But I am grateful to him for even the simplest *waah-waah*. On a beautiful night when we were high on ideas last year, I shared some nuggets from this book with Saurabh Dube, a well-known, seasoned scholar who takes interest in the idea of the ordinary. To cut the long conversation short, he gave a twofold response: 'do not write to prove anything to anyone else, and do not romanticise the ordinary'. Funnily, it became part of the agenda behind this book, even though I have been relatively resistant to following any advice.

Priya Mirza is my best, and ruthless, critic right at home. She shows no mercy in tearing down anything and everything that I do or write or think. At times, I walk out with a heavy heart and then walk in with a bouquet of flowers to please her. That strengthens my love and respect for her, almost like someone suffering from Stockholm Syndrome. I thank her for counting all the good and bad in this book and saying in the end, 'The book has an argument that enables us to live a life with reason!'

Lastly, a technical acknowledgement about the translated content in the chapters in this book may be pertinent. All translations of the content from vernacular language into English is by the author of the book unless stated otherwise in the prose. Sajal Roy from Dhaka helped with the illustrations, and Anakshi Pal provided help with the proofreading. Also, the editing of the manuscript received qualitative inputs from Aathira Ajitkumar and Shreya Chakraborti. I mostly agreed to the suggestions regarding the tone and temper of words and syntax in order to smoothen the performance of the prose. Since it was all done during a (viral as well as regime-borne) pandemic and evident (sociopolitical) vulnerability of humankind, I never shied away from 'sanitising' the narrative to the extent of even compromising on the punch of the performance. This is for the greater common good, so to say!

The rest is entirely up to anyone who is willing to jump off the madly rushing donkey of Mulla Nasruddin!

Notes

1. This was a profound critique of the bourgeoise conceptualisation of culture in which a skewed sense and practices of art and society prevail. See Herbert Read, *To Hell with Culture and Other Essays on Art and Society* (London: Routledge, 1963). However, while this strand of anxiety about cultural compartmentalisation is important, the chapters in this book also dwell on due intellectual sensitivity to the profoundly ordinary notions inherent in the larger body of textual and contextual cultural details. In this regard, one may like to get informed by a variety of attempts. For example, revisiting the medieval poetic epic *Padmavat*, Purushottam Agrawal enables us to read an early modernity in South Asia in which within ordinary experiences, love turns divine in spite of threats of aggression. Padmavati was more than extraordinary (within the realm of ordinary), and the tale is fraught with ambiguities. See Purushottam Agrawal, *Padmavat: An Epic Love Story*, introduction and illustration

by Devdutt Pattanaik (Delhi: Rupa, 2018). Likewise, we are not devoid of sincere attempts to make sense of the cultural politics vis-à-vis the ordinary in popular cultural texts. An eminent anthropologist Patricia Uberoi had set an insightful trope for discussing an enormous possibility of dealing with visuals, cinemas and ordinary social in Patricia Uberoi, *Freedom and Destiny: Gender, Family, and Popular Culture in India* (Delhi: Oxford University Press, 2006).

2. This book does not aim at partaking in theoretical, philosophical and even typically empirical research–based works dealing with the idea of experienced ordinariness. Instead, the aim is simple and light, that is, unravelling the author's experience (lived as well as beyond), though informed by a rich tapestry of discussions. Some of them will be resonant in various chapters in this book even though not subject to critical perusal. For example, Gopal Guru and Sundar Sarukkai have consistently engaged with the intricacies of experience, emotions and everyday life for over a decade, taking note of the ontological challenges and categories of location such as caste, gender and other markers of identification. See Gopal Guru and Sundar Sarukkai, *The Cracked Mirror: An Indian Debate on Experience and Theory* (Delhi: Oxford University Press, 2012). In continuity and creative rupture, they have added to the debate by curating a sensorium of the everyday social in Gopal Guru and Sundar Sarukkai, *Experience, Caste and The Everyday Social* (Delhi: Oxford University Press, 2019).

An anthropologist's theoretical, empirical and adequately personal journey through the trope of the ordinary is available in Veena Das, *Textures of the Ordinary: Doing Anthropology After Wittgenstein* (Delhi: Orient BlackSwan, 2020). As serendipitous as it may sound, while responding to the queries by the copy editor of my manuscript, I had a chance to read and discuss Veena Das's book in a panel discussion toward the public offering of her book. Needless to say, mine is a tiny dewdrop in the face of Veena Das's consistently evolved, splendid and curated culmination of scholarship.

3. Returning to the fundamentals in the wake of the pandemic was a point upon which philosopher Ramin Jahanbegloo agreed with me during a discussion on his book. See Galp Lok, 'Discussion on the book *The Courage to Exist* by Ramin Jahanbegloo,' YouTube video, 50:04, 22 December 2020, accessed on 20 February 2021, https://www.youtube.com/watch?v=eJQmepsLIbI. The book is part of a trilogy that Ramin has been working towards during the 2020 pandemic. See Ramin Jahanbegloo, *The*

Courage to Exist: A Philosophy of Life and Death in the Age of Coronovirus (Delhi: Orient Blackswan, 2020).

It was with this idea of return to the fundamentals that I began a series of conversations with a handful of scholars on a virtual public space called Galp Lok on YouTube. See Galp Lok, YouTube channel, accessed on 20 February 2021, https://www.youtube.com/c/GalpLok/videos. The idea is to return to the fundamentals in terms of themes, issues and events, as well as to return to the forms of knowledge including light-hearted conversations, witty book discussions or creative renditions of any kind.

4. See Michel Foucault, 'What Is an Author?', in *Language, Counter-Memory, Practice*, ed. Donald F. Bouchard. (Ithaca: CUP, 1977), 113–138. Also see Roland Barthes, 'The Death of the Author', in *Image, Music, Text* (New York: Hill and Wang, 1977), 142–148. These two famous interjections ought to be read along with an exciting debate between Sundar Sarukkai and Gopal Guru that rolls out the relationship between the authors and owner of experience. See Guru and Sarukkai, *The Cracked Mirror*.

5. In order to provide more muscles to this anxiety, one can undertake varieties of routes of reasoning. One of them is typically a combination of history and anthropology that unravels the overlapping critical dispositions of the subjects of modernity in South Asia. See, for example, Saurabh Dube, *Subjects of Modernity: Time-Space, Disciplines, Margins* (Manchester: Manchester University Press, 2017).

6. In case one intends to explore further, see Jean-Paul Sartre, *Existentialism and Humanism* (London: Matheun and Co., 1948), accessed on 20 February 2021, https://archive.org/details/ExistentialismAndHumanismBySartre1948EngTranslationPhilipMairet/page/n5/mode/2up.

Embryonic Intrigues:
On Something and Nothing

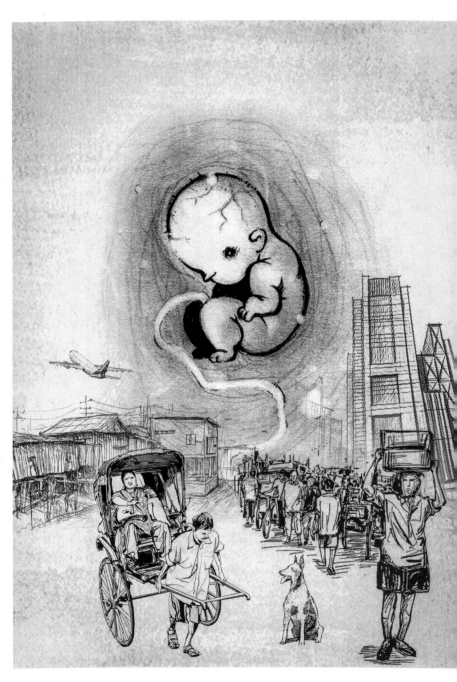

Illustration artist: Sajal Roy, Dhaka, Bangladesh

1

A Defence of the Ordinary, or Wishful Thinking

It is ridiculous to feel ordinary these days. A six-year-old child in Class One says innocently, 'I am not like some of those other kids who can do everything difficult. I give up easily; I am so simple and ordinary.' It sounds as if 'giving up' is the crime of ordinary people, while 'taking up' is the heroism of the extraordinary. If someone is willing to dismiss it as a non-issue since it is a child who says this, one can turn to fully blossomed, mature adults who would not shy away from proving to peers the speciality they possess. Everyone in the digital age is trying to prove something extraordinary on social networking websites, by flaunting contacts with well-known people and posting selfies with gurus, leaders and even authors of bestsellers. It looks like the world is eager to overcome ordinariness. In any walk of life, there are various degrees of war being waged against the ordinary. A man of religion turns into a crusader to assert the extraordinary importance of his faith. A woman of significance tries out every measure to hyper-emphasise a splendid mix of beauty and brain. Parents do not want to miss a chance and take meticulous efforts to enrol their child in the best school. Every morning, our newspapers report about violence; and if we practise reading between the lines, we find, a lot of those reports are actually about institutions and industries waging a battle against ordinariness. The reports of violence, and even our sporadic reactions, are all to widen the distance between our ordinariness and us. Governments want us to become extraordinary citizens and, thus, there are bills and laws to segregate 'we, the people'. Universities extol their position in this or that ranking and, thereby, distinguish themselves from ordinary varsities; the State aids further by creating the 'institutions of excellence' tag so that some of them can be held superior to ordinary institutions. Development agencies cajole us to work towards the dream of spectacular accomplishments. Schools infuse in children the value of extraordinary performance. Markets and advertisements force us towards high consumption of premium goods. Almost everything, from cinema halls to public toilets, from railways to public signage, seems to speak loud and clear that it is no longer sufficient to be an ordinary patriot; one ought to be partaking in posh and plush nationalism to be considered a good citizen. Even our national flag is subject to the battle against ordinariness.[1] The flag no longer has the modest appearance that we were familiar with. It is so enormous in shape and size that the national flag that emerged from the people's struggle, as we read in history textbooks, feels impersonal. The people's national flag that endeared to us all as school children has dramatically metamorphosed into something larger than life. Everything that one values, from traditional to modern, from local to global, from intimate to impersonal, is run through the litmus test to detect and weed out ordinariness or its equivalent—mediocrity.[2] In the game of perception and reality, anything ordinary is equivalent to zero, unlike a hero who has or aspires to unparalleled accomplishments. Thus, we encounter a pretty familiar rigmarole induced by various industries to ensure that even our experience of the ordinary turns out to be extraordinary.

This is the premise for this book that you may presumably have mistaken for a serious academic book with conclusive arguments. Each chapter herein indulges in a reasoned defence of ordinariness at various moments in life, despite the obvious odds. Yet, there is an explicit, though not always, hesitation to be trapped in academic seriousness. The book does not offer a clear compartmentalisation of the ordinary and the non-ordinary. Instead, it is a mess of various levels of ordinariness that unfold in discussions on emotions, education, relations and recreations inter alia. On many notes, the chapters will be optimally opinionated and judiciously judgemental while seeking to suspend conclusive conclusions. In the mode of wondering, the book attempts to show that ordinariness is a complex structure, experience and idea. Therefore, it all invites romance as well as scepticism at once; one cannot be either romantic or sceptical about ordinariness.[3] No plain formulation of good, bad or ugly could help in ascertaining it.

The ordinary is, hence, not so ordinary. As it turns out, it is always at the mercy of everything that can obscure ordinariness. There is a perpetual struggle that ordinariness has to wage. It thus unfolds in a melodrama of rivalling emotions in which the personal aspect cannot be held at bay. The idea of ordinariness shall be revealed through our personal association with it. In a way, the book reaffirms that the personal is public and adequately political. The enchantment of ordinariness does not allow the separation of personal ordinariness from the public and the political and, as soon as one intends to separate them, it assumes the significance of extraordinariness. Hence, nowhere shall this chapter, like the whole book, pretend to offer a scholarly answer. This is because the book does not separate the personal from everything that is deemed impersonal. That scholarly aspiration can be saved for some other occasion. Here the idea is to stay truthful to the ordinary in articulation and presentation, by playing with wit and wisdom, humour and sarcasm, barb and banter. So, let us explore the ordinary in engagement with works of art, fiction, popular narratives, personal encounters and experiences. Let us see whether we are there in those tales that unwittingly present the defence of ordinariness and whether those various tales help us in understanding what this basic concept, ordinary, means.

The various epics, myths and movies resonate with our personal life trajectories. The reel and real come together in one such tale called *Chitralekha,* penned by the renowned modern Hindi litterateur Bhagwati Charan Verma in the 1930s. The historical situation in which this novel made sense was in favour of exploring the distinguishable sociocultural identity of an India in the making. The novel presented a philosophically profound debate on right and wrong, vices and virtues, life and love. A filmmaker named Kidar Nath Sharma adapted the novel twice into cinematic work, first in 1941 and the second time in 1964. The second movie, hailed as a masterpiece, has an illustrious star cast with the three crucial characters played by Ashok Kumar as the celibate yogi Kumar Giri, Meena Kumari as the *rajnartaki* Chitralekha (a courtesan) and Pradeep Kumar as *Aryaputra Samant* Beejgupt, an affluent man of letters. Let us reduce a complex story into a plain and simple narrative. The suave and sophisticated man of letters, Beejgupt, from the upper echelons of society, is in love with the courtesan Chitralekha to the dismay of the moral authority of society. The ascetic Kumar Giri is requested to rescue the fallen Beejgupt from the clutches of Chitralekha; then the ascetic himself falls in love with the socially denigrated courtesan. The second cinematic adaptation also has innumerable insightful songs penned by the endearing poet Sahir Ludhianvi. About Beejgupt's romance with Chitralekha, a song in the film says, in the sonorous voice of Muhammad Rafi set to the music of Roshan, '*Man re tu kahe na dheer dhare*' (O my impatient mind, why not rest in patience). For Chitralekha's replies to the arrogant Kumar Giri's challenge on the issue of moral right and wrong, another song in the crooning voice of Lata Mangeshkar says, '*Sansar se bhage phirte ho bhagwan ko kya tum paoge*' (Escaping from 'this' world, what would you get of 'that' world?). All these songs complemented the unfolding plots of Verma's classical novel. The novel as well as its cinematic adaptations established a thesis on the idea of the ordinary. It was that ordinariness is dynamic—ordinary folks move from one layer of ordinary to another. One hears many voices in a polyphonic ordinary.[4] Ordinariness thus entails release as much as repression. The repression 'befalls' the celebrated celibate; the ascetic Kumar Giri is struck by a lustful love, a level of ordinariness, for the courtesan. The courtesan Chitralekha and her unrelenting lover Beejgupt turn out to be the true repositories of moral truthfulness; yet, they stay ordinary in love, longing both. From the ordinary relationship of a man and his beloved, we shift to the ordinary lust of a sage for a courtesan and, eventually, we see the return of the lovers to an ordinary union. In between, every intervention looks like the desperate attempt of various stakeholders to stop the ordinariness. Such is the immaculate dynamism of ordinariness in *Chitralekha*, as it is in our personal biographic narratives.

This template in defence of ordinariness was already established in a classic work of fiction that hinted at many facts way back in the first decade of the 20th century—Rabindranath Tagore's *Gora*. This was Tagore's path-breaking rejoinder to the Indian quest for racial extraordinariness. Before the moment of critical realisation, the protagonist Gaur Mohan seems to be at the zenith of racial purity amid other characters representing ordinary emotions. Among many who inhabit an ordinary world in the novel are Binoy, an idol-worshipping Hindu; Sucharita, the follower of the reformist Brahmo Samaj and Poresh Babu, the father figure with a generous and calm pose. The mother figure, Anandmayi, is an apostle of liberal values and compassion. Gora is committed to establishing the greatness of India in a pure Hindu race. Other characters join in debates with Gora at various stages in the narrative. Eventually, Gora discovers that he is not as pure-blooded as he believed. Crestfallen, Gora discovers his origin to be what was deemed inferior and impure and termed *mlechha*. The novel underlined the struggle between the ordinary and the non-ordinary, the superior and the inferior, in the sociopolitical scheme of judgement. An 'un-becoming' of a hero into a zero, decline from high to low in social hierarchy, may seem to be anathema in an anti-ordinary judgement. Tagore, however, taught us a lesson; that is, becoming zero seldom diminishes the significance of the protagonist. For, the un-becoming was a significant becoming of the protagonist. Being nothing or something without cultural jingoism was deemed commendable progress in the biography of the protagonist. Evidently, Tagore took a nuanced position in the heyday of reformist Hindu cultural nationalism in India by ennobling the ordinariness of his protagonist who was somewhat militant about his extraordinariness.

The same concept is more painfully realised when the impure son is on the verge of annihilating his mother, the source of his impure origin, in Acharya Chatursen's Hindi novel titled *Dharmputra*, published in the first quarter of the 20th century. The novel was adapted with the same title into the second directorial venture of the famous Hindi filmmaker Yash Raj Chopra (1961), in which actor Shashi Kapoor essayed the protagonist Dileep, born to a Muslim mother and brought up by Hindu parents. Dileep turns out to be a militant fascist sworn to decimate Muslims, and his first kill is going to be, by coincidence, his biological mother. Right then, his foster (Hindu) parents disclose the truth of his ordinary origin to Dileep. A catharsis of sorts happens when he learns that he is not a pure, extraordinary Hindu. The battle against the ordinary origin ends with the realisation that essentially everyone is ordinary, be they Hindu, Muslim or, for that matter, any caste or creed.

In one way or another, we have our own moments of painful realisation etched in our personal biographies. We have a *Gora* or *Dharmputra* moment that informs us about the routes, the passage of time and space through which we receive experience and influence. The route takes us away from our roots (traditions or established knowledge). Our origins do not become immaterial even as we acknowledge the influence of our experiences. It all only makes us feel ordinary, despite the crescendo of extraordinariness around us. Such is the fallout of the coexistence of roots and routes in our everyday life. It is true, even though we cringe: at the core, we are ordinary, made of ordinary sentiments, emotions, attributes, actions and reactions, intentions and even unintended motives. Ordinariness is sweeping, yet a glimpse of it demands a non-sweeping view. We cannot see the details of ordinariness in a hasty glance. A lot of the details of ordinariness are often taken for granted. We know that a fish breathes through water. Does it drink the medium through which it breathes? It would have been an existential problem in the aquatic world. They all breathe, eat, mate, copulate, live and die. Yet they do not see all the details of their everyday life. That ordinary everyday-ness is the spine that holds the book of life together—a spine in each anatomical arrangement; so crucial, yet so neglected. It stays neglected despite the occasional attempts at the yogic posture of shavasana in which you lie down on your back and let your body feel light and afloat. You examine your body inwardly and perhaps get a glimpse of some select parts of your spine too. You see it all with closed eyes. In the best of meditation, our endeavour is to see the exterior and interior of the body. We are mostly driven by the idea of stimulating something extraordinary in our bodies when we undertake such exercises. Even while taking a morning or evening walk, we tend to think that we have aimed at an extraordinary rejuvenation of the body and mind. However, we are mostly visiting, and revisiting, the ordinary spine of existence. Deep inside each body, there is an ordinary frame, a taken-for-granted spine. This ordinary thing is indeed more extraordinary than the sheen and shine that shows on our face and in the nimble activities of our limbs. Our mind may operate with the idea of extraordinariness. We are indeed exploring the details of the ordinary within as well as without. Those who love consumption do not seem to recognise the ordinariness that holds the seemingly extraordinary intact. The appearance of the best cars one sees is largely due to the fine chassis underneath. Only when one registers the vehicle does one realise the identification number of the chassis. Otherwise, once in a while, one recalls and rechecks the chassis number for official documentation. Mostly, one tends to admire the car for its look, functions of the switches and facilities and efficiency of the operation. The idea of the chassis remains dormant in our appreciation. But there is no car if there is no chassis. There is no body if there is no spine. There is no book if the central hinge, which binds the book together, is absent. *Ignored*, *dormant* and *hidden* are some of the common words characterising the ordinary. The ordinary is the hinge on which everything else depends. From banality to mundanity, from magnificence to excellence, from success to triumph, it all means nothing without the hinge called the ordinary. To sound a bit radical, let us say that the extraordinary breath of a yogi is nothing without manifold ordinary breaths flowing day in and day out. Every yogi seems to know the threefold passage of breaths. Imagining these passages to be like veins, they were named *Ira*, *Pingala* and *Sushumna* by the ancient yoga teachers. These teachers never cared to capitalise on their knowledge. They stayed ordinary and gave us the knowledge of yoga ordinarily. We learnt from them that the breath in Ira runs through one nostril and that in Pingala through another. Sushumna seems to enjoy a mystical charm in which *prana*, the most sublime breath, runs only when the ordinary flow in Ira and Pingala is smooth. Every yogi relishes the idea and imagination of prana flowing in Sushumna. Is this of significance without the ordinary breath in Ira and Pingala? If the two nostrils are blocked, imagine, what possibility of playing with Sushumna exists? Most importantly, if we have no idea of the countless breaths throughout the days and nights, without our practised work at Ira-Pingala-Sushumna, what kind of play with prana exists? That is the irrevocable ordinary breathing, with or without yogic framework. It is these ordinary breaths that can earn us yogic awakening in everyday life, or so envisaged Sri Aurobindo![5] He did not do so merely out of fancy but because he knew the enormity of ordinariness and everyday life. Only a yogi with profound thinking such as Sri Aurobindo could anticipate the importance of the hinge in an efficient structure. However, he did aspire, like many minds with similar insights, for experiential spirituality. The latter, the goal, may sound like something extraordinary, available to only very evolved humans versed in the yogic art. But it was seldom at the price of ordinary perceptions, sensations, intuitions and, over all, emotions. Throughout the texts and treatises on yoga, we learn this simple idea: *do not repress; release*. This does not mean the sacrifice of ordinariness. It means passing through various phases of ordinariness—release from one stage of ordinariness to another, from another to yet another. Thus, one reaches somewhere that may seem quite extraordinary to all those who have not duly passed through the stages. But even that destination, seemingly extraordinary to the outsider qua spectator, is blissfully ordinary for the one who has gone through various phases.

The Buddhahood that the enlightened Buddha attained is that sublime ordinariness. Despite all the reservations about university-bred scholars and sociologists or anthropologists, we learn a great deal about the idea of the ordinary from them. For example, the way an eminent anthropologist from South Asia, Gananath Obeyesekere,[6] has invited us to think of our experiences of a particular kind is worth seeing. He said that we operate with visions that we get with our state of consciousness or subconsciousness. It need not always be a high variety of meditation performed by a seasoned seer. Ordinarily, we live life with a practical sense of rationality as well as visions and values. In this light, one can also reread the Buddha story. The whole biography seems to create orbits of ordinariness through which the Buddha passes. The extraordinary conception and birth enter the realm of the ordinary as soon as a corporeal existence is identified with Siddhartha. The ordinariness of having a family and relations is shed in the pursuit of an answer to the existential question: Why is there pathos? There is a pursuit of penance and hardship that seems spectacular as the Buddha is reduced to a skeleton, and that is when he renounces the penance to start the ordinary existence of a mendicant living off alms. The story gets more orbits as the Jataka describes the demon Mara's attack, the desire and the dread of death working to dissuade Siddhartha. Then dawns, very modestly, what is called the bodhisattva. There is no big fanfare, no series of animals sacrificed, no great ritual performed, no elaborate priestcraft or shamanism and no unquestionable holy book. Buddhahood is the incredibly ordinary process of release from one orbit of experience to another and yet another. One is invested everywhere and lost nowhere. One keeps moving and then, in retrospect, realises the release from various orbits as well as the struggle one had to wage against the forces that tried to scuttle our release. That is the wholesome story of ordinariness.

It looks very likely that one orbit of experience may clash with the other and yet another one. One level of ordinariness may collide with another. More importantly, the orbits of ordinariness may be at the mercy of the machinery that is working day and night to make everything glamorous, memorable, countable and a little more than merely ordinary. Yet the ordinariness remains intact for a return, retrospection and re-evaluation. To understand this, one need not spend long hours in libraries. One need not start poring over the tomes of what is famously known as the 'philosophy of phenomenology' or the philosophy of very ordinary, everyday life. Phenomenologists try to help us understand the details of ordinary, everyday life. Hermeneutic philosophers, while dealing with the complexity of meanings, and existential philosophers, who showed us not only absurdity and banality but also a possibility of humanism embedded in the details of everyday life, do the same. They do it, obviously, in the language of philosophy. There are limits and possibilities in the philosophical language. It is not so easy, as everyone says, to follow the linguistic modes, styles and articulations in these philosophical works. Hence, one seems to turn to the TED-talkers, gurus of all ranks and leaders of various orders. From the spiritual gurus to the management and love gurus, there are so many stakeholders. At times, some of the teachers in universities also pose as secular gurus, some Marxist and some others with the label of liberals, and now there is a variety of rabid nationalist gurus. There is truly a demand for gurus who can tell things confidently and clearly. There is no ambiguity, all clear answers and, hence, they are gurus. All such prescriptive answers with prophetic clarity are in demand. Seldom do such prescriptions leave adequate space for free will. Each of them will say 'I will show you the path' and show a path, and the followers of each seem to have started to walk on the shown path. This is an extraordinary act of faith, of actions, of consequent reactions, of purchasing power and of expenditure and consumption. In this spectacular event in the biographies of ordinary people, there is a casualty. The worst-hit victim of this spectacle is the ordinary core of every human being. We have ensured a complete escape from the ordinary core. Elsewhere, the psychoanalyst Erich Fromm called it an escape from freedom.[7] The freedom comes from that source of the ordinary embodied in humans. That source enables everyone to rely on the basics, hinges, spine and chassis—all ordinary. We tend to surrender our core to anyone who promises us emancipation, salvation, bliss and freedom. Anyone who can make these promises with the best articulation conquers our enabling and inherent ordinary core. And why not! We cannot read those heavy tomes of philosophers about which the university academics glibly talk and make us feel inferior. We cannot decipher the nuggets of wisdom written in even lighter texts since we have a strange shortage of time. We read even our news only on social networking websites such as Facebook or Twitter. We have acquired monetary resources and our industries induce us to consume everything possible. We are financially empowered and informed consumers convinced of salvation in shopping malls. So why not purchase packaged meditational exercises from the gurus of our times and seek an extraordinary sense of spiritual transformation? There is evidently a level of extraordinariness involved in arriving at something so ordinary—the spine, the hinge, the breaths and the chassis! Obviously, in this scheme of spending, buying and consuming, all the cherished ordinariness is seldom ordinary. After coming back from an ashram or a meditational retreat or such camps, do we hear anyone saying, 'It was a wonderful time with my ordinary core'? After writing well-memorised or smart answers in an exam for which they work so hard, students tend to forget everything they read, learnt and wrote. The process of learning is so painful that it is better forgotten. That learning did not connect with the ordinariness of the learners. All those who burnt the midnight oil to learn and prepare for exams cannot consider it all related to their ordinariness. You just cannot afford to declare something ordinary because you did it with such effort and after spending so much money and time. Instead, we tend to make a spectacle out of our experience, be it learning or spiritualism. It is almost like showcasing the curios one collects on a tour of famous tourist destinations. All the souvenirs collected on a tour actually reflect our tendency to escape from the ordinary. In an organised tour, we do not wander like Alice in Wonderland.[8] Tourists have a map ready for reference of the tour, leaving little to trial and error, curiosity and wonder, and surprises and shock. A bucket list is followed in order to consume, enjoy and make merry, to tick mark everything in the mode of 'seen it-done it'. We seldom undertake an exploration of a Sophie's world[9] on a tour of coastal regions or mountainous terrain. We do not wander like the great minds of the 20th century did; for example, Rahul Sankrityayan[10] deemed *Ghumakkadi*, literally meaning wandering, a practical device of learning and narrating the learnt. A peripatetic thinker of sorts, Sankrityayan did not shy away from changing loyalties, identities and affiliations; he became communist and Buddhist with equal ease in the process of wandering. He returned home only to narrate stories of the seen and unseen, heard and overheard. The accounts he gave us were full of ravishing details of people and places ordinary in style, tempo and core. This is unlike our tourism, in which everyone returns from these retreats with a few selfies, some memorabilia and a lot of fatigue. All of this is, however, laced with pride—been there, seen that, consumed that and brought back home the souvenirs for our drawing rooms. We spend extraordinarily to arrive at an imagined extraordinariness and return with a more strengthened sense of being extraordinary. The escape from the ordinary core, solemnised once again, only reaffirms the value of ordinariness. Likewise, every time we return from meditation retreats, we solemnise our escape from the ordinary core. If we truly persist with the ordinary core, we would not be able to make a hullabaloo about what we experienced. We would be quiet in the quietness, still in the stillness, amused at the amusing details around us, angry where we should be angry and loved where we should be loved. This is so terribly ordinary a feeling that no effort is needed other than being oneself.

This book unravels facets of ordinariness in the context of life and lived experience in the mode of ordinary ruminations. The mode of thinking and writing in the chapters of this book may remind you of *vitanda-vada*. In this mode of talking, reasoning, arguing and writing, a creative paradox unfolds; this is very common among folks across cultural contexts. *Vitanda* connotes arguing for the sake of argument, and *vada* means a logical thesis that will generate *prativada* or an antithesis. This idea is inherent to a particular branch of philosophy called *Lokayat*.[11] Some commentators describe Lokayat (literally meaning people's way of seeing) as a kind of vitanda-vada. The philosophy of Lokayat is mostly in various fragments, with references to it scattered across epics, ancient texts and rejoinders. There is no consolidated body of philosophy of Lokayat the way we find texts on other orthodox philosophies such as Mimamsa, *Samkhya*, Nyaya and Vedanta. It became thus easier for commentators to write off the significance of Lokayat in the history of Indic philosophy. But following a convincing reading of Lokayat by the noted philosopher Debiprasad Chattopadhyaya, one understands that vitanda-vada of the Lokayat is, in fact, a strength of this mode of talking, reasoning, arguing and writing. There could be a more engaging reading of Lokayat elsewhere; suffice to say, the chapters in this book seek to create a vitanda to disclose various encounters between the ordinary, non-ordinary and extraordinary. It seeks to underline the layers of the ordinary, in which common sense and not-so-very-common sense stay together. The Lokayat way of seeing the world assumes significance in this book, since it was associated with ordinary folks who thought about practical interests, everyday life and everything that was either a non-issue or taboo for the ennobled philosophers in the Indic past.

This is pertinent to reiterate a few of the curses and benedictions inherent in this book, hinted in the preface as well. Dipped in polemics, sound with romance, enthused with utopian ideas and yet ready to underline the dynamics of ordinariness, these lightweight chapters do not promise to fulfil the intellectual lust of academics. However, many chapters in this book hold academics and scholars culpable for marginalising ordinariness, even in the discussions they curate on the issues pertaining to the ordinary. Such allegations are left suspended since there is no absolute trial seeking for a final judgement. However, this book adopts a conscious politics of pronouns in the mode of experiential narratives. At times, it is difficult to claim singularity of authorship of the experiential narratives. Any reader may feel biographical proximity with the anecdotes and experiences narrated in this book. Hence, the speaker in the book changes hats, speaking in first person, with multiple sets of pronouns. Frequent switches from one pronoun to another curate a modest drama of conversation on the idea of ordinariness and its various avatars. The pronouns, such as we, you, I and they, all seem to join in as the first person, without following the linear distinction between I and you or we and they. The currents and countercurrents of ordinariness tend to defy the basics we learnt in textbooks of grammar. This may amount to certain obstacles to familiar styles of presentations, and each such obstacle is grabbed as an opportunity in this book.

This is akin to each obstacle to the release from one orbit of ordinariness being only a catalyst. Each force of suppression only augments the aspiration to overcome. Hence, each of the chapters moves back and forth between taking note of the escapes and indulging in the ordinary. It is through such dilemmas that we envisage hope for release from suppressions. Ambivalence is perhaps more of an intimate companion of the ordinary. This is all located within a particular mode of seeing the ordinary. Ram Roy Bhaskar, a contemporary philosopher, is renowned for propounding the idea of meta-reality by reading texts such as the Upanishads and the Gita, along with the *Masnavi* of Jalal ad-Din Muhammad Rumi, the medieval Persian poet and scholar of Islam. Roy Bhaskar[12] helps us to create a turf of ordinariness by showing aspiration for 'emancipation' integral to 'everydayness'. The ordinary encapsulates the reality, where we operate with our egos, and meta-reality, which makes us transcend our egos. The spiritual seeking thus is very much within the realm of the ordinary, which poses challenges too. Reading Rumi's following verses, titled 'Only Breath', therefore, enables us to understand the folk endeavour to transcend the various layers of ordinariness:

Not Christian or Jew or Muslim
Not Hindu, Buddhist, Sufi or Zen
Not any religion or cultural system

I am not from the East or the West, not out of the ocean or up from the ground
Not natural or ethereal
Not composed of elements at all
I do not exist
Am not an entity in this world or the next
Did not descend from Adam and Eve
Or any origin story
My place is placeless, a trace or the traceless.
Neither body of soul
I belong to the beloved
Seeing the two worlds as one
and that one call to and know
First, last, outer, inner, only that breath breathing human being.[13]

This is the scheme of ordinariness throughout this book, which asserts everything that one is not, and it all leads one to find what one could be.

Notes

1. Though the objective is not to systematically engage, it is worth a mention that I am informed by a historically rich work on the national flag by Sadan Jha, *Reverence, Resistance and the Politics of Seeing the Indian National Flag* (Delhi: Cambridge University Press, 2015).
2. A fascinating analytical account that captures a range of ordinary aesthetics beyond institution-induced divides is in Avijit Pathak, *On Social Constraints and the Great Longing: An Essay on the Human Condition* (Delhi: Aakar Books, 2014).

    For the dynamics of tradition and modern, without reaffirmation of any monolith, one can return to Saurabh Dube, *Subjects of Modernity: Time-Space, Disciplines, Margins.* (Manchester: Manchester University Press, 2017).
3. For the doubleness of the ordinary, see Stanley Cavell, *In Quest of the Ordinary: Lines of Skepticism and Romanticism* (Chicago: Chicago University Press, 1988). Recently, Veena Das built upon Cavell's formulations in making the ordinary available for anthropology and ethnography. See Veena Das, *Textures of the Ordinary: Doing Anthropology After Wittgenstein* (Delhi: Orient Blackswan, 2020).

4. The polyphony of ordinariness is duly an implication of the processes through which artists are brought into contact with global issues, exposure to mediums and the making of novel art-articulations, as it were. The comic book retelling of the mythological tales involves acts of re-visioning, resulting in the surfacing of many ordinary voices. In this regard, it is worth browsing Roma Chatterji, *Graphic Narratives and the Mythological Imagination in India* (Delhi: Routledge, 2019). Also see, Roma Chatterji, *Speaking with Pictures: Folk Art and the Narrative Tradition in India* (Delhi: Routledge, 2012).
5. See Aurobindo, *Collected Works of Sri Aurobindo*, vol. 12, accessed on 12 January 2020, https://www.aurobindo.ru/workings/sa/23/index_e.htm.
6. See Gananath Obeyesekere, *The Awakened Ones: Phenomenology of Visionary Experience* (New York: Columbia University Press, 2012).
7. This is premised on perhaps one of the most irresistible contributions to understanding human psyche in modern times. See Erich Fromm, *Escape from Freedom* (New York: Avon Books, 1964).
8. This is to hint at the ever-fantastic children's fiction duly useful for adults too. See Lewis Carroll, *Alice's Adventures in Wonderland* (Boston: International Pocket Library, 1865).
9. Jostein Gaarder, *Sophie's World: A Novel about the History of Philosophy* (London: Phoenix, 1996).
10. See Rahul Sankrityayan, *Ghummakad Shastra* (in Hindi) (Delhi: Rajkamal Prakashan, 1949), accessed on 10 January 2020, https://archive.org/details/in.ernet.dli.2015.539291/page/n3/mode/2up.
    Some of the significant engagement with the life and works of Rahul Sankrityayan have been done by scholars such as Prabhakar Machwe (in Hindi), Alka Chudal, Sanjay Srivastava inter alia.
11. For further exploration on Lokayat, see Debiprasad Chattopadhyaya, *Lokayata: A Study in Indian Materialism* (Delhi: People's Publishing House, 1959). A more recent exposition of the philosophy is Ramkrishna Bhattacharya, *Studies on the Carvaka Lokayata* (Cambridge: Cambridge University Press, 2012).
12. See Roy Bhaskar, *Reflections on Meta-Reality: A Philosophy for the Present* (Delhi: SAGE, 2002).
13. Mewlana Jalaluddin Rumi, 'Only breath,' accessed on 10 January 2020, https://allpoetry.com/Only-Breath.

2

Seeing, Ordinarily, the Seen and Unseen

What could be the right way to see the ordinary? I mean an appropriate way of seeing that which is too close to us to see—the ordinary! One way could be the age-old scientific realism or its near equivalent, positivism, in social sciences. This will, arguably, lead to the truth that could correspond with reality as it is out there. This is popularly known as correspondence theory of truth. Another way could be a hermeneutic, constructivist approach, which need not necessarily dwell on exact empirical evidence. It could entail an iota of critical articulation and careful affirmation or, in other words, contestation and negotiation, in the way of seeing our world.[1] There is a chasm of truth and lies in various known approaches in social sciences. Each approach crusades in an epistemological war, or something like that, to arrive at a truth claim. As far as ordinariness is concerned, truth and falsehood, fact and fiction, and objectivity and humanism tend to intricately merge. Hence, the approach to ordinariness summons an appropriate ordinariness in the way of seeing. What follows is an attempt to unspool that ordinary way of seeing.

When we were in school, we heard this from one another, in Hindi: '*Jhooth bolna paap hai, nadi kinare saamp hai, wahi tumhara baap hai*' (Lying is a sin, and if you commit it, remember that there's a snake by the river, and that is your father). It was horrific to imagine that the endearing man who cares for you so much would actually turn into a snake if you lie. We thought of not lying, but we heard yet another rhyme in school: 'Johnny, Johnny / Yes, Papa? / Eating sugar? / No, Papa / Telling lies? / No, Papa / Open your mouth! / Ha ha ha!' This sweet paradox sealed the fate of true and false, seen and unseen, evident and intuitive, factual and fabulous. One lied, without having to deal with father as the snake by the river. We have tales in support of our sociocultural practice of telling a lie while valuing the truth, and they make us believe in the romance of truth and lies. Our very vivacious Johnny was a winsome child named Krishna, also fondly called Gopal, *Makhanchor*, Madhav and so on. The mythologically profound tales about the childhood of Krishna are telling. His foster mother Yashoda was anxious about the child's notoriety for stealing freshly churned butter or milk cream. The neighbourhood women had complained too. One day, Yashoda caught him red-handed, or rather, cream-handed, for there was cream smeared on his lips and hands. Krishna relentlessly pleaded not guilty and gave several plausible reasons why he was innocent or, rather, why the seen proof, the evidence, was not trustworthy. Then his mother asked him to open his mouth for a more careful examination of the seemingly evident truth. He did so, and she saw the the whole of creation (or as anthropologists say, religio-mythological cosmology) in his tiny mouth.[2] Lies led to the ultimate, absolute truth, or someone could say that the partial truth leads to an impartial one, and so on. But the interplay of the seen and the unseen gets complicated. Ordinarily, our way of seeing entails the interplay of black and white, dark and light and, if one is willing to take it, of vice and virtue. The ordinary scheme of seeing did not change. This is despite Lata Mangeshkar and Shailendra Singh humming lyrics penned by Anand Bakshi to the tune of Laxmikant–Pyarelal, while a couple of lovers danced, in Raj Kapoor's runaway success melodrama *Bobby* (1973): '*Jhooth bole kauwa kaate / kaale kauwe se dariyo*' (If you tell lies, a black crow will bite you, and you should be scared of it!)

Be that as it may, the chapters in this book employ this way of seeing in which the interplay of seen and unseen, heard and unheard, said and unsaid, truth and lie, and fact and fiction is central. After all, vitanda-vada in the style of Lokayat would expect an iota of agnosticism. The latter, however, is not a synonym of disrespect. Hence, there is due acceptance of the enchantment of ordinariness in this book. At times, it sounds irritating since you know that a lie is being countered with another lie to construct the truth! Despite disagreements, we, however, notice that the unseen is as strong as the seen, in this way of seeing.

I tried telling the staunch supporters of the empirical sciences that their 'seen' is ever 'unseen'. None of my friends in journalism took it kindly either. Everyone seems to be operating with a juridical mindset, looking for evidence-based justice. But this is an age-old puzzle in old philosophical texts too. You see a rope and it turns out to be a snake or vice versa. The ancient seers seemed to agree in principle about the uncertainty in inferences and interpretations. What is seen is always in the process of becoming, with many unseen things buried in it. Therefore, nothing is absolutely seen. No empirical evidence is conclusive. However, the practitioners of empirical sciences have to satisfy their masters and have to show that the seen is truly seen it and, hence, believed as such. A mirage is not trusted, since it is contingent. So is the desert, but the desert can be trusted since is relatively stable, and so on. In this whole game of seen and unseen, the assumption is that the truth is more powerful than a lie. Let us ask ourselves if this is so. Particularly in a time of fake news, which is more powerful? It may sound cynical and horridly truthful. Lies spread like wildfire, and if they are detected and trashed as lies, they resurface in new forms sooner or later. Lies are creatively slimy; the truth is too arrogant to be creative. The truth ought to learn a lesson from lies if it has to survive. No one will buy the truth just because of that old Sanskrit adage '*Satyam Shivam Sundaram*' (Truth is godly and beautiful). Ordinarily, we agree with the adage and also add another Sanskrit dictum to it: '*Satyam vad, priyam vad*' (Speak the truth that is sweet). Despite this, ordinarily, we consume everything that may not be the truth. Such is the intrigue of ordinariness, in which the truth and the lie exquisitely interact. The crusaders of truth or believers in '*Satyamev Jayate*' (triumph of truth) should understand this ordinary interaction of truth and lies and supply some due creativity to truth. Likewise, the seen and the unseen interact in our ordinary thinking, reasoning and understanding.[3]

When we say 'seen', we also tend to operate with a hierarchy of sense organs. Sight obviously occupies a higher grade than other senses such as hearing, smelling and touching. For a long time, hearing and hearsay have been strongly associated. What is 'heard' is suspicious, unless it is an answer heard by a researcher as reply to a meticulously framed research question. Unless the researchers say that they have heard narratives during ethnography, they are not taken seriously. Academic peers get upset that the researcher, the seeker of knowledge, is operating with heard testimony, and such testimony is likely to be a cock and bull story. Rumours and gossip, which an anthropologist like James Scott underlined as the hidden transcript of the people, are to be cast aside in the business of seeing. They can be, at best, juicy footnotes in the larger thesis. At best, one could feel generous and accept all the spurious varieties of truth as a result of the Rashomon effect or Rashomon syndrome. The latter owes its origin to the classic of the Japanese master filmmaker, Akira Kurosawa, titled *Rashomon* (1950), which presented to us a riveting debate on truth and lies—the evidence of one narrator as the non-evidence of another. We tend to think that absolute evidence is only one, the absolutely seen, and everything else are merely implausible stories evoking truth claims by chance. In this whole tussle of the seen and the unseen, a lot gets lost.

On the contrary, one 'hears' a gospel, a nugget of wisdom, 'Satyam Shivam Sundaram', and we accept it without 'seeing' Satya (truth), Shiva (godliness) or Sundar (beauty). *Homo narrans*[4] were characterised by the ability to narrate and listen in oral traditions. Hearing this leads to believing that one need not see the truth or the embodiment of truth that is Shiva or everything that you consider beautiful. Truth, god and beauty are to be heard, felt and intuitively realised. It is not surprising that the Prophet Moses heard the messages from God while sitting in Koh-e-Toor, the cave in the mountain Toor. All the followers of Islam believe in what the Prophet heard in the serene calmness of the cave. This is more elucidated in Chapter Fifty-Two of the holy book Quran. Allah spoke to the chosen one, the Prophet Moses, and the spoken words are recorded in the holy book for all to understand and follow. Hearing aids in visualising. The idea of a world that is dear to Allah comes to be seen through what one heard from the messenger of Allah. Let us move on to another beautiful instance. Sanjay, a wonderful character in the epic Mahabharata, sits with the emperor Dhritarashtra and gives a running commentary about what he sees happening on the battlefield of Kurukshetra. Neither can Dhritarashtra see due to his physical limitations, nor does Sanjay see the battle literally, again due to his physical limitations. Sanjay is far away from the battlefield. He sees everything clearly, but not with his physical eyes.

In all such instances, a believer may think that the Prophet Moses, Sanjay and other such epic characters have an extraordinary ability. Hence, they see through the heard messages and visuals in words. Is it so? Ordinarily, we are all able to see things while we hear. We do not follow an anthropologist's check-list, 'been there-done that'. Yet we visualise through heard testimonies, anecdotes, folklore, songs and mythological tales. Sanjay described the war from a vision he saw in his mind of the battlefield. Everything he narrated was taken seriously by Dhritarashtra. Good gosh! This will be considered heretical in the empirical sciences as well as contemporary common sense. To take it further, the great bard Ved Vyasa narrated the tales of the Mahabharata to the scribe Ganesha. Apparently, the scribe had stipulated a condition: if the narrator paused, Ganesha would stop writing the tales. The narrator, who spoke from memory and spontaneous recollection, agreed, but only after putting his own condition to the scribe. Ganesha shall not write without understanding everything that Ved Vyasa says. A fine logical structure of hearing, understanding and writing is seen here.

In all these instances, hearing helped to see. This was a veritable act of seeing, not a literal and linear process in which seeing means correspondence with things out there. This is a deeper act of seeing, which unfolds in our lives pretty ordinarily. When we hear mythological stories of gods and goddesses flying from heaven to planets, we almost see them in our minds. Perhaps, a good heard description of the gods and goddesses are sufficient for us to imagine them. Hence, our early sculptures of gods and goddesses did not care so much about clarity of features. We were very comfortable with the *nirakar* (without shape and attributes) form of Shiva. Any stone in the physical world could become a Shiva linga. Millions of devotees of Shiva made their temporary Shiva linga with mud clay. It was a liberating regime of seeing, in which one was not at a loss as far as clarity of seeing with physical eyes was concerned. One was fine with vision that let one see with the eyes of the mind, and, in this seeing, hearing was a conjoined twin. Along with the hearing came in details about smell, fragrance, aroma, taste, palate, touch and so on. All such details that we heard played an important role in what we saw without being prisoners of our physical eyes. What could be more moving than the visually impaired poet Surdas's love for Krishna, whom the former never saw. Surdas heard, felt, smelt and touched his beloved god, Krishna. Prabhakar Machwe, a renowned literary critic in Hindi, underlined this important facet: Surdas's poems and songs had many references to eyes. He never lamented or alluded to his visual impairment. Surdas apparently courted blindness, as per many interpretations. The various names of the method of deep immersion, be it devotion, love or playful association, aided in this variety of seeing. Many names from the medieval tradition of devotional poetry could emerge as instances to corroborate this proposition. Mira saw Krishna; what was the quality of this seeing? Kabir saw Ram; what was the quality of this seeing? The quality of seeing led them to their respective realisations. Tulsidas's Ram was seen in one way and Kabir's in another. There is an inherent variation within this way of seeing too. It is not to be mistaken as a monolithic intuitive way of seeing. Mahatma Gandhi saw the text of the Gita in one way and Bal Gangadhar Tilak in another. For one, it became a source of inspiration to practise non-violence; it propelled the other to a vigorous defence of dharma suitable for a nation in the making.

In works of fiction, too, we encounter good discussions on the way of seeing. The ordinary way of seeing carries forward the charm of mundanity heard, touched, smelt and felt in everyday life. A milestone in modern Indian literature named Phanishwar Nath 'Renu',[5] who wrote in an uncanny vernacular version of Hindi and is read in modern Hindi literature today, executed a similar way of seeing in his literary craft. Take, for example, his novel *Parti Parikatha*. Rich with the description of scenes and situations, river and villages in the river basin, people and their practices, and history and mythology, this novel brings about a beautiful realisation about our ordinary way of seeing. Renu shows that we see through the sound produced by insects, trees, livestock, reptiles and the gushing, overflowing river. We see the characters and their woeful accounts by hearing their hiccups, murmurs, whispers, sighs and giggles. Renu makes everything visible through his words, even the sound of the train, motor vehicle, wind and various sounds emitted by human body such as hiccups, burps and other kinds of unpleasant bodily sounds too. The inherent enchantment of that world unfolds. There is no compromise on the details of this world or in the magic of the mundane in this world inhabited by the humans. If there is any progressive orientation, it emerges from such a mundane, ordinary, enchanting world. Hence, we are at ease with the proposed progressiveness. It is not a clichéd rhetoric or an intellectual cultivation in vacuum. The disarming devil that makes the narrative credible is in the details, and the details abide by no hierarchy of senses. If Renu and his *Parti Parikatha* are too outdated and in Hindi and, hence, inaccessible to the literati more conversant with English, a more contemporary work in fiction can be considered. A former anthropologist, Amitav Ghosh's works in fiction combine literary aesthetics with ethnographic as well as archival details. Tridib is an amicably peculiar character in *The Shadow Lines*, the uncle of the narrator-protagonist in the novel. One wonders why the narrator is so much in love with Tridib, who is like Sanjay of the Mahabharata. Tridib narrates stories about places far and wide with such confidence and details that it is unavoidably attractive for the narrator. No, Tridib does not give too many factually accurate details. In fact, he disarms your urge for factual accuracy but fuels your intense longing for more of his stories coming from god knows where. Tridib has not 'been there, seen them'; however, his accounts are far more arresting than a traveller's factually correct travelogue. He has not seen all those places and people that he tries to show the narrator through his descriptions. Sanjay of the Mahabharata has been seemingly reincarnated as Tridib of *The Shadow Lines*. They saw by way of what they heard, imagined and thought. Their seeing was more than merely seeing. It did not subscribe to what scholars have called monoscopic modernity, in which seeing meant only one thing, that is, seeing through your eyes. Thus, the modern proverb 'seeing is believing'[6] was a dictum of a new scientific-empiricist faith, a regime that valued extraordinary truth.

The monoscopic regime gets hardened in juridical discourse even though other kinds of material evidence are admissible too, such as fingerprints, DNA tests and so on. But they all tend to fall into the scheme of the evidence based on the logic of seeing. They need not all be seen with the physical eyes. But all of them need to bear the certainty that comes from eyewitnessing. Eyewitnesses are the real witnesses. Even better is a technologically mediated truth claim: photographic evidence in the court of law. This is despite the notion of *andha kanoon*—the lady of justice, supposedly of Greek origin, is blindfolded while holding the scales of justice. Known as Lady Justitia in Latin or the Greek Titaness Themis, she represents a divine order of justice in which her blindfold ensures impartiality. Commentators have underlined a paradox that this blindfold indeed amounts to more discrimination in actual practices in the courtroom. One way to read it, however, could be that the mythologically sensitive idea of justice does not require seeing who is the complainant and who the accused. It will colour the perspective of the juridical authority. The goddess of justice ought to be seeing with deeper vision and not with eyes, just like the prophet Moses or Sanjay in Mahabharata. Eyes can only help to see the pleading parties, evidence and facts. Emotions of the pleading parties can interfere with the efficiency of eyes. In principle, this is true and, hence, there is the nobility of something peppy such as *andha kanoon* or the law's blindness. It is also true, like in the film *Andha kanoon* (1983, directed by T. Rama Rao) starring Amitabh Bachchan and Rajnikanth, that miscarriage of justice is also due to this explicit blindness. Justice suffers, be it in the modern court of law where the lady of justice is blindfolded or in the court of the emperor Dhritarashtra, who is physically blind. Despite everyone advising him to see by hearing their words, Dhritarashtra only saw what his ambition, fatherly weakness, showed him. With or without physical eyes, ordinarily, folks have their vision coloured by their vested interests and emotions, ambitions and goals, motives and purposes. Seeing is thus seldom an innocent verb. When Dronacharya decided to conduct an examination of all his students, he asked them to target the eye of a wooden bird perched atop a tree. All princes lined up with their bow and arrow and took position. Dronacharya asked them all what they saw. Yudhisthir, the man known for his steadfastness to dharma, saw everything, including his other brothers, teacher, tree, leaves and the bird's eye. So did the others, except Arjun who saw only the bird's eye. Dronacharya was satisfied only with Arjun's answer. Arjun shot and hit the target, the bird's eye. Everyone saw through the lens of their respective values, interests, ambitions and emotions. Seeing is always coloured, even though it is presented as blindfolded. Gandhari is epitomised for voluntarily sacrificing her eyesight by blindfolding herself after she married Dhritarashtra, the visually impaired king. Deep ethics of care and parity emerged from Gandhari relinquishing her eyesight. She saw with her compassion and sacrifice. There came a time when her son Duryodhana was going to Kurukshetra to fight the battle of the Mahabharata against the Pandavas. Gandhari knew that Duryodhana could not conquer his brothers. She decided to do him a favour—to look at her son with her eyes. The belief was that her glance would make Duryodhana's body invincible. She asked Duryodhana to come naked before her. Duryodhana did appear naked though with a loin cloth on his private parts. Gandhari's glance did turn Duryodhana's whole body undefeatable. She, however, lamented the idiocy of her son. He did not like to be seen fully naked. As a result, Duryodhana's body under the waist became his Achilles' heel.

Ordinarily, seeing and not seeing, showing and not showing, take place through sets of interests, emotions, ambitions and purposes. Seeing with or without eyes leads to an understanding that involves manifold senses such as taste, smell, touch and so on. Ordinarily, there is no fixed scheme of seeing, no hierarchy of senses. There is a polyphony of seeing. The seen is phonic too. In the middle of all this, there is unseen aplenty. In the remainder of the book, we encounter this sublime interplay of seen and unseen, heard and overheard, seen and heard, and unseen and unheard at various scales. Thus, no one shall complain about the inherent conspiracies, rumours, gossip and everything that the insightful anthropologist James Scott considered part of hidden transcript elsewhere. They are all integral to chapters across this book. Engaging with the issues of emotions, intrigue of relationships, mediations of market and media, enigma of education, fluidity of faith and rigidity of religion and notions of living and dying and enchantment in cultural texts, the chapters in this book shall stand by the holism of seeing. While a new way of seeing is operationalised therein, a set of provocations and propositions appear for due consideration. This approach to ordinariness makes the matter truly ordinary, to say the least.

Notes

1. Elsewhere, this line of thinking informs an understanding of modernity. See, for example, Saurabh Dube, *Subjects of Modernity: Time-Space, Disciplines, Margins* (Manchester: Manchester University Press, 2017). See also Avijit Pathak, *Indian Modernity: Contradictions, Paradoxes and Possibilities* (New Delhi: Gyan Publishing, 1998).
2. Elsewhere, this is an instance of '*maya-lila*' (illusion of truth and false and play) underlined as a premise to understand the idea of performance. See Richard Schechner, *Performance Theory* (London: Routledge, 1988).
3. There is an idea of 'showing seeing' aimed at altering the scopic regime in W. J. T. Mitchell, 'Showing Seeing: A Critique of Visual Culture,' *Journal of Visual Culture* 1, no. 2 (2002): 165–181.
4. See John D. Niles, *Homo Narrans: The Poetics and Anthropology of Oral Literature* (Pennsylvania: University of Pennsylvania Press, 1999).
5. I am informed by a seminal reading of Renu by Sadan Jha, 'Visualising a Region: Phaniswarnath Renu and the Archive of the "Regional–Rural" in the 1950s,' *The Indian Economic and Social History Review* 49, no. 1 (2012): 1–35. Moreover, an interesting reading is in Kathryn Hansen, 'Renu's Regionalism: Language and Form', *Journal of Asian Studies* 40, no. 2 (1981): 273–294.
6. Unlike this scientific dictum, seeing is believing also connotes a continuity between hearing (stories in South Asia) and seeing the characters of the same (heard stories) appearing in the motion pictures. See Chidananda Dasgupta, *Seeing Is Believing: Selected Writings on Cinema* (Delhi: Penguin, 2008).

When There Was Nothing

Illustration artist: Sajal Roy, Dhaka, Bangladesh

3

Lullaby, Tales and Play in the Kindergarten

Tulsidas, a medieval poet who is accredited with one version of the epic, the Ramayana, wrote:

> *Bhaye prakat kripala, din dayala, kausalya hitkari, harshit mahtari, muniman hari, adbhut rup vichari*
> (Thus arose the lord, with mercy and compassion to the suffering, before a gladdened mother Kausalya; thus appeared the lord in the heart of sages, as they ruminated on his divine splendour; thus was the resplendence of the lord, his winsome eyes, dusky body, with four ornate hands)

It sounds extraordinary when it is sung with due devotion. But when you think of the words, the illustration they present and the emotions that unfold, it will all appear common. Which mother and the folks around a newborn baby would not feel the same way? Divinity or not, a newborn baby brings about the same jubilation. Sex and gender do not matter, until it is entered as a consideration.[1] It is entered only due to a social mathematics that anticipates all strange consequences so well in advance that even gods will be shell-shocked. Two levels of ordinariness instantly unfold. One is very biological, coupled with emotions, and the other is deeply social and coupled with another set of emotions. This ordinary feeling that is inclined to celebrate and does mathematical calculations at once is bizarre. In the midst of all this complexity around an infant that the adults create, there is a relation that unfolds. Arguably, it is in this relation that the ordinariness of humans survives. This could perhaps apply to princes and paupers, haves and have-nots, alike.

It may be your own infant or that of your elder or younger siblings. There may be a friend's child whom you love and like to spend time with, while also attending to errands. As a labour of love or for more,[2] as a slightly grown-up child or as a new adult who is yet to get caught in the rut of career and competition, we have had our brush with what is popularly known as babysitting. It has never been a walk in the park to attend to a baby's ordinary everyday requirements. From birth onwards, for a good number of months, the incessant wiping, cleaning and changing diapers could make parental life hectic. Just recall the runny vomit that comes from a baby's upset stomach or a baby who cries incessantly for the want of a simple burp after the feed. We may list many more such activities that make babysitting a proper chore and even drudgery for many parents. Commonly heard words such as babysitting and baby care connote professionalism of some sort, and in the same series, there comes day care and childcare, leading us to various industries associated with babies. I am sure that one day there will be further compartmentalisation, and experts such as nappy dryer, diaper changer, baby feeder, infant walker, bicycle trainer and so on will rule the world of babies—just like there are dog walkers and dog trainers! Parents do not want to waste their quality time doing baby chores. Every parent is into star parenting or aspires to it, spending time with babies without the drudgery of child-rearing. Washing soiled nappies or toilet training will soon not be a part of parenting. The service industry will make it easy. Yet one wonders, would there be night-care services for babies, like there are day cares? Many parents complain about having sleepless nights due to whiny babies. Some of those parents, disoriented due to lack of sleep and being underfed since babies leave little time, would vote for such a service sector. On the whole, we witnessed the clamour of discomfort among metropolitan middle-class parents in the absence of service providers (from informal service industry) during lockdown after the outbreak of the pandemic in India. The situation was more or less similar in other parts of the world too. In such a situation, some parents boasted about the renewed relationship that they began to foster with their babies in such a situation. Soon the boasting was replaced by whimpers and complaints. It is not easy to do parenting chores unless we step down from the new pedestal of parenthood. Failure to live in the ordinariness of relationships is owed to the capacity to purchase and consume services.

There is a meaning beyond the popular words about our relationship with babies. The meaning comes from what we do, just like, to be is to do. Beyond romantic illusions, dealing with a baby is an exasperating job. The two worlds, of adults and babies, seem to be in conflict. The baby's expectations are often misunderstood or not understood at all. For sure, babies cannot get the slightest hint of clinically clear adulthood and, as adults, we are too hasty to heed any expectation other than our own. We want babies to eat, play, sleep and be toilet-trained and we want them to do all these the way we deem fit. We expect them to wean when we want them weaned. We expect them to walk when we want them to walk. We expect them to talk when we want them to talk. One has heard parents lamenting, 'My baby is this old and has not got all its teeth! My baby has not started walking the way other babies of the same age do. My baby seems to be a slow learner; look at the baby of the lady next door.' It is mostly our expectations and wants that we plant on the babies. The infants react sharply, and so do toddlers. The biography of growing up becomes a tussle between those parenting and those being parented, the growing up and the grown-up. In this ominous tale, there is only one victim: the ordinary joy of undergoing what appears as drudgery. The aesthetics of ordinariness is swept under the mysterious carpet under which Harry Potter's magical broomstick cannot reach. If only a few of those lullabies or some of those queer activities we do in front of babies to regale them could acquire the aesthetics of ordinariness! Remember becoming a monkey because the baby liked monkey business. Recall the song of which you knew only the first line and yet you sang by adding your own words of woe and wisdom. Those songs made the baby experience the comfort and compassion in your parenting. You may laugh at such songs due to the strangeness of words, phrases, rhythm and melody, but those are the classic examples of the beauty of ordinariness.

Every child has its body clock, which we can only slightly rewind. The problem begins when we try to rewind it dramatically according to our convenience and our own timetable. A baby hints winsomely. A smile flutters across their faces when the hints are discerned promptly. Do you recall when your baby hinted to you about the need for a nap? The hint may be clear if you could read the face of the baby. Eyelids look heavy, lips move slowly and breathing becomes slightly tempered. At times, these hints are confused, for the baby may feel two different needs at once. The need to be fed as well as lulled to sleep might appear together. Excitement about an image or a toy or a running tap may occur right at the time the baby feels an urge to go to bed. How do we handle it? Mostly, we tend to pass the buck on fathoming a cantankerous baby. We want our partners to step in since we have failed. We do not merely fail to understand the baby. It is a more pathetic failure to stay ordinary with the baby and juggle a few ideas and attempts. If not this, that may work. If not that, yet another option may do. Even though we think we have tried, we have only tried to free ourselves from the guilt of not trying. We did not rejoice at the chores of attending to the baby. We judged our efforts towards these chores in terms of success and failure. We want to be successful in the chore of babysitting, somehow, and, hence, there is frustration. A baby crying and resisting your efforts is not part of the package that you thought you signed up for. You do not wish to handle a resistant baby; you only want a baby who can do exactly what suits your scheme of things. If we step aside from our judgemental scheme of things, we would be able to overcome our sense of pleasure, pain, success and failure. Only then can we see that a whiny baby is as sweet as a smiling one. A resistant baby is as disarming as a conforming one. In the end, when the baby has gone off to sleep, you sense the dawn of a paradise. The faint fragrance of the baby pervades the household. One rests in peace with that fragrance and looks at the twinkling face with utmost happiness. In parenting a baby, the parents get parented.

Many a time, singing a lullaby to a baby is a revealing moment. Parents get lulled while singing, but the baby stays awake. Yawns coming from the big mouths of the parents begin to look like a toy and the incoherent singing, a funny sound. The baby will obviously have a good time. The parents get frustrated because there are plans for the time after the baby goes to sleep. Such planned activity seems antithetical to a baby's mind, and babies make sure that plans collapse. No matter how perfectly you think out everything, you soon detect a snag. You sing the same lullaby more loudly, and it is funnier than before. Babies demand more improvisation than you can do. A new rhythm ought to be invented, some new wording must follow and a novel melody must overcome both, the singing and the listening. When it happens, ordinary creativity engenders mundane aesthetics. A work of art that cannot be made available for a curated exhibition is created. There is no chance of fruitful commerce for this art. It happens and dies away, graciously, without any apprehension for longevity. Singing a lullaby defies the formats of the act, the language of music and the notes of melody. It happens so simply that even the singer might forget it the next time he or she is trying to replicate it. It is exasperating that one sang it so well just yesterday, those words and hummed symphony. But one cannot repeat the same act a day later. Fine replication is an adult idea, which fails to work when one is dealing with a baby.

Putting aside the scheme of the adults, parenting brings about magical moments. Try and recall a precious moment that may have happened to even those who often fail to join in the baby's scheme. It is that moment when you fathomed the baby's urges correctly or, just by coincidence, you brought your baby to the bed when the baby actually wanted it. The bliss of a harmonious holism descends. It seems the two, the cared and the caring, have joined in a melodious orchestra. Effortlessly, a rhyme occurs on the lips, following a note spontaneously reverberating in the mind. The hum and the lull seamlessly join in the delicate hem of relationship that turns vivid in such a moment. This is so ordinary and yet such an aesthetic experience.

I recall such moments, and so do my fellow parents. How does a child feel when she defeats her father? Every child desires to vanquish the father and mother figure. It is an ordinary aspiration, yet a much needed one. The joy of pushing around a visibly stronger-bodied man who is also a caring father is instrumental to the child's psychic experience. It is, however, not the same as the Oedipus complex. There was too much sexuality in the story of Oedipus. A child's ordinary aspiration to playfully vanquish an equally playful father is irrespective of the mother figure or any feminine figure. There is an experience of the aesthetics of paradox in it. A child feels more vulnerable when a visibly less vulnerable person called father or mother is always upright, tight and a little too bright. A goofy father or a perplexed mother, though visibly trying hard to be steadfast, adds psychological strength to children. More often, parents pretend to be goofy so the children can derive fun and pleasure.

I have seen some ordinary and, hence, important fathers, and I have heard their accounts.[3] They play each part of their role as father fully well. They discipline without punishing, control without constraining and set free without losing touch with the child. They maintain non-intrusive contact. They are fathers who turn visibly child-like while joining in the children's games. Just imagine the feeling of a child about something like this: my father or mother, rock-solid support, is a vulnerable human like me. This is the paradox that a child longs for, which keeps the father's human value alive too. After all, fathers are vulnerable humans too. They too have weaknesses, failures and ordinary natures. They need not do everything they preach. The fallibility of fathers maintains ordinary humanness. Or have the fathers decided to give up on their humanness? If so, they should be really doing all those things they promise to quit, and yet they continue, though stealthily. But, as we see, the fathers promise and fail to keep the promise, like ordinary humans. Many of us include our children's wishes in our new year resolutions, and we blissfully ignore many of them throughout the year. It is one thing to promise, another to keep those promises. Fathers and mothers have not fulfilled all those promises, and they cannot since they are essentially human. They will falter. If they are able to come to terms with their humanity, they will admit to their children that they have faltered. The children will then acquire the insight that to err is human! It is equally human to be rock solid, unfazed and even fazed.

Behold the children playing with their parents, mother or father or both. Though, rarely both parents are around to play with the children, thanks to the metropolitan lives and expectations and aspirations in double-income families. Had they been around, the day-care industry would not have thrived. But when they are, or even when either of the parents is, the children squeal in abounding joy. When a parent loses in a game, children start exhibiting a qualitatively superior kind of confidence, strength and love. When a defeated parent admits failure, the children inherit the gifts of grace, humility and affection.

I am very poor at playing proper games with my children. I never played when I was a kid, or if I did, even as a child, I always lost in most games that children of my age in my time and location played. This makes it more or less natural for me to continue to lose in the games that children play these days. I can invite empathy from you for what I experience as a parent. I feel my children give me time to relive my life that is otherwise likely to get lost. It is due to the children around that I can sing some of the songs that I ceased to sing when I grew up. The irritating habit of making music with all kinds of oral expressions would be a lost art if I did not have this clapping and cheering at my strangely produced live music. I do not know how to play the harmonica. We have two harmonicas at home. My daughter watches and hears me playing the harmonica though she has no idea or interest in the notes of music. A random session on the harmonica triggers immense joy and playfulness too. Of course, learning the notes is important, and playing by following the rules of the game is useful. Not knowing them, however, should not stop one from playing the instruments. At worst, one would produce cacophony. Children, unlike their adult partners, the parents, do not see a sharp distinction between cacophony and symphony. The euphonic value is the most important thing, to begin with. Parents who have the habit of enjoying the ordinariness, the humanness, will join in the pursuit of euphonic value—the sound of the music! The incidental connection with the famous 1965 Hollywood film *The Sound of Music* is duly suggestive. With children, we should be experimental and playful rather than perfect and pokerfaced. The children can arrive at the fine distinctions of the musical notes later, in another genre of playing on the musical instruments. But for parents and children to remain one, as humans, with human vulnerability, it is necessary for them to fail equally, rise together and fall gracefully and humbly. Losing with these children brings about a feeling of parental bliss, not sophistication, discipline, punishment or control. A mother feels motherly by getting defeated in a game with her son; a father feels more fatherly by sportily losing in a game with his daughter.

So, where is the Oedipus complex in it?[4] I seriously think it was the personal problems of the psychoanalyst that got projected in the reading of the Oedipus behaviour. What is the guarantee that

Dr Freud did not attribute his own childhood experience to the mythical figure known as Oedipus? Experts will contest or concur with it, and Freudian psychoanalysts, if any are still left, will hate such a proposition. Who will dismiss the scientificity of clinical psychoanalysis, whatever is left? In this regard, some psychoanalysts in South Asia could be a few exceptions.[5] They perceived the cultural and intellectual challenges to the European model of psychoanalysis. Nonetheless, let us forget about the professional field of psychoanalysis and return to another mythical instance. Many of us have heard the basic story. The primeval parents, Shiva and Parvati, decided to test their children, Ganesha and Kartikeya. The divine parents thought that their divine children have acquired sufficient skills and now it should be seen as to who does what with those skills. The parents set them free, asking them to go around the world and come back. Kartikeya took his peacock and set out on the voyage, while Ganesha mulled it over in the freedom that his parents had granted. He looked around and at his accompanying mount, the mouse, and started his journey almost at snail's pace. In little time, he took a round of his parents and declared the job done. He reported to his parents that he has seen the world since his world is his parents. Kartikeya returned too with the exciting details of the world that he had witnessed. Two different schemes of profundity, according to two different ways of seeing, emerged. Kartikeya's seeing the world meant one way of coming of age, while Ganesha's meant another. The parents assured them both of their respective accomplishment. Let us leave scope for interpretation. You decide which one to prefer as a proper model of coming of age—Ganesha's model or Kartikeya's. For the parents of the two children, both stood equally well. At times, it is conducive not to adopt a rigid model from mythology. However, one can elicit broadness, flexibility and equanimity. The ordinariness of parenting perhaps enables one to suspend heavy-hearted comparisons and conclusions about children. We anticipate them to be as immaculate as an imagined idea of adulthood popularised by various advertisements and popular soaps. Neither is adulthood so perfect nor can childhood be. So, be that as it may!

Notes

1. On this note, one cannot resist recalling a nuanced anthropological account by Leela Dube, who had brought into consideration the gendered experience of growing up in a Hindu household with reference to her biography. Anthropology and biography seamlessly met and opened new horizons of exploration in kinship and gender studies in India in Leela Dube, *Anthropological Explorations in Gender: Intersecting Fields* (New Delhi: SAGE, 2001).
2. This may remind some of us of a more interesting reasoning in an all-time relevant masterpiece by Gillian Rose that blended personal experiences, memoir and philosophy to make sense of the vulnerability of love, to the extent that an unsettling wisdom prevailed: to live, to love, is to fail. See Gillian Rose, *Love's Work* (New York: New York Review Books, 2011).
3. A theoretical analysis of this is available in J. Bowlby, *A Secure Base: Clinical Applications of Attachment Theory* (London: Routledge, 1988).
   . For a very technical data research in Britain, devoid of human feelings, see Mai Stafford, Diana L. Kuh, Catharine R. Gale, Gita Mishra, and Marcus Richards, 'Parent–Child Relationships and Offspring's Positive Mental Wellbeing from Adolescence to Early Older Age,' *The Journal of Positive Psychology* 11, no. 3 (2016): 326–337.
4. In this regard, an intervention by Girindrasekhar Bose, the pioneer of psychoanalysis in India, is worth revisiting. See Anup Dhar, 'Girindrasekhar Bose and the History of Psychoanalysis in India,' *Indian Journal of History of Science* 53, no. 4 (2018): 198–204.
5. It is worth pondering upon some of the interesting readings in an unusual collection of essays in Manasi Kumar, Anup Dhar, and Anurag Mishra, eds., *Psychoanalysis from the Indian Terroir: Emerging Themes in Culture, Family, and Childhood* (London: Lexington Books, 2018).

4

Anger, Love and Intersections: A Scheme of Ordinary Emotions

A poet named Malik Muhammad Jayasi, during the time of the emperor Sher Shah in India, exquisitely summed up a debate in his epic poem *Padmavat*:

Prem-ghaw-dukh jan na koi; jahi laagai janai pai soi[1]
(Only those who experience love, suffering and pathos know how it feels).

There is no alternative to this simple wisdom and, hence, excluding one emotion for another is merely intellectual hogwash. Such inclusions and exclusions are done by us; we may have preferences for select emotions only for our intellectual satisfaction. Ordinarily, emotions unfold without any such scheme. Only they know, as Jayasi said, who live through them. Those who only think of emotions can seldom fathom the depth and breadth of emotions.[2]

Let us recall a classical cinematic work. Satyajit Ray's Apu trilogy, based on Bibhutibhushan Bandyopadhyay's novels, is a modern epic in world cinema; we discover so many new facets every time we watch it. The second film, titled *Aparajito* (Invincible, 1956), in the trilogy encapsulates the ordinary arrangement of our emotions. The child named Apu lives in a village with his widowed mother. It is a spartan life with terribly limited resources, yet the boy manages to excel in his studies at the village school. Through his schooling, the child brings a semblance of joy to the life of his struggling mother. But the problem arises when Apu aspires to go to Calcutta (Kolkata) for further studies in college. He seeks to persuade his mother. This is not so easy due to the dearth of monetary support as well as his mother's longing to keep him by her side. In fact, it turns out that the mother's emotional longing for the son was far more important. She did not want to let him go, but she has to give in to Apu's persistent pleas. Heavy-hearted and with a glint of tears in her eyes, the mother bids adieu. The son discovers a whole new world of friendship, struggle and aspiration in Calcutta. The boy holds the tiny dream of a self-sufficient tomorrow close to his heart. He comes back home only during the vacation in college. In the first few visits home, he has a lot to narrate to his mother, who could see the excitement of the city in her son's eyes by just listening to him. She wants a reaffirmation every time Apu comes home that she is still of some significance to him. Gradually, as it is with growing boys, Apu did not have much to relate to his mother. Coming home becomes nothing more than a perfunctorily performed duty. Once when Apu is still in Calcutta studying in college, he receives a message informing him about his mother's serious illness. He takes the first train back home, runs across the field from the railway station to the house and, as soon as he enters the house, starts calling out for his mother: 'Ma, Ma!' He does not find his mother anywhere inside or outside the house! Then his maternal uncle appears, who breaks the news to Apu that his mother is no more! Apu's world comes crashing down, and he slumps to the ground crying out for his mother. The beholders feel the affect the scene produces, but this is not where it ends. Apu's veritably frozen body on the earth and crescendo of crying rising to the sky receives a compassionate one-liner from the uncle: 'Don't cry, this is what happens to everyone in the world.' The film ends with Apu continuing his meaningful crying.

The social world may ask you not to cry, and learned priests or wise relatives may try to help you out of this particular emotion that makes you cry. But you do not stop crying, and you better not. You never cease to long for your loved one, feel possessive of them and feel reluctant to let them go away, temporarily or permanently. We must cry our heart out when we are pained. Moreover, we must ignore all the terrible dictums that make us shy about crying, including the one that says 'boys don't cry' or even an advanced one, 'big boys don't cry'. I vividly remember my uncles and aunts telling me, as well as my father, on the death of my mother: don't cry! We both took turns to go to the washroom and sit there for a while, crying. I used to rush to desolate places where I could be myself and cry as hoarsely as possible. A space to myself—where I can say clearly that I am in pain—is so important. In the same breath, let us also admit that overcoming melancholia, taking it in stride and getting on with life are equally ordinary outcomes. In the same way that we are ordinarily overcome by melancholia, we ordinarily overcome it too. So we let it all unfold, so long as we are ordinary.

In human history, many changes are reflected, good and bad. They are changes in the nature and scope of culture and society. Often textbooks inform us about the conquest and decline of empires and kingdoms. Spectacular changes have been chronicled and documented. In the midst of the variety of changes, the basic ordinary core of human existence was impacted too. We delegitimised some of our human attributes, our emotions. Somehow, we have created an unreasonable hierarchy of emotions. Someone did it at some point of time. It kept changing in the history of human emotions. Yet a few basics became too solid to be challenged and, hence, we seem to be helpless about it. We just cannot appreciate emotions that spontaneously appear in our everyday life. For example, we tell each other that anger is bad and happiness is good. Love is good and hatred is bad. Vice is to be abandoned or, rather, symbolically killed. Virtue is celebrated, almost at any cost. This is kind of untoward in human sociocultural history. Emotion can seldom endure purity, just like value (vice or virtue) is always in flux. Love is susceptible to doubts, and so is hatred. Both can have almost an uncanny romance, reminiscent of the elegance of mingling darkness and light. An illustrious trope of ordinary emotions emerges from all this criss-crossing. Ironically, we are skilled and socialised enough to obscure our vision of this trope of intersecting emotions. The trope of emotions in which tragedy and romance unfolded at once is no longer valued except in the genres of expressions such as theatre, literature, cinema and performance art. The industries of advertisement and consumer services have dented our ordinary sense to such an extent that we think of emotions in neat binaries—either love or hatred, for example. We are more interested in giving credit to one emotion over the other. We are skilled at comparing and contrasting to find out which one has better utilitarian value. Admitting love over hatred serves a better chance to gain prestige, profit and profundity.

One can hear another saying, 'I hate you'. It is, however, difficult to hear someone saying, 'I love hatred as much as I love the emotion of love'. We are evidently not honest about our emotions. In the lack of emotional truthfulness, we seldom want to imply that we are likely to get carried away. Instead, the emotions counted as superior in a time and space by a secular or religious authority have become our valued emotions.

It is like university academics in America or even in some parts of Europe who have declared, mostly unofficially, that networking is a more important requisite than critical intellectual dialogue. It is beginning to show among the university academics across South Asia too. Networking, a kind of attempt at forging professional relationships known as collaborations, thrives on the supremacy of select emotions. No, this is not at all about the adage 'Love thy neighbour'. This is not love without explicit or implicit objectives, plans and purposes. The utilitarian instrumentality of networking makes it distinguishable from any holy adage. This is not love either. An emotion like love cannot be sustained by pretence for long. This is purely for business. Take yet another example from academic practices. Every researcher goes to the field for research, asking questions and observing the respondents. It is not that the researcher does not lose patience, but it is never to be shown. It is not that the researcher does not feel exasperated at the answers given by the people in the field research, but it is never to be revealed. It is not that the researcher does not feel hungry, frustrated, tired and so on. It is not that the researcher does not feel like telling the people in the field research, 'You suck!' But it must not be said. Such a wonderful camouflaged emotional self of the scholar in the making! One wonders whether they are training to be truthful scholars or emotional thugs. Why do we do such a thing? We perform 'fake emotions' without qualms, in the university as well as in our everyday life. At least in this regard, scholars, experts and lay people are the same. We behave like emotional thugs or emotional liars. Do we consciously decide to be split personalities, feeling one emotion while expressing another? We selectively express our emotions. Each teacher does it, and so does each student. Each husband does it, and so does each wife. If they do not, all hell breaks loose. If one truthfully expresses emotions, one is a deviant in the book of social norms, an outlaw according to the law book, an eccentric according to the definition of civility and abnormal according to the so-called book of scientific definitions of normal behaviour. One cannot freely emote, even though one is living in times inundated with emoticons on the phones!

Getting angry is surely an anathema. You can be anything but angry. Speaking sarcastically is not right. If you turn dispassionate and irreverent, that is it. Get ready to be charged, socially and legally too. Even if you decide to be indifferent, you are held culpable for many wrongs around you. All your teachers, in school and colleges, from home to coaching centres, teach you about the harms of being emotional. The education industry seems to be committed to debilitate our freedom to be emotional. Be it emotional intelligence or emotional foolishness, we are guided by the notions perpetuated by teachers, counsellors and therapists. When you fall in love, almost like love at first sight, your near and dear ones begin to tell you about the parallels between foolishness and emotions. You are told that the heart is stupid and the mind is to be heeded.[3] Curiously enough, your own body is divided into these two regions, as though there is no dialogue between the throbbing heart and thinking mind. It seems as if the mind always says the right thing and the heart always means something hazardous. If this is the scene, then demonising selected emotions is much easier than said. Anger is very easily cast in the same light as evil and other sinful feelings. Love and lust are meticulously separated from each other, causing a great deal of consternation. Many generations of humanity suffered this socially constructed matrix of emotions. Perhaps this is not true for the whole of humanity. Whether we liked it or not, our parents did not shy away from telling us the truth, and it was all emotional. They expressed their anger, without an iota of realisation that anger is usually accompanied by love. It is difficult to extricate parental anger from their love. They expressed compassion, without an iota of realisation that compassion is immediately in company of pity. It is difficult to detect where parental compassion becomes their pity.

Emotions are dramatic and, hence, they occur in close subsequence, perhaps too rapidly. This is what Krishna told Arjun in the battlefield of Kurukshetra in the Mahabharata. Emotion is never monochromatic.

It appears with variegated colours, and one of the colours, or many, could be a counter-emotion of the emotion that is being articulated by the person who feels it. The unsaid emotion is as important as the said emotion. The non-verbalised emotion should not be ruled out just because one has not taken the pain of looking at it. Hence, Krishna commands Arjun to see something more attached to his emotion of pain at the thought of shooting arrows at his kith and kin. Arjun begins to see that his pain is accompanied by the urge to seek justice and to avenge the humiliation and injustice, and he thus embarks on the mission. Some of us, devout and unreasonable, thought that it was all because Krishna showed his cosmic, larger-than-life image to Arjun. The Samkhya philosophy, one of the six orthodox philosophical traditions in ancient India (which was hardly the India of today), emphasises the reason and rationality of Krishna working on Arjun's mind. Yet, we simply accept the idea that Krishna revealed his cosmic form and, therefore, Arjun decided to abide by the command of the divine charioteer. Never mind that the truth is that the whole of the Bhagwad Gita is a treatise on the validity of human emotions, and a reasonable Hindu or, for that matter, non-Hindus interested in understanding the deeper meanings should read the Gita taking the emotions into account. Then, eventually we should ask ourselves, do we really understand what emotions mean according to the Gita? This need not be answered immediately. What is a question if it is answered then and there? There is a need to revisit the Gita umpteen times before one decides to answer the question, for a treatise on emotions is as complicated and enchanting as are emotions.

There is another way of showing the legitimacy of emotions of all kinds. The civilisational history of ancient South Asia presents another way of thinking about the significance of all human emotions, which could curtail our common sense against select emotions. A sage named Bharat is believed to have written a treatise called the *Natyashastra* in ancient times (1st century BCE to 3rd century BCE).[4] Scholars of performance studies often study this treatise. However, it is broadly a theoretical work on the performance of emotions, *a rasawali* or a compendium of *rasa*s. In Bharat's *rasawali*, emotions are paramount in a society based on caste or varna hierarchy. This is, however, not to be mistaken as the absence of relation between caste and emotions. There are other scholars who may prefer to hyper-emphasise the caste hierarchy in Natyashastra too. Needless to say, we encounter caste-based emotional reactions aplenty in everyday life too. But the centrality of emotions in Natyashastra does not let the sense of hierarchy prevail. Bharat listed eight rasas, and Abhinavgupt added a ninth one. They are equally important for the enactment of *bhawa*s (enactment and expression of emotion). A character could play out a combination of the most suitable emotions according to a situation or the requirements of a character/role. The listing and description of the fine qualities of emotions enable us to interpretatively think—a hero, like an antihero, could take any combination of emotions. The judgement was not based on what emotions one chose but instead on how one performed a chosen combination of emotions. How deeply one looked angry was more important than the legitimacy of the anger. How convincingly lovable one could be was more important than the legitimacy of the love. If one had to feel disgusted, it was important to not mince words in expressing disgust. The hero could be a hero without killing the importance of an antihero in this scheme. Unlike our socially constructed hierarchy of emotions, in Natyashastra, no emotion is inferior nor is there any superior emotion. All are equally relevant. Love cannot express hatred, and anger cannot be represented in absentia. This meant that the character of Ram is as exciting and imaginative as that of Ravana. Even though the end shows the conquest of Ravana by the *Maryadapurushottam* (the embodiment of righteousness) Ram, we never discredited the emotional characterisation of Ravana. As the audience of the tales of the Ramayana, we also fell in love with the character of Hanuman, the monkey who seems wiser than most evolved men, against Darwin's theory. We only followed the ordinary trope of emotions when we watched Ramlila or heard *Ramkatha*s, the traditional performances that narrate episodes from the Ramayana. Hence, the spectacle of Dussera, in which we burn the effigies of Ravana and his Lanka team, seemed a little ridiculous to us even though we rejoiced in the fanfare. We always asked whether we can ever discredit the emotions of the antiheroes!

If a Ram's anger is fair, so is that of a Ravana. After all, a brother has a legitimate reason to be angry at his sister Surpanakha's nose being chopped off. Does not every brother feel obliged to protect his sister? If that sounds too patriarchal to your 'informed ears', let us reframe it. Siblings feel protective about each other. The occasion of Raksha Bandhan on every *purnima* (full moon night) of the month of *Sawan* (roughly August) playfully reminds them about the emotional obligations between siblings. If there is no such festive occasion, every now and then siblings playfully learn about caring for each other in everyday life. So, Ravana's anger is equally legitimate. Besides, it is part of a cultural common sense among Maithili-speaking folks versed in their folklore. Hence, a modern Maithili litterateur Hari Mohan Jha created a folksy character called Khattar Kaka in the 1940s, who asked the same questions as in the folk songs: How is Ram a maryadapurushottam if he doubted and banished his wife because others complained?[5] No emotion is innocent. No one is free from accusations. Yet every character in mythology or real life seems to take up select emotions.

So, it was fine when Vijay decided to be an angry man in most films starring Amitabh Bachchan (which included hits like *Zanjeer, Deewar* and even *Shakti*). We all identified with this angry young man and sought to see some angry young women too. We happily got to see both genders essaying the emotion of anger in a duly historical framework. It was fine to be angry when we were disillusioned with the promises made in a newly independent India. Much before that, we wanted to be angry and blast bombs, like Bhagat Singh did to make 'the deaf' hear us.[6] Bhagat Singh famously called the unheeding British the deaf who needed an explosive argument in order to hear a point. We tried out the same emotional strategy when our own rulers failed us. We began to mobilise our energy for a new demand. We wanted *azadi*, freedom from all bondages. Then we were declared outlawed by the State. Such is the permission to be selectively emotional. You can be emotionally nationalist, but you cannot be emotionally patriotic. You cannot be emotionally constitutionalist. You cannot be in love so much that you begin to seek freedom. So, to be emotional is to be ordinarily free, in spite of the regulating agencies putting up prohibitions.

Though the regimes of power guard against emotions, the realm of poetry offers a candid picture. Rahim Khan-e-Khana, the poet during the time of the Mughal emperor Akbar, said prophetically:

Rahiman dhaga prem ka / mat todo chatkay / tute pe phir na jure / jure ganth pari jaye[7] (Rahim, the thread of love shall not break; once broken *and joined*, knots appear in the thread).

Indeed, this was the idea of sublime love without knots. Our interpersonal love relationships are mostly knotty, in some way or other, with layered emotions. Layers of emotions in interpersonal love carry confusion as well as clarity. Even though it is knotty, folks manage to carry out relationships with confidence and clarity. The poetic imagination of Rahim allowed him to take note of emotional intrigue so deeply that he also wrote about the passage through which devotees and god (or goddess, as you may please) cannot pass together. For a verse like this, Rahim Khan-e-Khana was also called Rahim Das, joining the league of the medieval *Bhakt* (devotional) poets. The verse says,

Rahiman gali hai sankri / dujo na thahrahin / apu ahai to hari nahi / Hari to apun naahi[8]
(The alley is too narrow to take both, god and devotee; either of the two can pass).

The poet who spoke Sanskrit, Persian, Arabic and Braj with equal ease underlined the need for the sacrifice of the devotee's ego to cross the alley with god. Such is the lightness of emotions, knotty in the first instance and an obstacle in another if loaded with ego. Emotions can make one ambivalent, of this world or of that. It is through such ambivalence that one can arrive at Rahim's poetic ideal. The ideal of sublimity would be far-fetched if one does not see through emotions. To do so, one has to be free from regimes of censorship.

It is in such a scenario that we return to the freedom to be emotional. This is very much in the register of the ordinary. We are ordinarily like this, emotional and truthfully emotional. Emotionally, and ordinarily, we do not follow the hierarchy of emotions while enacting them. Only in the vaunted preaching about values and valuables do we succumb to a variety of hierarchy of emotions, manufactured and circulated by various forces. In performance, thankfully, there is little choice than to get carried away in enactment of emotions. More often than not, in hindsight we realise that we can hate as passionately as we can love. Hatred is not inferior to love in our scheme of performance in everyday life. An ordinary person in everyday life does not selectively perform emotions. I recall someone deeply immersed in the experience of pathos telling me, 'You will not understand since you are not wet!' Here, wetness alluded to immersion in emotion, much akin to what Rahim, the prophetic poet, suggests earlier. Wetness cannot be intellectually fathomed despite utmost empathy. Emotions are like that wetness, felt and performed, without any external director's mediation. Or is that too much wishful thinking? Let us hope that it is not.

Notes

1. See, for the full poem, Malik Muhammad Jayasi, 'Padmavat,' Hindi Kavita, accessed 20 December 2020, https://www.hindi-kavita.com/HindiPadmavatJayasi1.php.
2. While this is a poetic conclusion, for what could be an intellectual qua philosophical conclusion, one can take a quick glance through an encyclopaedia entry, *Stanford Encyclopedia of Philosophy*, s.v. 'Emotion,' accessed 20 December 2020, https://plato.stanford.edu/entries/emotion/. Just like one need not be humorous while speaking of humour, it seems one need not be emotional while speaking of emotions. About humour, this was a starting point for Eagleton. See Terry Eagleton, *Humour* (New Haven and London: Yale University Press, 2019).
3. On this note, one can recall the holistic growth that the philosopher J. J. Rousseau envisaged for his character Emily who, in the company of Sophia, realises the unison of heart and mind. See J. J. Rousseau, *Emilius or a Treatise of Education* (Edinburgh: J Dickson and C Elliot, 1763), accessed 20 December 2020, https://www.google.co.in/books/edition/%C3%89milius_Or_A_Treatise_on_Education/PglXAAAAYAAJ?hl=en&gbpv=0.
4. There are various translations of the text. I am referring to Bharat Muni, *Natya Shastra*, trans. Manomohan Ghosh (Calcutta: Asiatic Society of Bengal, 1951), accessed 20 December 2020, https://archive.org/details/

NatyaShastra/natya_shastra_translation_volume_1_-_bharat_muni/page/n15/mode/2up.
5. See Hari Mohan Jha, *Khattar Kaka* (Hindi) (Delhi: Rajkamal Prakashan, 1971); and Hari Mohan Jha, *Khattar Kaka'k Tarang* (Maithili) (Patna: Shekhar Prakashan, 2011).
6. For more along this line, see S. Irfan Habib, *To Make the Deaf Hear: Ideology and Programme of Bhagat Singh and His Comrades* (Delhi: Three Essays Collective, 2010) and Chaman Lal, *Understanding Bhagat Singh* (Delhi: Aakar Books, 2013).
7. See, for more, 'रहीम के दोहे | हम हिन्दी भाषी' [Dohas of Rahim], accessed 28 January 2021, hindibhashi.com.
8. See 'रहीम के दोहे (भाग 2)' [Dohas of Rahim part 2], accessed 28 January 2021, https://hindibhashi.com/हिन्दी-साहित्य/कविगण/रहीम-के-दोहे-भाग-2/.

5

Lotus, Mud and Fear of a Sex Beast

Bunty is the bewildered child protagonist of a Hindi novel titled *Apka Bunty*, penned by the famous novelist Mannu Bhandari. The boy grows up with many complexes in a tension-ridden family with separated parents. Think of any other child in the neighbourhood, whom you could name anything, including Bunty as per your convenience. Such an imagined or real child, just like Bunty, happens to get a glimpse of his naked parents one night. The world turns topsy-turvy, every passer-by seems naked and the child is too aghast to deal with it. In the child's imagination, nakedness begins to be integrally associated with something sinister from then on. So is sexual intimacy, and that too of your own parents. Everyone was a child with more or less similar encounters, and everyone may have an iota of similar tribulations.

We have killed the ordinariness of sexual union of bodies by adding such spectacles to it that even partial nakedness can give nightmares to kids. This should not be taken as advocacy to indulge in private sexual acts in front of the children. It is actually about informal, family-based enculturation on the issues of love, intimacy and even sex. This is necessary because many of our children grow up interpreting even a simple exchange of kisses as a potential cause of pregnancy. We have seen this in many films as well: an adolescent asking another one, 'Won't I get pregnant if I kiss?' Hence, the idea of controlling such a dangerous union dawns upon us. The most infantile form of control is repression until desires violently erupt like a volcano, creating utter helplessness in adolescence. Across civilisations, this is heard. It reverberates as a collective anxiety across the timeline. Modern or otherwise, there is this fear of a horse without a lead! Body without bodice! Desire without morals!

Hence, in some form or other, this story is recapitulated. A chariot needs horses, which could have abounding energy, and a charioteer who can control and give direction to the horses. Blinders and horse tack are put on the horses so that they cannot see sideways. This is to ensure that they look straight ahead and focus only on the short distance immediately before their eyes. There is a fly mask or fly cap too, which covers the muzzle and ears to protect them from intruding flies. In the name of protection, though, it is ensured that the horse's senses are under control. There are also horseshoes to protect the hoof of the horse from grime on inhospitable terrain. We know why we want this protection—so that the horse obeys the charioteer's command without any resistance. There could be occasional resistance, feeble or strong, that the charioteer needs to tackle. After all, how can one ensure a complete erasure of possibility? Also, some horses are what are called *adiyal ghoda* in Hindi or the adamant type. So, the job of the charioteer is pretty challenging despite all the normative technical arrangements to ensure that the horse obeys commands. Hence, the charioteer is supposed to be the zenith of wisdom, master of the senses, able to stay detached and sincerely committed and so on, despite the fact that one runs out of phrases to describe a do-gooder. The charioteer is the embodiment of his or her own set of fallibilities for which there are invisible blinders, caps and shoes for protection. Anything used for protection is actually serving a double purpose, the other one being control.

Humans have thought for ages that the horses and charioteer both are part of human personality. Therefore, the job is tougher. If not protected and controlled, humans would be inclined to perversion.[1] In the historical epoch that was the dawn of modern industrialisation, old norms gave way to new ones. Everything that seemed easy and normal yesterday became spurious, disturbing and almost pathological. Human drives and instincts also slipped under the scanner of the morality-mongers. Ordinary folks began to doubt their ordinary ways of leading lives. The simple imagery of horse and charioteer was not helpful. The old wisdom did not seem to effectively protect and control. Everyone craved a new set of wise advisers. Then came a doctor named Sigmund Freud,[2] followed by many and not followed at all too. The doctor pinpointed the real stuff—the pulse of the people vis-à-vis the sexual core of humans. Any and every problem of modern life took him a notch deeper into the dark chamber of human secrets. With the decline of old authorities, the newly found authority of the doctors gained prominence. It was realised, slowly and steadily, that humans are sex beasts to be properly guided lest they turn into invincible sex monsters. This realisation was not for reviving the old morals that coerced people into accepting old norms. The old morals ennobled the values that led to imagining the private (sexual) and public (asexual) as two distinct domains. It was not ordinarily, or usually, like this in reality. But the figment of imagination under the regime of old morals concealed the ordinariness of humans in which private and public, home and world, personal and social, individual and collective coalesced. The domain of folklore and oral traditions is a testimonial to the way undivided domains of experience existed for the ordinary folks. But the urbane world had its own prophets who disregarded the traditions of the ordinary as spurious and rife with superstitions.[3] Instead, the realisation that humans may turn into sex monsters led to new formulations, new doctors, novel authorities and mechanisms of control. The new doctors sought to bring about an understanding of the beast, to begin with, and then the method 'to tame the shrew', so to say. One does not need to be well versed in Shakespearean drama. The drama had also attracted feminist scholarship to critically reflect on the constitution of femininity vis-à-vis subduement and demureness! One could see it unfolding in ordinary lives, offstage, every day.[4] The idea was to find a new way of protecting and controlling horses and charioteers. The same old anxiety, recast into the language of new times, sought for new solutions and ended up with the perpetration of more anxiety.

Away from the anxiety-driven way of seeing desirous humans, there were some who longed to fathom the aesthetics of human will, wish and wonder. Many such approaches ought to be recalled. One of them explicitly dealt with the crisis. A paradigm of psychoanalysis propounded by Sri Aurobindo is worth a mention. The axiom was: you cannot understand the lotus by analysing mud! With this axiom, one begins to formulate new questions: which one is the real self of humans, the mud or the lotus? Should we look at the lotus and the mud separately or together? Many such questions exist that could lead us to add more dimensions to human personality than what appears in the anxiety-driven approaches. Dr Freud had already said that he could not find anything worthwhile in the vast experiences of the mystics. For him, such experiences are to do with the infantile state, where feelings were repressed. Unfortunately, from this viewpoint, someone like Ramakrishna Paramhamsa was only a case with 'some' repression. Against this, there comes a way of thinking and seeing that allows one to celebrate Paramhamsa as an exemplary model of experiential freedom. It summons course correction in psychoanalysis and in our prevalent way of seeing. Hence, it is imperative to remember what Sri Aurobindo said in his discussion on integral yoga:

> The psychoanalysts look from down up and explain the higher lights by the lower obscurities; but the foundation of these things is above and not below.... The superconscient, not the subconscient, is the true foundation of things. The significance of the lotus is not to be found by analyzing the secrets of the mud from which it grows here; its secret is to be found in the heavenly archetype of the lotus that blooms for ever in the Light above ... you must know the whole before you can know the part and the highest before you can truly understand the lowest.[5]

There are many ways of making sense of the aesthetic profundity of the lotus. The spiritual seers showed us the relation between the cosmos, soul, *vidya* (knowledge) and Brahma through the lotus. One can be a little ordinary in the way one sees the interplay of lotus and the mud, infinite 'other-world' and finite 'this-world', divine spiritualism and mundane, everyday life.[6] Perhaps, that is when each petal of the lotus starts blossoming with meanings. Then the lotus is in various parts, integrated as a whole and yet suggesting meaningful fractions. We can see further that there would not be the lotus without the mud, though there could be mud without the lotus. Such is the power of the omnipresent mud. Though the cosmic lotus is equally omnipresent, it can become invisible if one does not know how to see it. It is the omnipresent mud, seldom out of sight. Mud can be seen with the best or worst way of seeing. Whether you see like Freud or Sri Aurobindo, there is always mud around. It is another thing that the doctor will spend all his life analysing the mud and yet would fail to get at the lotus in the centre. One can see the omnipresence of the mud as a source for the blooming and blossoming of the lotus. The seemingly contrasting background of mud adds more significance to the lotus, and the presence of the lotus renders the mud into something more than merely 'muddy mud'. The material beauty of mud is reflected in the nonmaterial significance it holds. This is almost like each element in chemistry had more significance in alchemy. Chemistry reduced, for example, carbon into one element with set characteristics. Alchemy maintained the mysterious (or miraculous, as they believed) possibility of the same element. Alchemy was not obsessed with order and chaos or rational procedures that could be replicated. It was primarily inclined towards romancing with the elements of nature and exploring the extra-material significance of the matter. Without qualms, alchemy presented a mix of metaphysics and science. Even if there is apparent metaphysics behind chemistry, it is strategically muted, so that we can believe in the supremacy of science over proto-science or pre-science.

Therefore, Paramhamsa is more than a doctor's diagnosis.[7] Any 'patient', in the same vein, is more than all the reports of diagnosis put together. Any social deviant is indeed more than the label attached to him or her. Any man or woman reduced into one identification or a set of identities is a little more than what the whole world says. But doctors will not admit this since there is no way you can call a person a patient as soon as you admit this. Paramhamsa reveals this through his ordinary acts in his biography. It may have been a mystic's extraordinary vision. Paramhamsa would enact everything to make them ordinary. The visions, attachment with the goddess Kali, love and devotion and mundane activities of caring, attending to and feeding the goddess would appear as though they were effortless actions in a social life. This is such an arresting magic of mundanity soaked in emotions. In the dead of night, Paramhamsa would hear the goddess running across the alleys naughtily, like a young girl, casting shadows in the moonlight. He, the seeker, would run after the dark silhouette of the goddess, as though a child after the mother. The ecstasy of meeting and the melancholy of separation unfolded with the very simple act of feeding a cat. Considering that everything around, from temple to the cremation ground, was fused with the divine energy, this was very much a place to forge a relationship with the cat. Feeding the cat and chitchatting as though it were more than a mere feline companion discloses the devotee's compassionately broad outlook. There are tales about Paramhamsa's compassion for cats and monkeys and that he used instances and imageries of these animals in his discourses.

The social order could not take the seemingly insane tendencies of a seeker. Since Paramhamsa was refusing to follow the conventions, defying the markers of identity such as sacred thread, he seemed to be a threat to the logic of order, control and protection. The truth is that he was simply an ordinary lover, a devotee who longed to diminish the separation between himself and the divine.

Let us return to more ordinary kinds of lovers who maintain a very corporeal interest. These are the kind of lovers who could be protagonists in the *Kamasutra* by Vatsyayan, performing sexual acts and poses full of pleasure and desire. Implicit in the detailed description of the poses is an articulation of wisdom. Instincts are not for suppression. They are for playing out your desires in the fairest possible manner. Hence, categories of fair and unfair hold significance even for the instinctual play. The author of the *Kamasutra* meticulously lays out those categories of right and wrong sexual unions, methods and fulfilment of desire. This is without deleting the details of pleasure, erotica and sensuousness. The lotus seeks to rise through the petals in the very significant mud because, along with dharma (right conduct) and *artha* (social and economic progress), kama (sexual desire) is also important for the lotus to fully blossom. More than the celebration of mud, Vatsyayan had an eye to the aesthetics of carnal pleasure stemming from the muddied ground. Unlike post-Hollywood humanity, Vatsyayan did not have a narrow vision of basic instincts. It was not a matter of moral concern, unlike now when we have an abundance of imageries communicating messages pertaining to instincts and yet we tend to conceal it as something terribly private.

Sex education programmes, unfortunately not so seriously executed across the schools in India, seem to be guarded about the details of mud, petals and lotuses. It is fine to impart biological information about the hormonal changes, responsibility of the bodily organs and safety in sexual acts. Sex is discussed as a soft target of human weakness, a possible problem. It is something against which we are told to be watchful. The information imparted in schools does not complete sex education, since it seldom arrives at the life of love, sex, intimacy, indulgence and potential violence involved with sexual acts. Most sex education programmes fall short of the important wisdom on release, responsibility and rights as far as sexuality, sexual desires, instincts and enactment of them is concerned. It does not lay out the reasons why a child should understand various kinds of expression of love. For example, a kiss need not always be sexual and a touch need not always insinuate something bad. The taboo is kept intact and, hence, morally avoided but secretly sought. A strange kind of value education seems to overpower sex education. Many children grow up abhorring the values imparted to them as part of the value education programme. On many occasions, they experience contradictions between value education and sex education in schools. Official documents, the policy perspective, too reek of disdain for the word *sex*; they seem to suggest that sex and values are two separate entities and that values are supposed to control sex. It is not surprising that the secret seeking, away from value surveillance, turns out violent, inflicted upon oneself as well as others. We nearly nip the lotus in the bud, leaving behind very muddied mud. The point is to bring poetry and art along with biology.

Notes

1. Let me paraphrase Karl Popper's criticism of modern science and its epistemology (and, of course, of positivism). It was inherently paradoxical in that it, on the one hand, had trust in human ability (to know and be free), and, on the other, it was suspicious of human ability (to really know and be really free). Such a duality existed since the Greek philosophers began to ruminate on freedom of humans and their ability to know the truth. See Karl Popper, *Conjecture and Refutation* (London: Routledge & Kegan Paul, 1963).
2. For the purpose of introductory lectures, see Sigmund Freud, James Strachey, and Angela Richards, *Introductory Lectures on Psychoanalysis* (London: Penguin, 1973).

3. The cultural history of colonial South Asia brings forth several instances of the educated cultural elite looking down upon the knowledge and performances of the ordinary folks. For example, *ganika*s from the olden times became *tawaif*s and nautch girls in the course of history, and their performances were deemed dubious. See, among others, Lata Singh, *Raising the Curtain: Recasting Women Performers in India* (Delhi: Orient BlackSwan, 2017).

    Some of the representative texts informing us about the cultural politics of elite social reformers in colonial India would include Radha Kumar, *History of Doing: An Illustrated Account of the Movements for Women's Rights and Feminism in India, 1800-1990* (Delhi: Zubaan, 1993).

4. One should be invited to think whether or not the 'Beauty Myth' is also a way to 'tame the shrew'. It may be required to revisit the famous Naomi Wolf. See Naomi Wolf, *The Beauty Myth* (London: Vintage Books).

5. Quoted from 'Bases of Yoga,' Sri Aurobindo, accessed 20 January 2021, http://sri-aurobindo.in/workings/letters/0023/022294_e.htm.

6. My purpose is not to exactly replicate it; hence, I am not presenting a systematic reading of this immensely significant discussion on the issue of spirituality and divinity from a psychologically sensitive perspective, such as in Sudhir Kakar, *Mad and Divine* (Delhi: Penguin, 2009).

7. An insightful discussion is in Sudhir Kakar, *The Analyst and the Mystic: Psychoanalytic Reflections on Religion and Mysticism* (Delhi: Penguin, 1991).

6

Jokes, Abuse, Friends, Enemies and Something Called In-laws

Generally, we have a long list of friends in our youth when we have sufficient time to hang out. That invariably shrinks to a short list when we grow up, categorised into close friends, distant friends and even nodding acquaintances. Our youthful associations with various friends offer us myriad anecdotes, the ordinary wisdom of everyday life. Let us recall some forgotten or faintly remembered friends and nuggets of ideas that shaped up in their company.

We begin to recognise many such friends in the act of recalling. We are still friends, so to say, but mostly through our occasional exchanges of greetings and wishes on one of those smartphone apps. In college, right before the turn of the millennium, none of us had the luxury of possessing even a primitive type of phone. To make an intended pun, forget about us, the bachelors, even our married fathers did not. Fathers and mothers too had to meet up in real time and space to enjoy the feeling of friendliness. The facility of face-to-face communication looked symmetrically and evenly available for both, children and parents. We used to engage in lively banter without the aid of dead emoticons. We saw emotional expressions in raw forms, with lively guffaws and deadly offences through our jokes getting serious and seriousness getting jocular. Every evening we used to go on random walks, sometimes with the excuse of buying some vegetables from the market, an errand on which our mothers used to set us. We did buy vegetables, along with our important *line-baazi* or *line-marna* (a practice among the youth of looking at girls and longing for romance) and exchanging notes about 'who is up to what'.

I recall a specific friend who was a regular companion in my youth, but now there is no hope of hanging out. An interesting incident took place one fine evening when we were coming back from the market with some cauliflowers in the *jhola*, a fabric bag usually stitched by our mothers. My friend overheard someone calling out for him from across the road. It took my friend a while to note that he was being addressed with abusive words by the man, a relative stranger. The stranger came closer and continued with the vile abuses: 'Where are you going away? Take me along; I am ready to marry your sister.' My friend, to begin with, was slightly amused. In a moment, however, I saw my friend's face reflecting mixed emotions, trembling and smiling. Before I could really fathom the situation, my friend gave in, and he kicked this abusive stranger. In another minute, I saw the stranger getting thrashed by my friend in the middle of the road. The passers-by crowded around to enjoy the scuffle, which ended before I could understand anything. We later figured out that the abusive man was the neighbour of the household into which my friend's sister was married. My friend's sister was like a sister-in-law for the abusive man. The stranger was thus merely following the cultural template meant for the *devar–bhabhi*[1] (brother-in-law and sister-in-law) relationship. There are plenty of sexually loaded humorous tales about devar-bhabhi across cultural contexts in South Asia. Many of those tales have also provided a template for pulp fiction and low-budget cinema in vernacular languages. The thrashed stranger, the devar, was seemingly more culturally informed than my friend who took instant offence. Finally, the man dusted himself off and said with a grimace on his face, '*Saale* (wife's brother/brother-in-law), if you don't want me to marry your sister, let me take her out on a date once.' The word *saale* originally indicated the relationship between *jija* (sister's husband/brother-in-law) *and* saala (wife's brother/brother-in-law). Like devar–bhabhi, this relationship too had a great share of joking and hilarity, as can be seen in manifold folktales and popular cultural texts such as cinema and pulp fiction in vernacular languages. But *saala* or *saale* is also used as an abusive word in a patriarchal society to target a girl's honour.

Most abuses indeed target women to infuriate men. One can read in this the principle of patriarchy that lowers the status of women in male-dominated societies. But then some abuses similarly ridicule and offend male folks too. Songs from across cultures are known to target even long-dead ancestors: for example, did your grandfather have no virility to (re)produce you? There are so many other abusive lines that will indiscriminately disgust men and women. Like my friend, many of us have our ears so socialised to urbane, sanitised mannerisms that we cannot take these abuses any more. How could we, since we remember being punished for abusing each other in our school days? When I mimicked the bully of the neighbourhood and said the same abuses, my elder sister whacked me so hard that I completely forgot the joy of abusing. One can sacrifice such an allegedly illicit joy. One cannot ignore, however, a simple question: why do people abuse and why are there different consequences? Abuses engender both laughter and offence.[2] In the anecdotal remarks earlier, we detect deeper issues—collision of cultural orientation in making sense of cuss words! The man who addressed my friend as 'saale' was simply following the age-old cultural mechanism to start a conversation with my friend. The reactions of my friend, on the other hand, hinged on a cultural orientation based on urbane, disconnected, sanitised and safe growing up. A word for a relationship thus became a word of abuse. Perhaps, the changed reception of words anchors us into diverse layers of ordinariness, to which we can return later in this essay.

Meanwhile, it is wise to reiterate that abuses (meant to offend rather than relate) are in vogue due to patriarchal or regressive sociocultural values. They are offensive because it is not acceptable in a sane and civilised society. But the tribe of anthropologists did not buy this politically correct, overly simplistic idea. They explored and came up with the idea of 'joking relations',[3] particularly referring to the tension between wife-givers and wife-takers, folks who are related by marriage (affinity rather than direct blood line). The discussions of anthropologists enable us to understand kinship, a larger network of relations along the bloodlines as well as along the lines of affinity, including the tension of in-laws. Abuses appear as relational words and safety valves in such tension-ridden relationships. Folks back then were not like us. They aspired to maintain relationships, even though it was through words of abuses. In the kinship network, words of abuses were distinguishable from abusive-offensive words. In the age of smartphones, we seem to have lost that sense of distinction between relational words of abuse and anti-relational abusive-offensive words. Such abusive and offensive participants in social media, devoid of relational significance, are fairly called trolls. They use cuss words without any sense or intention to forge or maintain relationships. Their abuses are aimed at intimidating rather than forging intimacy in the target audience. So, either we have turned oblivious to abuses or we use them strategically, invariably keeping our anonymity, to attack and offend, rather than strengthen and perpetuate relationships. Just like a jija–saala, jija–saali (the female equivalent of jija–saala) or devar–bhabhi, there were other relations in kinship networks in which words of abuses were deployed by folks to generate lightness, intimacy and hilarity. Any such usages could become purely abusive if employed out of context with vested interests. For example, there were *nanad–bhaujai* (husband's sister/sister-in-law and brother's wife/sister-in-law), *sasur–damad* (father-in-law-and son-in-law), *saas–bahu* (husband's mother/mother-in-law and son's wife/daughter-in-law). The usages of the words of abuses indeed reflected the perpetuity of relationships in kinship networks.

However, in a changed scenario with our sanitised sensibilities and singularity of meaning of words of abuses, we are no longer comfortable with them. By and large, we take pride in showing in public our clean face and tongues exorcised of the ghosts called abuses. After all, we want our parents and neighbourhood uncles and aunts to say about us, 'Such a nice upbringing, such a wonderful schooling, so well mannered.' Such self-censorship works against the ordinariness of relationships between friends and foes or between siblings and in-laws. A sense of fear prevails to such an extent that most such relationships make one poker-faced to the other. At times, we call this sense of fear political correctness and, hence, we have ceased to admire each other's face or even to pass a light comment such as 'You are looking beautiful today!' You can forget about saying, 'Why are you dressed like the nouveau riche?' or 'What have you eaten today that you are flaring up at jokes!'

When mothers-in-law were in the practice of joking with sons-in-law, they managed to say much that would not be acceptable when sober and sane. When there was still that space, many daughters-in-law managed to return barbs to the parents-in-law, even though doing so was considered rude. One may have heard, thankfully in this lifetime, a bahu telling her saas, 'Let alone table manners, your son does not know the much-needed bedside manners.' Innuendoes were less offensive even though there was a series of counter-attacks; for example, 'Look at the big mouth of this tender bride. Looks like her father drooled over every samosa.' A sasur may have pointed out to a damad, 'Don't be so fragile, man.' In fact, the moment they greeted each other, they exchanged witty barbs (sugar-coated offensive remarks) which at times turned into barbed wit (hard-hitting and unpalatable hilarious remarks). Witty barbs and barbed wit worked hand in hand in tongue-in-cheek exchanges between relatives in kinship. This does not mean that they never felt bad about any comments. A damad or a bahu sulking for what was light humour at the price of their pride was common. Likewise, a sasur or a saas showed on many occasions that their egos were no less weak. They too sulked whenever they were hurt. Abuse-filled relations were yet to become abusive relationships. Hence, each sulking side maintained a private chamber where they could nurse their grievance, a *kop-bhawan*, literally meaning a room where the angry person spent time alone. It only invited some more witty remarks from the offending party, thereby, opening the possibility for the sulking one to make a more effective rejoinder. Either this exchange diffused the tension or exacerbated it. It did amount to more severe consequences, such as dialogue in siege, a halt in communication in the relationship for a while. That was the cultural format of relationships, providing ample space for intimacy, hilarity, offense, perpetuity of communication, abrupt halt and then its resumption.

There are commonly heard abuses not only in affinal kinship or relations by marriage but also in blood relations. Many anthropologists only looked at marriage-based kinship to make sense of the abuses. But what about a mother calling her son *saradhuwa* (the word originates from *shradh*, the post-death funerary ritual, and it literally means wishing a person dead)? In villages as well as small towns, mothers are known for getting exasperated with their sons and daughters. While they had colourful abuses for daughters, they had macabre choices for sons. My favourite is *taati-bala* in the context of Maithili-speaking mothers in the north of India. It literally means the person who is lying dead on the wooden bed prepared for cremation. By calling a son taati-bala, a mother wishes him to be a dead person lying on the cremation bed. Daughters mostly received sexualised abuses, curiously enough more in private than in public. These were gendered abuses citing sexual specificities of female targets.

Let us return to the general situation, away from kinship networks, in which friends abused one another. Male or female, these friends who are not related by blood or marriage had far more nuanced usage of abuses. Cuss words such as *kutte-kaminey* and *sale-harami* are almost punctuation marks in the conversation of friends. If they were too sanitised, they did well with the colloquial abuses like *kukur, chant* and even *chutia* and so on. Needless to say, each of these cuss words can be traced back to folk society and kinship networks too. But then, friends employed them in a relatively shallow manner. When they called each other saala, for example, they did not mean to indicate a relationship between wife-giver and wife-taker. Friends used the abusive words to deepen their level of comfort and relationship through seemingly frivolous fun. It all sounded casual and, yet, it was consequential. The buddies exhibited a knack for experimenting and creating novel abuses. Many of the abuses, one can say, are additions to human folklore. The point is, however, the growing illegitimacy of folklore in general and abuses in particular. We do not want anything that has the potential to offend anyone. Yet, we want to launch offensive strikes on enemies. We have heard, seen and read about the *jawans* (armed forces personnel) on duty across borders hurling abuses at each other when they are not hurling grenades. One can say that the aggressive parade with ridiculously performed anger and orchestrated hostility for each other in Wagah along the Indo–Pak border is a continuity to this. Abuses are performed, showed and seen.

A funny sequence in the 1991 blockbuster *Saudagar* (Merchant), directed by Subhash Ghai, had two very well-known thespians Dilip Kumar and Raaj Kumar, both known to have worked together after a long gap. The film had an extended sequence of the two actors abusing each other, playing characters with sworn animosity. These characters are actually old friends turned enemies due to accidental events and plots making them mutually hostile. Rumour had it that the particular scene became longer than expected by the filmmaker because the actors playing these characters were also known to have had some rough patches in their relationship due to which they did not work together after their earlier movie *Paigham* (The Message, 1959). Neither wanted to be a mere recipient of abuse from the other. Both continued to return abuses. The beauty of the prolonged scene, however, is in the series of abuses through which each character underlines the love turned sour. As long as they abuse each other and articulate their vows to kill each other, they are in a relationship. Adjectives, otherwise mere straightforward expressions, such as *jahil, ganwar and pakhandi* (uneducated, rustic, ostentatious) acquire abusive value in the scene; this underlines the invention of more sophisticated varieties of abuses that would replace the conventional ones. Animosity is a kind of relationship that should be respected. Even though it is about seeking to offend each other, one feels connected. The real distancing is when the characters turn mutually indifferent—no abuses, no reaffirmation of the vows to kill each other. Then it is only a deadening silence and opaqueness, perhaps suitable for sanitised political correctness but not so for the cultural canvas of relationships.

There is always a chance that the real killing will be through words. A bullet may not inflict the lasting pain and injury that words can. Many profound poets said this long ago, and we can easily recall them from memory. Putting the insightful medieval poet Kabir's proposition[4] into words:

Aisi bani boliye, man ka aapa khoye / auron ko shital kare / aaphun shital hoye[5] (Say such a word with poise and peace that you calm others as much as you calm yourself).

Many of us perhaps misunderstand Sant Kabir's proposition. This was not to dismiss the ordinary practice of joking, abusing and expressing witty sarcasm. Kabir himself did not compromise on his witty sarcasm when he had to comment on the institutional fallacies of organised religions by saying:

Kankar-pathar jod ke masjid liyo banaye / ta chadhi mulla bang de / ka bahro huyo khudaye[6] (A mosque is erected with bricks and mortar, atop which the priest shouts out the call for prayer. Is God really so deaf?)

These couplets echo in the illuminated chambers of our memory, if we care to hear. Kabir does not spare Hindus either as he says,

> Pathar pujein Hari milen / to main pujun pahar / ghar ki chaaki kou na puje jaka pisa khaye[7] (If worshipping a stone gets you to God, I will worship a mountain; so ironical these worshippers are, they do not worship the millstone from which they get their grains ground).

The saint poet Kabir's enormously confident intellect enabled him to present a sarcastic critique of the two religious practices of Hinduism and Islam. One can imagine how critical Kabir may sound to Hindu and Muslim worshippers. But would anyone disagree with Kabir's sarcastic critique? The answer is likely negative. If Kabir did this, so did the ordinary folks. If we press our memory to serve us well, we have heard them telling each other, ridiculing Kabir with subversive wit: '*Kabirdas ke ulte baani / pehle khaani tab asnani*' (Such is the awkward way of Kabir, fill your stomach before taking a bath).

The poets may have indeed reminded us of the reasons behind balanced communication that refrains from offending anyone. If balanced articulation is one kind of ordinary wisdom, so is the idea to laugh at each other and at oneself. Abuses, like jokes, worked to serve this ordinary wisdom. Unfortunately, we all became susceptible to offence since we lost sight of ordinary wisdom. We do not want to laugh at others, nor do we like others laughing at us. This is not only today; evidence of the decline is in an episode of the Mahabharata. The Kaurava brothers are invited to see the splendour of the castle that the Pandava brothers possess. The castle has magical twists and turns. Where you see a mirror, it turns out to be a pool of water and vice versa. As a result, the visitors are colliding here, tripping there. Duryodhana trips too, and the onlooking Draupadi, the empress of the castle, laughs at the bewildered Duryodhana. Not only does she laugh, she also passes a comment: '*Andhe ka beta andha*' (The blind son of the blind father). This stings the visiting guest, the eldest of the Kaurava brothers, Duryodhana. Many interpreters suggest that this sealed the fate; the war was inevitable after this. It is true that this is not the only reason why the Great War, also called *Dharm-yuddh,* happened. But this certainly reveals the consequences of the declining tendency to laugh at each other, abuse each other and rest in peace with this ordinary human habit.

It was not so shocking then to see a protest against the usage of a particular cartoon in school textbooks. The genius cartoonist of modern India, R. K. Laxman, gave a hilarious depiction of the snail's pace at which the designated group headed by the maker of the constitution, B. R. Ambedkar, was finalising the constitution.[8] The first prime minister of India, Jawaharlal Nehru, was shown whipping the slow snail in the cartoon. The protest pointed out the anti-Ambedkar connotation of the cartoon and demanded that it be removed from the textbook. This was not new, as the history of Indian politics reveals several occasions when so-called Gandhians did not take it kindly when a joke or a hilarious comment about Gandhi made it to the public debates. Let alone sharing creative abuses, the ordinary tendency to joke about gods, goddesses, historical icons, role models, leadership and public personalities has lost ground too. Just imagine the reaction of the loyalists of the Congress party in the trying time of the Emergency in 1975 to a sarcastic, jocular and nearly abusive Hindi poem by a famous poet, *Jankavi* (people's poet) Baba Nagarjun. It was penned right when the atrocities of the regime were gaining currency. As youth growing up in the Hindi heartland of India, we recited the poem so much so that it became part of everyday lore for some of us. Based on memory, the poem goes:

Kya hua aapko? Kya hua aapko?
Satta ki masti me bhool gayi baap ko,
Indu ji, Indu ji, kya hua aapko?
Bachpan me Gandhi ke pass rahi,
Tarunai me Tagore ke pass rahi,
Ab kyo ulat diya sangat ki chhap ko?
Kya hua aapko, kya hua aapko?[9]

Whatever happened to you, Indu ji?
Drunk with power, you forgot your father
Your childhood was spent in the company of Mahatma Gandhi

And your youth in that of Tagore's
Why have you forgotten everything you may have learnt from them
Whatever happened to you, Indu ji?

The spirit was more or less the same when the litterateur Hari Mohan Jha created a fictional character known as Khattar Kaka, easily identifiable with an average, ordinary, Maithili-speaking elderly person. Jha presented a subversive, humorous and riveting critique of almost everything under the sun through this endearing and upsetting character, Khattar Kaka. This was way back in the 1950s, when India was undergoing its Nehruvian tryst with destiny and when it was envisaged that scientific temper would be cultivated along with traditional ethos. For example, to paraphrase, once when an interlocutor asked Khattar Kaka about the supremacy of Vedic literature, he took no time in declaring, 'Yes, the Vedas are very important, but they should not be read by young students since they have vivid descriptions not suitable for the youth.' Kaka continued his pithy explanation on the indulgence of the Aryan gods in everything that is deemed taboo for mortal humans. Amid hilarity and sarcasm, one gets to hear a witty elderly man's antithesis to everything that is normative.

One wonders whether Hari Mohan Jha, Jankavi Baba Nagarjun, Sant Kabir and such articulate embodiments of wisdom who came up with subversive ideas would have run for their life in the face of a lynch mob chasing them in today's milieu. In such a time, it may be reassuring to see that school children at times do not shy away from bad-mouthing teachers, parents, friends and so on. It is called bad-mouthing because we have declared jokes, abuses, sarcasm and subversion as normatively illicit. It may appear disgusting, unacceptable and downright immoral, but all such usages point to the fact that repression of ordinary abuses and jokes have led to more violent and unbridled reactions. We have lost our sense of humour and the humours of our senses, ordinarily our repository of wit and wisdom! We can wishfully hope that 'friends' come together to retrieve the forgotten.

Notes

1. In a different context, Smita Jassal has explored the nuances of devar–bhabhi relationships through the Bhojpuri songs sung during the festival of Holi and changes in the ideas and practices in the time of cassette culture. See Smita Tewari Jassal, 'Taking Liberties in Festive Song: Gender, New Technologies and a "Joking Relationship"', *Contributions to Indian Sociology* 41, no. 1 (2007): 5–40.
2. Through nuances underneath, language is employed as a vehicle to exchange abuses and offence, and it is considered impolite in general. Many fail to see the anthropology in it and thus resort to semantics alone. See Jonathan Culpeper, *Impoliteness: Using Language to Cause Offence* (Cambridge: Cambridge University Press, 2011). Perhaps the relation of power and language is seen in this regard too, rather than following the template of *raj-kavya* (power-poetry) that Pollock profoundly noted in the wake of Sanskrit cosmopolis. See Sheldon Pollock, *The Language of the Gods in the World of Men: Sanskrit, Culture, and Power in Premodern India* (Berkeley: University of California Press, 2006).
3. One of the oldest takes on it in classical anthropology is A. R. Radcliffe-Brown, 'On Joking Relationships,' *Africa: Journal of the International African Institute* 13, no. 3 (1940): 195–210.
4. More elucidated and erudite readings of Kabir are in Charlotte Vaudeville, *Myths, Saints and Legends in Medieval India*, compiled by and with an introduction by Vasudha Dalmia (Delhi: Oxford University Press, 1996). Much before this, Rabindranath Tagore had compiled and introduced Kabir to English-speaking readers in Rabindranath Tagore, *Songs of Kabir* (New York: Library of Alexandria, 1915).
5. See, for all such couplets, https://www.kahatkabir.com/magazine/90/kabir-ke-dohe-hindi.html, accessed 25 January 2021.
6. See https://www.kahatkabir.com/magazine/literature/624/neeti-ke-dohe-kabir.html, accessed 25 January 2021.
7. See https://www.kahatkabir.com/magazine/literature/624/neeti-ke-dohe-kabir.html, accessed 25 January 2021.
8. See Ritika Chora, 'Intolerance Wins As NCERT Textbooks Are Back, but without Six Cartoons', *India Today*, 11 September 2012, accessed on 25 January 2021, https://www.indiatoday.in/india/north/story/intolerance-ncert-books-cartoons-br-ambedkar-115745-2012-09-11.
9. See http://kavitakosh.org/kk/इन्द_जी_क्या_हुआ_आपको_/_नागार्जुन, accessed on 25 January 2021.

7

Defiance, Rebellion and Protest: From Embryo to Artificial Intelligence

A mathematics professor was almost on the verge of killing a student who professed her commitment to join in the debate on an issue that was a bone of contention across the nation. The professor kept asking questions without expecting any answers: why are you debating on something not related to course work, why do you not leave it to politicians, what is the meaning of such education that makes you speak against the law, who is provoking you, why are you so gullible and so on. The student replied with a poised smile, 'Sir, I can educate you on all these questions if you join me in the debate!'

Many educators and educational administrators do not seem to consider debate as a part and parcel of education. By and large, learning and debating or arguing have been divorced from each other in the popular imagination. Hence, we hear this allegation from people around us as well as from the political leadership. Why are these students protesting? Do they not have to use their time in studying instead? Why such politics of students? These questions reveal our limited understanding of the idea of protest and our ignorance of what education is supposed to be. These questions arise from a bizarre imagination of education upheld by professors who became professors due to dubious credentials, and administrators of the institutes of higher education who became administrators due to their known ignorance of what university and education stand for. They tend to speak in the tongue of rabble-rousing wannabe leaders and slogan-shouting political spokespersons. The rabble that is ever-ready to go on a rampage determine the imagination of nearly everything today. What imagination of education have they upheld? They imagine education to be like a coaching centre. Like in coaching centres, students are expected to be automated creatures attending classes, taking exams, striving for good grades. They deem such education fit for what they call nation-building. How would the students build a nation if they do not simmer with the issues burning the whole nation? If the youth do not reason with the reasonable issues that hurt them most as common citizens and ordinary folks, then how would they contribute to nation-building, and what kind of nation would they build?

Moreover, this line of questioning also underlines our fear of youth, which has a history. The head of an institution was heard saying that these youths cannot reason, so they have no right to debate! With such a low opinion of young people, administrators like this have wrought havoc on the institutions they administer. Many ennobled professors, ennobled because they hold administrative positions by hook or crook, support such nefarious ideas. They look down upon the youth to get the sleazy pleasure of looking up to their self-proclaimed authority of reasoning. Thus, they premise all their allegations on a sanitised notion of education in which youth, and even their teachers, are not supposed to be thinking, debating, disagreeing beings. They imagine institutions as a means of schooling the youth into servility and docility. Ivan Illich, a theologian and insightful educationist, wrote against this in his famous rumination on deschooling society in the 1970s.[1] But these new breeds of self-proclaimed educationists have not heard of Ivan Illich, nor do they seem to have read Mahatma Gandhi's proximity with Illich's ideas. In the late 1970s, Ivan Illich visited India, and he spent time in Sevagram where he talked about Mahatma's hut. Such was the proximity between the two minds.[2]

In the absence of an iota of idea about the vision of the educationists, it becomes easier to separate the youth-led protests from a rich history of human civilisation and political movements. Do we remember that many movements of historical importance in world history were students' movements? These movements, even though we may disagree with the types and methods of protesting, ideology and politics, brought about revolutionary changes. Never mind. The idea is not to give history lessons. It is simply to state that to protest is human. It is one of the most ordinary tendencies of humanity. We learn to cry in protest from birth. Therefore, youth-led protests in the most organised forms ought to be perceived in that light as well. This is much needed since there is a rant against outspoken youth. Political parties, stakeholders in the status quo and others have already popularised the idea of 'Urban Naxals' for a variety of young persons and their mentors who tend to speak out. One wonders what the child who showed the mirror to the naked emperor would have done if he or she were called an 'Urban Naxal'! This label would have nipped the growth of the child in the bud.

A newly born baby slides out of the mother's womb smeared in amniotic fluid, and the first thing that we all look forward to is the baby's cry. An obstetrician's ears are up like restless antennae to hear the baby cry. If the baby cries naturally, there is a sigh of relief. If it does not, an effort is made to make the baby cry to ensure that the lungs resume normal function. The crying baby sends out a beautiful message unless declared otherwise by the doctors in the labour room. The plain and simple message is that things are fine. Poets may very well read between the sound-lines of a crying baby. It may be taken, or someone will say mistaken, for the first articulation of protest by the newborn against this process of letting the baby out into the precarious world. For the baby, the womb is far more secure than the world monitored by the best healthcare systems. Almost everything felt safe and sound in there; almost everything feels unsafe and unsound out here. There is no escape; the baby has to cry. This is a melodious expression to every parent until crying becomes a tactic of an attention-seeking baby. Every time the baby cries, we get a signal. We check for the nappy's wetness or scrutinise the bedsheet or see whether the baby is hungry. Babies cry to communicate. Even the most nagging babies communicate and can do so only by crying. That is the only language, or one can say, the most primaeval language of humans. One learns since infanthood about the significance of crying and, thereby, of loudly and firmly protesting. The vehement and violent crying of a baby, particularly when in utter discomfort, is a reminder of this.

Folks in disagreement could be in utter discomfort too. They cry out their opinion as loudly and hoarsely as possible since the authorities are not listening. They defy, decry, protest and rebel. It is a normal human tendency, and thank the stars, or whomever one trusts most, for these series of acts of defiance, protest and systematic crying. Just imagine a populace that takes everything quietly. It will be horrible, like living in a society of dead people. Also, one should celebrate the fact that law, despite its aversion for disorder, subscribes to the idea of protest as one of the crucial rights of humans. It is the most respectful attitude to the ordinariness of humans. Then, why do we hear such reservations when the youth in schools, colleges and universities protest? It is not only political regimes that deem youth protest reprehensible. University administrations, which will have illustrious academics with research publications on a wide gamut of progressive issues, express dismay about student protests too. Even in the classroom, teachers in higher education exhibit an intolerance to questioning by students. Further, the best way to silence, in the classroom set-up, is to point out the under-informed or misinformed nature of a student's question. Likewise, political regimes, too, consider the youth misguided if they walk out of classrooms and join in the protests in the streets.

Let us return to the growing baby. This is the time when all the fundamentals of personality shape up. From memory, we can recall a lesson we learned when we had read William Wordsworth. No one can disagree with the poet's prophetic articulation that the child is the father of the man. Let us correct the androcentrism inherent in large parts of the classics and say that the child is father and mother of the man and woman, even though William Wordsworth or many of his devout readers may feel irritated. This line is from a famous poem titled 'My Heart Leaps Up' or 'The Rainbow', known to have been penned in 1802. The poem reads as follows:

> My heart leaps up when I behold
> *A rainbow in the sky:*
> So was it when my life began;
> So is it now I am a man;
> *So be it when I shall grow old,*
> Or let me die!
> The child is father of the man;
> And I could wish my days to be,
> Bound each to each by natural piety.[3]

The poet may have been merely interested in showing the process of formation and journey of a child to personhood. Many readers of the poem suggest this by literally reading the naturalism of the poem. But there is more than that encapsulated in the poetic dictum. The child assumes the parental role also because it delivers a second innings for the father and mother. In this second innings of life, the father and the mother revisit their own becoming as well as unbecoming. They get a second chance to reshape themselves and return to the tales and songs, notions and norms that they unconsciously imbibed when they were infants. Nostalgia, muffled in purpose and conscious rationality, come to work in the process that Wordsworth's poetic insight underlines. The poem certainly evokes more than naturalism. There is a great deal of realism at work in the poem, which acknowledges and persuades us to acknowledge the essential ordinariness of humanity, inclusive of childhood and adulthood. The joy of youth that is central to the poem cannot be separated from the youth's tendency to protest. Or do we have a sinister idea that joy has nothing to do with protest? If so, we are logically as well as romantically in the wrong. A couple of centuries later, the musicians Brian Wilson and Van Dyke Parks returned to the catchphrase 'The child is father of the man' in their famous album *Smile*, for which Wilson won the Grammy award. The lyrics of the song were as follows:

> Child, child, child, the child, Father of the man, Father of the man / Easy, my child, it's just enough to believe / I believe, I believe, I believe / Out of the wild into what you can't conceive / You'll achieve.[4]

The song sought to complicate the poetic romance that was in Wordsworth and show the untenable belief that succumbs to scepticism. The adult forgets everything of having been a child, including the tendency to protest. It is all about recalling the forgotten.

The child grows up into adolescence, the most troublesome time according to popular common sense. Even psychologists do not lag in this common sense. This is the time for the coming of age, to begin with, as a threat and eventually as romance. Nonetheless, the tendency to cry out a protest or two stays in the scheme of becoming. The most intense expressions of defiance unfold in the raw energy of adolescence. Parents, aunts in the neighbourhood and the teachers in school may not find it tolerable. They may complain about the rawness of energy expressed in adolescent behaviour. Invariably, such behavioural expressions are considered acts of defiance. Even counselors in the schools deem the emotional expressions of adolescents as irrational outbursts. To regulate the defiance of teenagers, everyone begins to comment on each behavioural facet. From school to home and neighbourhood, they employ many mechanisms to gag the giggles, laughter and guffaws. In many ways, everyone tends to condition the simple acts of communication as though they were potential acts of defiance. Nothing escapes the monitoring gaze of parents, teachers and anyone even slightly older than the teenagers. From pitch of voice to the way of walking, dressing, eating, singing and humming, everything becomes a reason for everyone to worry about.

However, all of them fail, more or less, and that gives a good reason to celebrate. The girls still manage to chuck the book of norms out of the window; the boys still fantasise about female teachers and neighbourhood aunts without caring for moral lessons. Both boys and girls have the joy of banging the door shut on the faces of their parents more than once despite the dire consequences. The best is when they seek to show the emperor naked by telling their parents at home that their perspectives suck. They make faces at and insult the uncles and aunts in the neighbourhood who were staring at them every now and then. They draw vulgar graffiti showing their class teachers in morally compromised positions in the school toilets. When they see a teacher inviting students to do a street play in which they have to raise slogans against social evils, they throng there with their eyes filled with the light of hope. We have seen many of these kids marching in peaceful protests against the felling of trees, displacement of the urban poor and degradation of the environment due to poor models of development among other things. We have seen the photographs of school and college students joining in large numbers in candlelight marches to India Gate. The sceptics may say this is hardly a movement, this makes little impact and that these kids are totally out of control. But the truth is that the energy that has always been immanent gets channelised with a cause in mind. The cause may be the only difference, but the energy, tendency and instincts were always there. It evolves into more organised, informed and fairly strategised protests when the youth reach the universities. It is but natural to see educated young people protest against diverse issues, the decay of universities, decline in education facilities, the heavy-handed State and inequality of various kinds.

One wonders whether the rank and file of spokespersons in society and polity have forgotten the basic nature of education as well as the instinctual preparation of humans that is inclined to protests and critical thinking. These spokespersons cry gallons of tears, mucus running from nostrils, to disapprove of youth protests. We have heard them saying something as ominous as 'Education is a waste of public money'. It merely discloses the intellectual lunacy of statist and technocratic thinking that perpetuates a linear relation between study and employment. They also seem to be unaware of recorded and less recorded histories of youth. On many occasions, students from modern schools and non-modern *diksha viharas* (educational institutions in ancient times) have arisen in protest. All of us may have heard the story of the diksha vihara where the famous teacher Chanakya taught. The story of Chanakya overthrowing the Nanda dynasty and creating a new line of kingship should not be forgotten. Coming to more modern times, Surya Sen was an endearing and evocative teacher who organised a revolt with schoolchildren in Chittagong in colonial East Bengal (Bangladesh). That revolt is famously known as the Chittagong uprising in colonial history. At the time, the powers that be deemed the students' revolt led by Surya Sen as a terrorist attack on the official armoury.

Moreover, many university teachers in postcolonial India had closely worked with political groups without being labelled Urban Naxals by their own people. The nature of education is such that an educated person develops a critical mind to reason with issues and take a stand. Teachers and students come together in protest against capital punishment and various kinds of objectionable laws passed with ulterior motives. They protest; hence, they are citizens. It is a misapprehension created by the State and the market for all of us that education means getting ready for employment alone. It is also about getting ready to take a stand after critical reasoning and creating novel dreams, utopias and the possibility of a better future. It is no wonder then that even though one may disagree with the method and implication, many educated youths joined the Naxalbari uprising in the 1960s.

The peasants' movement in Bengal attracted youthful believers educated in some of the premier universities in India to the struggle for justice. There was a fatal fallout resulting from this armed uprising, and what could be better documentation of the loss and pathos than the telling tale by one of the most remarkable writers of post-Independence India, Mahasweta Devi. The novel titled *The Mother of 1084*, also adapted into a film that earned rave reviews and critical appreciation by the filmmaker Govind Nihalani, presented the journey of a mother named Sujata into the experience of her deceased son Brati. Everyone considered Brati a bright student. No one knew that his education enabled a perspective, a vision, of a better world. Who can deny that education is supposed to do this? With this awareness, Brati joins the Naxalites, who were participating in an armed struggle. An emotionally distraught mother discovers the details of the struggle, the beliefs of her son, the politics of the movement and anti-movement forces. The pathos of a mother who lost her son does not obscure her understanding of the position her son had taken.

Those who hastily employ the phrase 'Naxal' should learn about the origin of the word, the history of the movement and the quintessential role of education. It was not a position taken in ignorance; instead, it was a perspective and vision coming from education that was accepted with full awareness. Then, why this hue and cry? Protesting with a vision is the earliest thing that begins to unfold in a growing child, and this comes from the very infantile stage of childhood, about which we have heard the realistic romance of poets. Hence, the ingenious poet William Blake wrote in the late 18th century, about a schoolboy:

> I love to rise in a summer morn,
> When the birds sing on every tree;
> The distant huntsman winds his horn,
> And the skylark sings with me:
> O what sweet company!
>
> But to go to school in a summer morn,
> O it drives all joy away!
> Under a cruel eye outworn,

> The little ones spend the day,
> In sighing and dismay.
>
> Ah then at times I drooping sit,
> And spend many an anxious hour;
> Nor in my book can I take delight,
> Nor sit in learning's bower,
> Worn through with the dreary shower.
>
> How can the bird that is born for joy
> Sit in a cage and sing?
> How can a child, when fears annoy,
> But droop his tender wing,
> And forget his youthful spring!
>
> O father and mother if buds are nipped,
> And blossoms blown away;
> And if the tender plants are stripped
> Of their joy in the springing day,
> By sorrow and care's dismay,
>
> How shall the summer arise in joy,
> Or the summer fruits appear?
> Or how shall we gather what griefs destroy,
> Or bless the mellowing year,
> When the blasts of winter appear?[5]

The idea is not to present a poet's romance with childhood. It is to underline the silent protest that the schoolboy begins to articulate early on, with his deafening sigh, explicit dismay and drooped tender wings! If this is so with the schoolboy or schoolgirl, why do we frown upon the youth? After all, the child was and invariably is the father and mother of the man and woman. If the regimes of power do not want to see protests, all they need to do is to legalise and institutionalise the heinous crime of foeticide! Then there will be less of other kinds of crimes. If there is still some protest left due to cultural orientation, which there will be since culture always has subversive components, they can employ arsenals and armies to carry out a pogrom, genocide and then they can hope for the end of protests. Ah! It is a fool's hope, since there will be trees and flowers, grass and creepers, flora and fauna, giving a call for protest too! A pandemic is also no less than a call for protest against our ways of seeing, living and being, if and only if we care to listen.

Notes

1. See, for more, Ivan Illich, *Deschooling Society* (New York: Harper & Row Publishers. 1971), accessed on 26 January 2021, https://archive.org/details/DeschoolingSociety/mode/2up.
2. See Ivan Illich, 'The Message of Bapu's Hut', accessed on 26 January 2021, https://www.mkgandhi.org/museum/msgofbapuhut.htm.
3. William Wordsworth, 'My Heart Leaps Up,' Poets, accessed on 1 January 2021, https://poets.org/poem/my-heart-leaps.
4. Brian Wilson, 'Child Is Father of the Man,' Lyrics, accessed on 1 January 2021, https://www.lyrics.com/lyric/10270213/Brian+Wilson/Child+Is+Father+of+the+Man.
5. William Blake, 'The Schoolboy,' Poetry Lovers Page, accessed on 20 January 2021, https://www.poetryloverspage.com/poets/blake/schoolboy.html.

There Was Something

Illustration artist: Sajal Roy, Dhaka, Bangladesh

8

Flirtatious, Lustful and Committed: An Ordinary Romance

Three intricately related ideas plague us: If you are truthful, you never lie. If you are trustworthy, you never deviate. If you are committed, you never shun responsibility. There could be multiple such formulations, all hinting towards a misplaced ideal. Such an ideal is misplaced because it does not take into account the humanness of humans. It is a misplaced ideal if it is a sermon delivered from a moral high ground so far above ground level that one cannot see the dewdrop-laden blades of grass and rejoice at the sight of seemingly insignificant and beautifully significant tiny wildflowers. From such positions, we can only admire high and upright, tall and tight, mighty and right. Such an extraordinary perspective celebrates only an extraordinary entity. The rest of the things seen from such a perspective would be either nonentities or mere perversion. Interestingly, at times, perversion may also metamorphose into an extraordinary characteristic, and then it is not publicly known as perversion until someone complains about it. A good number of men like or envy a successful womaniser, even if temporarily. A womaniser, a figure we may have seen in our university life, is somewhat a chivalrous man with suspiciously sweet demeanour, strange tenderness and enigmatic charm and has a way of disarming most people. Everything that can make some of us feel creeped out may be turned into the spell of a womaniser—sweet, soothing and seductive. We are familiar with the female counterpart of a womaniser too. Though the world of desire is patriarchal enough to mute the narratives of female counterparts, we can still hear fragmented articulations in folklore, popular culture and live spaces of pubs, parks and parties. There is no barrier of political correctness when it comes to feelings. With no barrier, one never knows where one takes an about turn and joins in admiring even boldness and beauty in perversity.

This is the making of something extraordinary out of something commonly human.

Flirtatiousness is yet another ordinary feature of humans. Flirting may regale us in our youth before we commit to one relationship and settle down in happily ever after mode. We are fine with flirtatious friends until we have translated friendship into the institution of marriage and kinship. Acceptable amorous advances that we once enjoyed suddenly begin to feel like a taboo after committing to one person. One can aggressively justify this by saying that change is natural. 'I did this before marriage; how can I do it now that I am committed to one person after marriage?' This dilemma arises since the idea of institutions such as marriage and family is perpetually conceived from that moral high ground. Too much premium attached to marriage undermines the human, ordinary everydayness of it. Likewise, too much stress on the idea of family results in violence in the relationship. Therefore, we ought to understand that it is not simply an ordinary change that we refer to when we say or quietly feel how we could like some other person when we are already committed to one in the institution of marriage. Everything allowed before marriage becomes bizarre, at least in public cognisance. This happens to such an extent that it is horrifying to imagine a husband being flirtatious even with his wife, let alone any other woman. One instantly falls many notches lower in the eyes of people, and of children if they have already come of age, if a husband even implies lustful desires towards his very own wife. As flirting is tabooed, so is lust. In fact, lust has a little more miserable life, since it is often pitched against the extraordinarily sublime notion of love. If you are in love, you are not supposed to harbour any lustful desires, not supposed to glance at the body parts of even your loved ones. You may be immediately dubbed a sexually frustrated man or woman. One hears this quite often: you were children and, hence, innocently infatuated with your school or college teacher. After growing up, there is supposed to be some biological miracle in your body. You are supposed to cease from doing everything you did despite the vigilance of all your guardian angels. We have imbibed these regulatory morals without understanding our ordinary tendencies. This leads us to a repressed self; many such selves constitute a repressed society.

That said, one can go on talking about the most violent manifestation of this repression that creates what we have lately heard of—a rape culture. A society without due understanding of the dynamics of desire usually fails to curtail the violence implicit in desire.[1]

I invite you to contemplate an interesting sight and experience with which many of us have grown up. This was well before gated societies with skyrocketing apartments became the norm. In most houses, there used to be something called a *roshandan* (a kind of ventilator, also known as fanlight, through which air and light could pass). It was usually located above the lintel or windows in the wall. Every day at some hour, sunlight streamed in through the roshandan and cast various patterns on the floor of the rooms or veranda. As children, we played with each beam, which changed its location inside as the sun moved outside. We used to imagine catching the sunbeams and collecting them in our pockets. It was all fake since we knew that no one can catch them. We allowed those sunbeams to rest on our eyes and nose. We also let them in our mouths and imagined swallowing them. All these funny acts, reveries of childhood, implied something profound. There is one sun when we go to the rooftop. There are many patterns when we come down the staircase and enter various parts inside the house. No one denies the significance of that singular sun, undergoing changes in colours as refractions show at various moments in the diurnal revolution. We rejoice, hopefully even now, at the sight of the singular sun, from the rooftop, in the park, in the hills and also from inside aircrafts sitting in that coveted window seat. Who has not tried making flickering eye contact with the beaming sun from a running train? As children as well as fully blossomed adults, we have had our brush with such mundane adventures. Once in a while, one feels like spending quiet moments gazing at the setting sun, with intermittent sighs of relief about the break from the grinding day. Yet, none of us usually discredit the many patterns of sunlight cast through the roshandan. Each pattern is an invitation, for playfulness and freedom, for imagination and story making. Every day, there is a cosmos inside the house constituted by the patterns, shapes and stories made of the sunlight streaming through the most neglected and ordinary part of the house, the roshandan. On occasions, we have seen the face of a worshipper in *sajda*, in namaz offered during the daytime. The beams of sunlight filtering through the roshandan add a sublime effect to the face, and the sajda assumes an unequivocal visual effect.

Flirting and lusting are like those patterns of sunlight, the origin of which is that singular sun we behold and worship. But the medium called roshandan, much like human desire, is equally important. If the medium is removed, we have to be content with the singular, superior sun, which is equivalent to the institution of marriage or commitment to one relationship or a wife or a husband. Though it may appear incorrect according to the grammar of gender politics, there is an interesting instance from folk cultures across South Asia. There was an institution of joking relationships, in which folks also cracked lewd jokes to obtain sexual pleasure. This instance was discussed in a previous chapter as well. Furthermore, in that template, casting lustful glances and getting reprimanded, both in ordinary joviality, was fine. Making flirtatious comments and getting either approved or disapproved was part of everyday life. There was a bearable and pleasant lightness of being without any external agency or regulatory mechanism from outside. Folk cultures of the world have permitted possibilities beyond socio-religious normative prescription and proscription.

As we matured, or so we thought, our notions of purity and pollution cast negative aspersions on anything related to desire. We had to prove to ourselves that we could distinguish basic instincts and evolved instincts. It is risky to appear un-evolved when other civilisations across the world are rapidly evolving from human to artificial intelligence. Everything related to the basic instincts were already suspected to be pertaining to the beasts. So we categorised flirtation and lust as undesirable activities. But could we weed them out? We could not. Industries are smarter and, in fact, more honest in admitting the persistence of desire. The cosmetics industry, the manufacturers of dreams of being ever young and virile, and condom manufacturers, among many others, have capitalised on human desires, flirtatious natures and lustful urges. Many capsules appeared in the market with the most seductive jingles, convincing men and women to want longer-lasting pleasure. This was an advanced version of the indigenous herbs sold at known crossroads or pavements in big and small cities.

All the desi (home-grown) sexologists had to gear up to a more advanced version of attracting clientele than just having graffiti advertisements by the side of railway tracks. Now they are listed on web pages, on which they put images of white-skinned men and women in intimate positions. The absence of coloured, brown Indians in those images on the websites of sex gurus reveals something deeper. Perhaps, Indians are no longer into the business of flirting and lusting. This is not true. Once in a while, we receive statistics on the large number of browsers in India searching for pornographic content online, thereby, placing India closer to some developed nations. Some years ago, India ranked fourth in the web traffic for online pornographic consumption, after the United States of America, United Kingdom and Canada. Newspaper reports[2] informed us that some of the most frequently used keywords were 'Indian porn', 'Indian wife', 'Indian bhabhi', 'bhabhi–devar' and 'Indian teacher' among others. We learn from various blogs and online media portals that Indian consumers of online pornography have a fairly cosmopolitan taste. Hence, they not only search for East Asian and Western porn but also zoom in on porn content along popular ethnic terms. The ethnic terms are related to places and regions. Sooner than later, Google leads you to one of those pages that deal in instinctual and anatomical desire such as prolonged sexual pleasure or the ways of strengthening genital organs. Some advertisements online sell oils, pills and herbs using bizarre images of genitals. The evidently enormous consumption and popularity of all such content indeed posit a challenge to moralistic blindness to the cultural underworld of lusting and loving.[3]

Desi sexologists also stick posters in the toilets of railway compartments and stations and public lavatories. They no longer simply promise to cure *gupt-rog* (literally, secret disease), since it is no longer a malady of a few. Now they promise to address an epidemic of normatively curbed sexual desires. Even something so unrelated as a soft drink went on to create the jingle '*Ye dil mange more*' (the heart wants more)! A model pours water from a bottle down her body to drive a message home: this bottled water is as pure as your instant erotic desire. Even cellular phone network providers began to add the idea of desire, persuading the consumers to talk more. Manifold stakeholders orient us to put into effect our desires. The entertainment industry presents a new tale, every turn of a decade or so, about the significance of being desirous. The industries have emerged as the most prominent supporters of the pursuit of desires in general. Particularly, the advertisements cajole the consumers to buy many versions of flirting and lusting, within or without institutions to which it is equally human to be committed. The industry-induced imagination persuades a man or a woman to desire more than what is available in socially legitimated institutions. A married man, seemingly loving towards his wife, may cast a glance of admiration at a passer-by without any qualms. He may feel guilty about it as soon as his wife catches him doing so. The purity and impurity, so to say, fit the scheme of being ordinary. But then, it goes without saying that industries induce a great deal of fake desires too. In a society where repression and oblivion of the nature of desire are common, it is easier for industries to capitalise. We are indiscriminately, and helplessly, haunted by strange, salacious and sickly seductive images.

As is the case with industry-induced desires, there is an invented humanity attached with the idea of flirting and lusting. Many stakeholders contribute to an audiovisual discourse in support of eating more, touring more, seeing more, touching more and, in the same series, ogling more and copulating more! It dwells upon the idea of deprivation and fans a sense of inferiority and superiority about who consumes how much! Larger-than-life spectacles are created about our instincts. Instincts common to humans, animals and maybe even in the vegetation around us seem to have acquired extraordinary appearances. Repressed in the regime of morality, the ordinary human instincts have radically overpowering manifestations in the regime of commerce. We are sandwiched between the two anti-human regimes. Either we ought to be foregoing what we are or we ought to become something that we are not. We are indeed not sexually obsessed, instinctually frustrated, bull-like creatures without any sense of commitment to values, aesthetics, ethics and care. Nor are we those idealised humans, ready to join the pantheon of gods in the temple called family, worshipping the singular sun alone. We are instinctually ordinary, fallible. Hence, we are ready to get attracted to various humans we come across, able to flirt, romance, lust and love and then return to the nest to happily discharge our commitment towards care, nurturance, love and compassion. We laugh at ourselves in hindsight. 'Ah! Can't believe I did that, but it was sweet!'

There is an enormous possibility in our ordinary instinctual arrangement if we are free enough to understand it. If it was not repressed, we would find release from one stage of ordinariness to another. More often, we are misguided by the economics of imageries, the industry-induced seduction. Since there is seldom a free conversation about such human possibilities, we remain trapped in confusion, guilt and instinctual drives. We may turn more truthful than ever before in the regimes of morality if we are free to take note of a possibly committed man or woman indulging in chance flirtations. Or is it too much to expect from the regime of morality that is too moribund to allow free reasoning?

Notes

1. It is in such a social condition that marriage and commitment are also seen through the problem of dependence. A technical data-driven analysis thus may not suffice in underlining the human angle of the issue, as seen in Steven L. Nock, 'Commitment and Dependency in Marriage,' *Journal of Marriage and Family* 57, no. 2 (1995): 503–514.
2. See 'Despite Ban on Several Websites, India leads Porn Consumption on Smartphones in 2019,' *CNBCTV18*, 2 January 2020, accessed 19 February 2021, https://www.cnbctv18.com/buzz/despite-ban-on-several-websites-india-leads-porn-consumption-on-smartphones-in-2019-pornhub-4980631.htm#:~:text=A%20new%20report%20has%20revealed,double%20to%2018GB%20by%202024.
One such report-based article is by Nandini Yadav, 'Despite Porn Ban, India is the Third Largest Porn watcher with Thirty Percent Female Users,' *FirstPost*, 25 February 2020, accessed 19 February 2021, https://www.firstpost.com/tech/news-analysis/despite-porn-ban-india-is-3rd-largest-porn-watcher-with-30-female-users-5721351.html.
3. Pornography is a much-talked-about process and product connected with marriage, personality and relationships. Among many representative preliminaries, the following is perhaps a more rounded one. See Daniel

Linz and Neil Malamuth, *Pornography* (Delhi: Sage, 1993). For the relation between pornography and various facets of modernity, the following is an appropriate compilation of essays. See Lynn Hunt, ed., *The Invention of Pornography: Obscenity and the Origins of Modernity, 1500–1800* (New York: Zone Books, 1993).

9

Match, Friendship and Marriage: Looking for Romance

Let us think of a familiar love story, one of friendship and relationships, that has influenced us when we were growing up. A boy and girl began to see each other. Each was from a qualitatively different social position, location and perspective. Yet each could hear their throbbing heart and singing mind, which they longed to share with the other. They fought where they should have fought. They disagreed where they felt it necessary. Yet they stayed together, for they valued friendship, love and relationships far more than anything else. The staying together allowed for spontaneity and possibility in the relationship. There was a healthy anatomy of the relationship that emerged and flourished. This did not go down well with their respective families. They were pushed to the brink, from where either they had to commit suicide together or they had to be annihilated by those who gave them birth. In such a story of friendship, love and relationship, we learned how the world could go against the ordinary ways in which folks come together, forge friendships, long for love and reaffirm relationships. Such tales have a notion of the 'ordinarily social' lovers who did not let social stratification and hierarchy condition their friendship and love. The ordinary 'social' became distinguishable from the usual 'social'[1] in the friendship of the lovers, for, they deviated from socially set norms of befriending, loving and even mating. Hence, an intolerant society wished them away as much as it wished them dead. The annihilation of those seemingly radical and ordinarily social lovers was the onset of what we see today in yet another realm of ordinariness.

In this experiential narrative, like in the other chapters in this book, the pronouns of reference get confused for a sense of conversation to arise. 'We', 'you', 'I' and 'they' all seem to join in as the first person—with due grammatical hazard. We have heard umpteen such love stories when we were growing up. A variety of stories from across cultural contexts, some with known authors and many without, conjured friendship, love and relationships in our imagination. Moreover, they instilled in us the value of being ordinarily social friends. If Shakespeare gave us the dramatic tale of Romeo and Juliet, the legendary Waris Shah penned for us the fascinating drama of Heer–Ranjha around the mid-18th century. Another Sufi poet, Hashim Shah, wrote many *qissa*s (performative poetry from the Punjab region) on Sohni–Mahiwal, Sassi–Punnu and Shirin–Farhad during the time of Maharaja Ranjit Singh. We also hear of the folk ballad 'Reshma-Chuharmal' that is performed in various parts of Bihar in *nautanki or naach* (folk theatre).[2] In all such tales, the lovers enter into a friendship due to the spontaneous experience of emotions despite the differences in their caste, class and such stratifications based on their sociocultural background. There could be various versions of these stories performed on various occasions. However, the basic theme is more or less the same: ordinarily social friendship, love and relationships must be annihilated. Everything that we grow up valuing is subject to 'extraordinary tampering' that represses one level of ordinariness for another one that looks little less ordinary and potentially extraordinary.

So many things about our friendship and love that we learn in childhood do not remain the same. In our teens, we generously made friends without caring for the other's social profile. In adolescence, we were ever ready to romance with familiar as well as unfamiliar people. We hung out with friends, no matter how pretty, strange and grotesque they seemed. Our youth enabled us to befriend and romance anyone indiscriminately.[3] The so-called turbulent time in our growing up is indeed the time when we seem most truthful to our feelings—so earnestly truthful that we did not hesitate to write a few love letters in blood! We were so curiously candid that we took little time in shedding tears, effortlessly and unwittingly too! This is much before you began to rationally hide your feelings, stifle your tears and swallow the lump of sadness that jammed your throat. The only rationale that we pursued was our instant emotional responses. This was when your mind and heart were in a holy nuptial knot, having constant conversation with each other on issues of everyday concern. This was when everything mundane, ordinary and simple was most cherubic for us. Across the ocean of adolescence, you metamorphosed into something like a sophisticated and skilled monster. We all wish to sweep everything formerly valued under the carpet, hoping it is never rolled up for sunning or cleaning. It feels safe that you or your parents have put all the memorabilia of your childhood and adolescence in a few cartons, which are safely parked in an attic or a cupboard in the study or in a godown or garage. Once in a while, you may visit them, selectively, and as soon as you feel embarrassed, you scurry back to everything that is glittery and golden. Who cares about that old maxim that all that glitters is not gold!

Your friendship glitters. Most probably, you are happily in a friendship since you and your friends have matching interests. You both eat beef or you both are against those who eat any non-vegetarian food. You both are infrequent smokers or you both hate anyone smoking around you. How funny is that? You and your friend both appreciate the same colour, same music, same cinema and the same kind of food. It is pathological sameness that you celebrate in your taste, preferences and even ideology. You are both for Marxism or anti-Marxism. You both are liberal or conservative or are both confused about liberalism. Even more ironic, you both are inclined to believe that fascism is the best remedy for the failure of liberalism! This is truly frightening. You have sweet little chats because you are similar, but neither is capable of getting into a conversation that can invite you both to lock horns in an intellectual duel. After all, you have grown up hearing from your parents and your teachers alike: do not argue! Everyone tends to deem argumentative behaviour as negative behaviour. We think only enemies argue against each other, like in the courtroom.

Any child disagreeing with the parents is declared a bad child with bad upbringing and bad behaviour. Sociologists call them deviants; psychologists cast them as delinquents; psychiatrists may dub it as some kind of psychosis. Gosh, no wonder why anyone who questions the establishment is immediately looked down upon as Naxal (the popular phrase 'Urban Naxal'), a source of terror! This is truly an anti-social scheme of thinking in which friendship is the most vulnerable relationship. It is anti-social since it gives more importance to sameness; even though, socially, we can seldom be the same!

The sameness is in the mind, not in the society. Socially, we are more inclined to ask questions, express reservations, highlight differences, connect divergent aspects, argue out positions and iron out perspectives. This is how, ordinarily, social could be different and distinct in dialogue. Social as a characteristic of society at large encompasses many layers of ordinariness. When referred to as ordinary social, we are hinting at a level of ordinariness pertaining to social, a noun par excellence. This is like those poetic epic characters mentioned at the outset, who were different, in the fold of ordinarily social and yet able to forge friendship and romance. We need not always turn to profoundly sophisticated thinkers on the notion of difference such as Jacques Derrida[4] or Judith Butler[5] to decipher ordinarily available ideas. Socially, we are more inclined to have conversations in which we have a chance, a better one, to know one another through our differences. We fear, in general, differences in conversation. Hence, no friendship is for conversation! No conversation means no emotional fluidity and intellectual flexibility. Tomes are written in praise of conversation. We may use them for writing an op-ed piece for a newspaper or for writing another brilliant research paper. But we do not allow ourselves a friendship for conversation.

Friendship is, ironically, for chitchat, sharing feelings with, as we often see, 'like-minded folks'. This is friendship for a range of instrumental needs, such as eating ice-cream, watching movies and 'hanging out'. This friendship certainly needs an abundance of visual testimonies, in selfies and photographs on Instagram and Facebook, as though there is no friendship unless visually reaffirmed on social networking sites. One can hear some people saying, 'Hey, we need to show the world that we are friends.' One wonders what kinds of friends are those people who never care to show off except when there are challenges and conflict. You may sift through your memory and find that fellow who fought against someone who uttered a bad word about you. Or someone who turned up unexpectedly to just say hello when you felt terribly lonely! There are no photographs, but you vividly remember that lost bond. At best, you hummed together, often ending up giggling in embarrassment. You wrote passionate letters of love and hatred, agreement and disagreement, sorrow and happiness, to each other, many a time without posting them. Such friends were in society yet independent of social conditioning. Such friendship, in the fold of an ordinary social setting, perhaps lasted longer than their lives.

The visually documented friendships of our times seem to have more tenuous longevity. It will last until you make your differences public. The further irony is that it may last a little longer and actually get converted into some sort of relationship if you convert each other into mutually useful resources. Say, for example, you start a business venture or a collaborative project or a network of like-minded folks interested in doing something together. Deadliest of all is when two people, like attracted to like, decide to settle down 'happily ever after'! Each is a useful resource to the other. The wife looks at the husband as a profit, and the husband thinks that the wife is capital. It may be the other way around too. It is not that this mechanical union is totally devoid of love, lust, sex and reproduction. It looks as sweet as the finest of chocolates, which begins to melt with a fluctuation in the temperature. The best chocolates cannot withstand the rise in mercury; hence, they either need to be put in the refrigerator or an air-conditioned environment. Emotional mercury, or mercurial emotions, threaten this sweet, chocolate-like, vulnerable relationship. It needs, inevitably, an eternally air-conditioned surrounding. The romance in this relationship cannot tolerate sweat and grime, the dust of time or a walk in the open park that obviously cannot have air-conditioning like that in a shopping mall. Curiously enough, the family around such a useful marriage is equally enigmatic. Relatives flock for benefits, as we do with chocolates, as long as they are in good shape at the right temperature. As long as the marriage is basking in temperate air-conditioning, everyone from the family is ready to join in. All helping hands come running when no help is needed. It all changes as soon as the temperature is out of control and the mercury starts shooting up. In some other conditions, the metaphor of chocolate will not work. Hence, one has to press for some replacement of metaphor, but the motive and consequences would be the same. Such friendships and marriages entail a good amount of spending time together, observing each other and then taking a decision. The man and woman may think of the certainty about the calculation. After all, both sides followed a proper scientific procedure, a rational calculation. No one doubts the method and magical output. Yet, one is not ready to own up to the consequences, unless the consequences are exactly as expected. If anything untoward happens, the blame game begins. A trail of bad blood, bad-mouthing, allegations and counter-allegations ensues. The mathematical neatness with which one entered such a friendship and marriage does not exist at the point of the exit. It seems the gate to exit is so narrow and the man and woman who were pronounced one, by ritual or by law, are in such haste that there is bound to be a scuffle. The entry was mathematically smooth, the exit melodramatically bumpy.

The complexity in finding the right match and deciding on marriage is heavily conditioned by intermediary agencies. Maternal uncles or aunts are no longer the trusted experts in finding a match. Those conventional matchmakers often fail to match the 'needs and expectations' of the two families from where the two significant individuals are ready to get into a conjugal relationship. Many a time, the families are only approving agencies. If they are not, there is supposed to be some kind of tussle between the family and the significant individual. Even uncles and aunts browse the matches proposed by expert agencies. Expert agencies and neutral matchmakers generate a list of potential matches. On what grounds? Sameness! The details from the matrimonial pages in newspapers and matrimonial websites vouch for this minimum criterion. They ensure that a doctor marries a doctor, an engineer marries an engineer, a professor marries a professor and a clerk marries a clerk. The aim is marriage between the same income group, same professional background, same class, same status, same religion and caste, same region and locality—the same identity in short. Not to say, this basic of sameness is the premise of the sociocultural mathematics of relationships. Such mathematics answers the question: who should marry whom? Furthermore, the sociocultural mathematics entails 'wordings of the world'[6] (categories and concepts) in matrimonial advertisements such as:

> a Tamil Brahmin, vegetarian, teetotaller, apolitical, classical music enthusiast, engineer boy would like a Tamil Brahmin, vegetarian, teetotaller, apolitical, classical music enthusiast, school teacher or professor girl!

There are many such advertisements, replacing Tamil with the regional-linguistic-cultural identification of other places. There could be something like the following too: *Samartha* Brahmin boy in central government service seeks a Brahmin bride who could be a full-time homemaker.

To some extent, the styles of matrimonial advertisements have qualitatively changed. They are made to look less vulgar about the basic criterion of sameness. Online portals have revolutionised the ideas of matrimonial advertisements. Here is an example of the way one of these websites, Shaadi.com, speak about themselves on its home page:

> Shaadi.com, one of India's best known [sic] brands and the world's largest matrimonial service was founded with a simple objective—to help people find happiness. The company pioneered online matrimonial advertisements in 1996 and continues to lead the exciting matrimony category after more than a decade. By redefining the way Indian brides and grooms meet for marriage, Shaadi.com has created a world-renowned service that has touched over 35 million people.[7]

The other websites rival in proving themselves as more trusted brands with glorious results. The point is that a brand is finding happiness for people! Why is it then a problem if happiness itself becomes a brand, a thing? Why is it then a problem if a relationship itself becomes a branded product, a thing? Any criterion set by such brands would be the most decisive one. No one can dare to drift away from the brand, the criteria, the idea of friendship and relationship nurtured by these brands. There is a sense of risk, insecurity and uncertainty without the most reassuring 'branded' service provider, the so-called experts. All this sets our mindset, according to which it is just fine to be like this, deriving a sense of security in branded products called matrimonial alliances. Equally expert service providers come into the picture if there is a matrimonial dispute: legal as well as nonlegal mediators through whom the man and woman speak. They do not speak directly; they cannot stand each other. They even avoid looking at each other's face during the dispute. They hold each other responsible for the failure of the project named relationship. Those who were once happily married do not seem to know how to happily walk out of the marriage. Mudslinging, abusive accusations and total breakdown of the semblance of conversation dominate. The annihilation of ordinariness is thus consummated.

The hilarity exacerbates when one hires a detective service to find evidence of the other's culpability. There are these 'expert service providers' too. One such service provider, Detectives India, writes on its web page on 'Matrimonial Investigations':

> Matrimonial dispute develop [sic] due to suspicious activities of life partners. Some marriages even breakdown [sic] due to suspicion. We help our clients in ascertaining various information pertaining to their spouses which includes cases of extramarital affair, adultery or any other activities. Further, our professionals understand these cases need to be probed very cautiously to safeguard the matrimonial alliance.[8]

Such services underline the utter helplessness in relationships gone awry. Doubting each other replaces the solemn oath of trusting each other. One looks at the other with love laced with suspicion. This is the conclusion of the mathematics of friendship, marriage and relationships built on the premise of sameness today. No expertise of any mediator can change the mindset. Instead, they seem to sustain the risk, fear and suspicion. This is indeed an extraordinary situation in which it seems a challenge to develop an ordinary relationship with equally ordinary varieties of love, trust, care and compassion or an ordinary friendship where we look at each other as humans with emotions, expectations, greed, selfishness and everything that could make us sensitive to our fallibility. In an ordinary relationship, we are not calculated as perfect resources for each other. The enabling effect of an ordinary relationship make the related folks live through extremities of time. With simplicity, one sails through rough waters. Who would not value a relationship that does not wither away in any weather, be it harsh as a scorching summer or as spine chilling as a wintry winter? There must be some remains of that ideal ordinariness in which we could have freewheeling conversations about who we really are. It was perhaps a longing for that ordinariness that made Amrita Pritam, the poet of ordinary feelings, write an ode to Waris Shah, the poet who narrated the tale of Ranjha in the story of Heer–Ranjha. Pritam's ode is actually an ode to the ordinariness obscured by the ominous politics of sameness. Let us borrow a translation of the poem, from Punjabi to English, by Nirupama Dutt,[9] to elucidate the lost ordinariness:

> Waris Shah I call out to you today to rise from your grave
> Rise and open a new page of the immortal book of love
> A daughter of Punjab had wept and you wrote many a dirge
> A million daughters weep today and look at you for solace
> Rise o beloved of the aggrieved, just look at your Punjab
> Today corpses haunt the woods, Chenab overflows with blood
> Someone has blended poison in the five rivers of Punjab
> This water now runs through the verdant fields and glades
> This fertile land has sprouted poisonous weeds far and near
> Seeds of hatred have grown high, bloodshed is everywhere
> Poisoned breeze in forest turned bamboo flutes into snakes
> Their venom has turned the bright and rosy Punjab all blue
> Throats have forgotten how to sing, the yarn is now broken
> Friends are lost and the spinning wheel has gone silent
> Boats released from the harbor toss in the rough waters
> The peepul has broken its branches on which swings hung
> The flute that played notes of love is now forever lost
> Brothers of Ranjha have lost the hero's devotion, his charm
> Blood rains on the earth, even the graves are oozing red
> The princesses of love are now weeping midst the tombs
> Today all have turned into Qaidon, thieves of love and beauty
> O where on earth do we go to look for a Waris Shah once more

Let us try to retrieve that ordinary friendship, love and relationship that made us cry when we heard a dirge and made us laugh when we heard lovers celebrate differences. As suggested earlier, there may be many folds of ordinary social. For example, one in which we count and calculate and the other in which we trust and live. Both may be duly interrelated. Notwithstanding, in this rumination, there is an attempt to emphasise on the one which nurtures simplicity of relationships. That fold of ordinary social in which such relationships flourished is perhaps still there under the obscurity of sociocultural mathematics, the sociology of stratification, the anthropology of kinship, the history of emotions and the poetry of feelings. Hence, we hum without qualms all those songs, such as the one by Amrita Pritam, to remind ourselves of the imperative of recalling the forgotten! Indeed, humming is a far more genuine and exquisitely ordinary start than framing a technical research question.

Notes

1. Here, social is not a qualifier for something else. It is a noun that ought to be subject to scrutiny the way it was in Gopal Guru and Sundar Sarukkai, *Experience, Caste, and the Everyday Social* (Delhi: Oxford University Press, 2019).
2. A fascinating research that compiled some performances to build up an argument on cultural labour in folk world view is worth a mention here. See Brahma Prakash, *Cultural Labour: Conceptualising the 'Folk Performance' in India* (Delhi: Oxford University Press, 2019). Alongside, it would make sense to read the folk songs sung by Maithili-speaking women that curate a cultural trope for reasoning with death in Dev Nath Pathak, *Living and Dying: Meanings in Maithili Folklore* (Delhi: Primus, 2018).
3. A trajectory of courtship in popular fiction in India also complicates the idea of mate selection. See an unusually exciting essay by Patricia Uberoi, 'A Suitable Romance: Trajectories of Courtship in Indian Popular Fiction', in ed. Shoma Munshi, *Images of the 'Modern Woman' in Asia: Global Media, Local Meanings* (London: Routledge Curzon, 2001), 169–187.
4. Derrida's systematic deliberation on the philosophical trajectory and notions of friendship could be essential for an academic deliberation. Some of the ideas in this essay may resonate with Derrida's, but there is a conscious attempt to avoid replication or technical citation. For further exploration, see Jacques Derrida, *The Politics of Friendship*, trans. George Collins (London: Verso, 1997).
5. In an interesting interview, Butler paved the way for rethinking friendship based on the idea of difference in the context of the queer. The idea of difference-based friendship in this chapter may concur with Butler, but there is a conscious distancing from sophisticated theory in order to maintain a conversational flow. To explore further, see Pheng Cheah and Elizabeth Grosz, 'The Future of Sexual Difference: An Interview with Judith Butler and Drucilla Cornell', *Diacritics* 28, no. 1 (1998): 19–42.
6. While an anthropologist tries to word the world, the act also gets worded by the world. This is the interplay of the self and other, if any. Wording of

the world, in this context, is meant to play with a titular phrase in Roma Chatterji, ed., *Wording the World: Veena Das and the Scenes of Inheritance* (New York: Fordham University Press, 2015).

7. 'Letter from Founder, Shaadi.com,' accessed on 19 February 2021, https://www.shaadi.com/introduction/index/letter-from-cmd.
8. 'Matrimonial Investigation', Detectives India, accessed on 19 February 2021, http://www.detectivesindia.co.in/matrimonial-investigations.html.
9. Nirupama Dutt, 'When Amrita Pritam Called Out to Waris Shah in a Heartrending Ode while Fleeing the Partition Riots,' *Scroll*, 14 August 2017, accessed on 19 February 2021, https://scroll.in/article/847004/when-amrita-pritam-called-out-to-waris-shah-in-a-heartrending-ode-while-fleeing-the-partition-riots.

10

The Teacher, the Taught and Traditions: A Dream Lost

The most puzzling remark I ever got as a teacher has been invariably of this kind: sir, you are a great teacher! I could never deal with this congratulatory judgement made by students. To confess the truth, it always upsets the teacher in me. It is truly a failure at my job if students end up saying such plain and simple things about the teacher that I tried to be. I usually try to be an ordinary and truthful human with the students and, usually, it backfires, since no one expects a teacher to be so ordinary. Once in a while, it does not, because the students decide to join in the conversation with a fellow human and not because I have ceased to be an ordinary human. There is nothing congratulatory about it. This is the most original format of the relationship between the teachers and the students, an ordinary relationship of ordinary folks geared to an ordinary goal—understanding. Hence, in Tulsidas's Ramayana, there comes a significant moment in the relationship between the teacher Vashishth and his pupils, the four scions from the kingdom of Ayodhya. Vashishth reminds his pupils that they are not extraordinary princes as long as they are students. They must not expect the kind of love and compassion they had at home. They ought to be ordinary boys in pursuit of knowledge, struggling with the basics, leading an austere life and practising the skills to understand the nuances. This is all to unfold with due ordinariness. In this framework, the teacher is not a miracle-maker either. If any miracles are to occur, it is as a result of the interaction between the teacher and the taught. Unfortunately, we dubbed teachers as miracle (wo)men and ennobled them. Now, we have declared them in the national educational policy document as 'service providers'. It only makes it possible for teachers to become treacherous if we reduce them into a mind fit for any of these labels.

Usually, teachers are looked up to by both parents and students as a noble source of light. To make matters worse, the administration and the State, media, elites and even intelligentsia seek to imagine teachers as extraordinary creatures. A slight error causes the looking up to transform into looking down upon so dramatically that one begins to doubt both, looking up and looking down. Either way, it sounds like fantasies through which we behold our teachers. The preferable part of a chosen mythology or wonderful tales from modern history aid in shaping and sustaining an imagination. There are equally big fantasies through which students and parents, society and state, and administration and environment tend to behold a teacher. It is nice to think up fantasies, dreams, utopias and such insights that allow us to make sense of our realities beyond time and space. Fantasies are more than mere realities, and no one can dismiss their significance. However, at times, or given a historical condition, it could often be that a dream becomes hysteria; fantasy gives way to fanaticism. Both the teacher and students suffer from this possibility a great deal.

Our traditions and societies do not seem to be kind to our teachers. The normative gaze judges a teacher in the most outdated fashion. We dehumanise our teachers in schools, in colleges and even in the universities where we are supposed to have come of our intellectual age. We mistake teachers for super-humans, just like Max Weber[1] mistook them to be entirely value-neutral in an ideal classroom situation. If Weber insisted on value neutrality, we tend to stress on teachers being value-loaded. Teachers are made of their ideologies and utopias, their facts and fantasies, and their poetics and politics. They are no superhumans, in the sense that they have also gone through socialisation in society and re-socialisation in skill training or university life. Teachers are bundles of values, and all values need not be unquestionable across time. They could be vulnerable like other humans too. No matter how safe they play, how reticent they are about their feelings, how calculative they are in their profession, they could be as gullible as other creatures in the midst of the game of life. Find me a single teacher who would not like to draw his or her salary and any teacher who would have no desire to be acknowledged for his or her work! It is difficult, since we all operate with material interest, and that is fine. There is an ordinary core to the extraordinary person we call teacher. Moreover, the vulnerability of a teacher makes him or her human. Thank goodness for this, or else the teachers would be no different from army lieutenants. Or have they become lieutenants of some kind?[2]

This is, however, not to suggest that one can absolve a teacher of wrongdoing, nor is the intention to valorise vulnerability to the extent of dwarfing the enormous possibility in the personality of our teachers. Such conclusions would be as erroneous as the expectations fantasised about earlier. If we have accepted teachers as humans, with skills to reason, empathise, learn and teach, grow and help everyone else to grow along, we have indeed allowed ourselves to see more in our teachers beyond the limits of eclipsed fantasies. It is time that we admit that the becoming of a teacher entails a process so prolonged that it gets difficult to ever declare the finality of the product. Teachers are, in other words, ever in the flux of becoming. It resonates with an idea that one of the greatest thinkers of education, J. Krishnamurti, gave us:

> What is a teacher?... The teacher is bringing about the unconditioning of the human brain; not only his own brain but the brains of the students.... In relationship with the student he is helping both the student and himself to free consciousness from limitation.[3]

There may be failures in the endeavour to become a teacher. The possible inclines and declines never disappear in the biography of a teacher. Hence, we should be equally tolerant and willing to understand the possible failures of a teacher too.

We ought to be thinking of those who are taught in the same vein. The students seem to be entirely at the mercy of the teachers. The word *taught* seems to mean yet another thing—the content that a teacher delivers. We say 'what my teacher taught me today'. We will come to that meaning associated with the verb 'taught' shortly. Before that, let us admit that students are made of various components coming from biography, history, society, polity, culture and civilisation. They are human too and, therefore, we have plenty of mischief, rude and rowdy behaviour, indifference to teachers' expectations and a challenge to the idea of administrative order. As long as this is the case, the students have the possibility of bringing in new motives, focuses, ideas, insights, stories and arguments. Students ride roughshod, effecting the affects, anger and hatred, love and affection, conformity and rebellion. This is so fascinating that all such effects, even though seemingly adverse, become tools for better creative outputs in the classroom. So long as these students' interjections are labelled as disturbances, the classroom would not be a site of excitement for both, teacher and the students. True, there is more than the romantic understanding of the students' fallibility and vulnerability in the classroom. There could be occasions when one or two students in a class size of forty could dominate the discourse. They may indulge themselves in the egoistic display of intellectual supremacy. Teachers are not meant for only two such students. They are for all forty and, therefore, there could be a little jarring pull of threads. It is very likely that someone may occupy the centre, leaving everyone else on the periphery. Someone may triumph in making a particular ideological, theoretical or philosophical perspective look like the single-most suitable way of thinking. This is, in general, the vulnerability of a conversation, and this is not necessarily a problem of the select students. This could also happen when the teacher's voice appears as the singular and superior one. Have we not come across innumerable teachers who were in love with their own voices? Only they knew what they were talking about when they spent hours without engaging with any of the students in the classroom. Every monologue need not be an engaging soliloquy. We see this in theatre as well as in the classrooms during the monologues of the lecturers. On all such occasions, when the teachers teaching is equal to talking in a kind of echo chamber, we witness the tussle of power in the classroom. The students crave for dialogue, but the teachers deliver only monologues. So, this fundamental is to be cleared. Both teachers and students are human and, hence, play out their roles through vulnerability.

Many great thinkers on education made us understand this very basic idea about the ordinariness of teachers and students and about the simplicity of the process of teaching and learning. The purpose is not to recount them all here in this essay. For the sake of convenient reflection, we can once again turn to J. Krishnamurti. His talisman called freedom was such an anchor to the conjoined world of both, the teachers and the taught. If both teacher and student do not feel free, there is little education. With so much importance attached to formal teaching and formal learning that is geared towards an excruciatingly painful system of examination, we make a serious compromise about the character of education in general. The strain on teachers and students is inevitable in the bureaucratic humbug that schools erect in the name of quality education. There is no space for anyone to breathe freely in such an arrangement, let alone reflective learning in repose. In the name of education, we have prisons in which both the alleged victimiser and victims suffer equally. The pathology of education robs the freedom of both, the teachers and the students equally.

This is the scenario in which education has been transformed into an extraordinary entity. Everyone lusts for this fetish, at any price. Models are set up in the megacities, and the country cousins rival each other in emulating them. Remember the small-town private school operating with the tagline 'English medium school'? They copy the blunders created in the big cities in big schools with big banners and big merchandise. How can there be any space for the growth of the mind, channelising of emotions and dialogues of teachers and students in this ingeniously engineered bureaucratic organisation called a school? The teachers have to abide by the rules and regulations coming from the management boards, the state and examination bodies. Yet, on festive occasions, such as Teachers' Day or Guru Purnima, we hear platitudes about *guru-shishya parampara*, the traditional system of teaching and learning premised on the teacher–student relationship. Any mention of such a tradition, thus becomes mere rhetoric for pride, prejudice and politics. Rhetoric does not deliver relationships. It may be, however, the other way round; there may appear some useful rhetoric in a thriving relationship between teachers and students. We have Greek intellectual history informing us about the emergence of powerful rhetoric due to such traditions of relationships between students and teachers. Of course, closer home too, we have several examples. Something so sublime as the poetry of Amir Khusrow during the time of the Delhi Sultanate in the 13th century took birth due to such a relationship, that of the teacher Hazrat Nizamuddin Auliya and the student Amir Khusrow. If a historian feels upset and says that Khusrow was already writing poetry before he met his spiritual mentor, Hazrat Nizamuddin, we will refrain from making a generalisation. The point, however, is that an ordinary love between teacher and student could result in dialogic relations such as those that enriched the poetry of Amir Khusrow. Elsewhere, in the context of transformative pedagogy, an ingenius educationist Paulo Freire[4] made a significant observation about love, relationship and dialogue. In love, the teacher and students enter into a dialogue with mutual respect. Such dialogues are not only to serve the instant teaching and learning. They also play an instrumental role in the transformation of an unequal society where inequality flourished due to age-old institutions and subjugation of the weaker groups. That is the context in which the relationship of the mystic mentor and poet Amir Khusrow makes deeper sense. The relationship was of such profundity that they sought for even posthumous proximity. The graves of Amir Khusrow and Hazrat Nizamuddin Auliya in the same premises, literally facing each other, are the testimonial of a tradition in which the teacher and the student entered each other's mind in a relational mode. The relationship brought out the creative impulses that we hear in so many qawwali songs even today. Aggrieved at the death of his beloved teacher, Khusrow is supposed to have recited:

Gori soye sej par much par dare kes / Chal Khusrow ghar aapne / Sanjh bhaye chahu des[5]
(With hair scattered over face, my beloved sleeps on the bed; let us go home, Khusrow, it is night all over the place).

This is not very different from what Krishnamurti had envisaged. An ordinary function of education, as it was in the example of Khusrow and Hazrat Nizamuddin, is to provide deeper liberation of the mind and spirit. In ordinary education, science and spirituality, intellect and emotions, and mind and body unfold together. There is no separation between text(books) and context (real-life experiences). If you have to think of formulating an educational policy document such as the National Curriculum Framework for school education to emphasise the relation between text and context, there must be something greatly amiss with the idea of education. Let alone teachers and students, even stakeholders with vested interests seem to be at a loss with the basic notion of education. Perhaps this is the reason why almost everyone and anyone claims to be an educationist today. Anyone can wax eloquent about education, as to what it should be, what it should be doing and what all those who deal with education should be doing. This is so since there is an utter fogginess about the ordinary phenomenon called education that demands ordinary practices, such as what the saint poet Kabir had in mind when he said the following:

Guru kumhar shish kumbh hai / Gadhi gadhi kadhai khot / Antar hath sahar dai/ Bahar bahai chot[6]
(The teacher is the potter, and the student a raw earthen pot; like the potter supports the pot with his hand on the inside and slaps it from outside to make it strong, the teacher shall be firm outside and mellow within when dealing with a student).

Ordinarily, it is a healthy practice to be firm and demanding, clear and communicative with students. With time, it has degenerated into a cruel regime of corporal punishment. Furthermore, it has degenerated to such an extent that if a teacher is firm, a student along with parents can go to the court of law and have the teacher behind bars for a year along with the fine of ₹50,000, according to the law in India. Since the ordinariness is obscured irredeemably, some traditional nuggets of wisdom may be ridiculed by many teachers, students and everyone who partakes in the extraordinary notion of education. Say, for example, how would one understand this articulation of Kabir:

Kabir hari ke ruthte / Guru ke sharnai jaye / Kahai Kabir guru ruthte/ Hari nahi haut sahai[7]
(If your god is against you, your teacher will help you out; if your teacher is against you, no god can be of aid).

Since God is also a prisoner of extraordinary temples, where the ordinariness of gods is jeopardised, why do we even listen to Kabir? The latter is obviously trying to tell us that your bad luck can be still redeemed if you are in a dialogue with your teacher. You can understand, rationalise and find a way to cope. But you have already diminished a teacher into a service provider; you would not have a dialogue with him or her. You might want to go to another service provider, a branded spiritual guru who would not facilitate a dialogue. Instead, such an expert guru would preach at you with clearly defined dos and don'ts. There is not a relationship in either of the cases which can liberate you or persuade you to explore and arrive at your own destinations.

An important realisation needs to be reiterated before we tend to think that traditions are putting the teachers on higher pedestals with greater responsibility. True, teachers have responsibility. But what kind of responsibility? It is not necessarily to coach and help a student obtain good grades or, as every parent in India may aspire for their children, to get 99 per cent. Instead, it is a responsibility to forge relationships between teacher and students, between text and context, between intellect and emotions, and so on. It is in this relationship that the ordinariness of both, teacher and the taught, shall unfold. This is where even a firm and strict, seemingly intimidating and yet intimate teacher comes into existence. Would the business of extraordinary educational vision give way to this ordinariness of education? The stakes of the shareholders in the business of education are too high to make one optimistic. However, pedagogues are supposed to be diehard optimists, so let us join them. I meant the pedagogues, not the pretentious scholars who tend to think too highly of themselves, as though they were really the owls of Minerva!

Notes

1. The two famous essays by Max Weber, famously known as vocation lectures, *Science as Vocation* and *Politics as Vocation*, should be closely read together in order to understand the Weberian deliberation. The mention of Weber's notions about teachers is only to further the conversation rather than a systematic analysis of his arguments. For further on vocations, see Max Weber, *The Vocation Lectures: Science as Vocation, Politics as Vocation* (Cambridge: Hacket Publishing Company, 2004).
2. This possibility emerged from the systematic critical reading by Michel Foucault elsewhere. There is no conscious attempt in this essay to speak through Foucault. Yet one can explore further to see the resonance in

M. Foucault, *Discipline and Punish: The Birth of the Prison*, trans. A. Sheridan (New York: Vintage/Random House, 1979).

3. J. Krishnamurti, 'A Teacher is Deeply Involved with the Flowering of Human Beings,' accessed on 19 February 2021, https://jkrishnamurti.org/content/chapter-45-teacher-deeply-involved-flowering-human-beings.

4. Paulo Freire aimed at developing a pedagogy in which love, respect and relationship characterise the dialogue of teachers and students. Such a pedagogy is a harbinger of much-needed transformative politics in societies where unequal relations wrecked possibilities. Explore more with Paulo Freire, *Pedagogy of the Oppressed* (New York: Bloomsbury, 2014). In the same vein, it is also worth pondering on Freire revisiting his central ideas giving more space to hope for social justice in Paulo Freire, *Pedagogy of Hope: Reliving Pedagogy of the Oppressed* (New York: Bloomsbury, 2014).

5. The poem is taken from an online archive, Kavita Kosh, accessed on 19 February 2021, http://kavitakosh.org/kk/चल_खुसरो_घर_आपने_/अमीर_खुसरो.

6. The poem is taken from 'Kabir,' Kavita Kosh, accessed on 19 February 2021, http://kavitakosh.org/kk/कबीर.

7. The poem is taken from 'Kabir,' Kavita Kosh, accessed on 19 February 2021, http://kavitakosh.org/kk/कबीर.

11

I Am Nothing, Just a Teacher: A Dream Found

Some odd organisations are in the business of selling awards for teachers. At times, the email invitations to join in the list of awardees are hilarious. Each addressee of such invitation emails is addressed as a potential awardee, and it showers bizarre accolades to woo the vulnerable egos of teachers. I am sure there are similar awards for other professionals as well. Every now and then, a letter comes to invite nominations for the awards. They request the addressee to nominate any teacher who they think deserves an award. Some of the addressees nominate their senior colleagues and, at times, they also nominate themselves. The nominated teachers are invited to receive the award in gala ceremonies held in five-star hotels or such posh locations. Almost every nominated teacher is declared a winner of the award by some strange jury. The winning teachers are then asked to pay fees in cash, ten, twenty or thirty thousand, depending on the grade of the awards. The winners return home with glorious awards, felicitation letters and mementos. At times, such award-winning teachers are given a red-carpet welcome in the institutions to which they are affiliated. Many of these winner-teachers are in private universities, colleges and even in public universities. They post photographs holding awards or flashing the letter of felicitation that says 'Best Teacher of the Year' on social media! These award ceremonies are annual events, and everyone in the teaching profession is invited to be nominated or nominate, with a price to pay. It looks like there are many takers for these awards. Some colleagues purchase such an award and diligently boast about it on social media pages—with beatific smiles and grotesque smugness on their faces. That is the reason for the frequency of the emails and the soaring charges for the awards. Should we conclude that teachers have become willing consumers of these awards? The purpose is not to answer such a difficult question. It is to take note of the hilarity of changes that have reduced the possibility for someone to be an ordinary teacher. Sometimes, these spurious awards are available for sale and, sometimes, genuine awards are instituted by government agencies towards which teachers are lured. Either way, an award-inclined teacher looks desperate to get rid of the inherent ordinariness of the vocation of teaching.

In universities across India, we see some teachers trying hard to accomplish the goals that they set for themselves, perhaps at the onset of their teaching careers. What are the goals? To become head of the department, dean, provost, pro-vice chancellor and even chancellor? Many share their photographs online, acting as though they are masters of destiny, with such captions: 'Today I became the head of the department. My mother always dreamt of this golden day, and I thank god for this great achievement!' Some teachers distribute sweets when they become the head of a department. Students and colleagues queue up to congratulate them. Subdued but noticeable fanfare ensues. If this appears too banal to the teachers with a scholarly disposition, let us not forget another variety of alluring carrot that dangles before the minds of scholarly teachers. They receive emails inviting them to send their books for award competitions. The scholarly teachers do it, or they ask their trusted students to do the needful. Many such academic friends post the images of awards that their books receive. Needless to say, some of those awards also carry prestige since they are bestowed by literary festivals or professional associations. However, the loud and clear bottom line is: behind every writing, thus, there is an imagined award.

Why should only these awards be ridiculed? There is a bewildering variety of behavioural manifestations of teachers who present volumes of testimonials on one singular tendency: no one wants to be an ordinary teacher. It is no wonder that even schoolteachers start doing things beyond teaching in schools. Some of us may have had the privilege of seeing those teachers in the good old days. Perhaps, the old days were not so good, for those teachers always complained of deprivation. They looked terribly ordinary, so much so that everything today seems extraordinary in comparison. As simply and primly dressed as possible, those teachers commanded immense respect. Clad in a pleated cotton sari or a nicely ironed salwar-kameez or in neat and clean dhoti-kurta, kurta-pyjamas or later even in shirt and trousers, those teachers walked into the classroom with firm yet friendly faces. They were strict about following their dreams and ideals. Many male schoolteachers rode their bicycles from their village to the schools miles away. The salary was so slim that quite a few of them also did farming to provide for their families. Teaching earned respect, not riches. The households of those teachers had a strange charm of simplicity, confused with poverty. The poor teachers, so to say, were large-hearted enough to feed a mango or a guava from their kitchen garden to their visiting pupils. They had their moments of frustration too. We have not yet forgotten, and certainly not forgiven them, for the cruelty they performed on our bodies. Caning was almost normative. Making a student kneel down for the whole class period of 40 minutes was nearly a routine. Embarrassing a laggard was their hobbyhorse. They seemed to be real monsters in our lives too. Much later, when some of us read Franz Kafka's diary,[1] we could instantly note the similarity of our experiences with the teachers of our youth and our fathers. These male authorities, in family and school, shared almost similar sternness and condescending attitudes. However, we related far more with the angst of the subject of a teacher's violence in the narrative of Rabindranath Tagore.[2] Many children used to tremble at the sight of the teachers notorious for caning or twisting the arms of a child who seemed even slightly out of place. We may easily recall some of those heart-wrenching moments when our friends wet their pants in fright of those teachers. A friend who teaches Hindi literature in a university shuddered as he recalled such encounters with teachers. He used a phrase in Hindi to humorously describe the teachers' violence on the student's body, *sharirik samiksha* (literally meaning physical analysis). Just like the child in Tagore's narrative who avenges his suffering by caning a pillar, mimicking the emotion and action of his teacher, we must have hurled a few pebbles in deep vengeance as high in the sky as we could with our small arms. Some of us used to simply hide in solitary corners, crying helplessly. Many students coped with the fear psychosis by simply bunking school. Such is the flipside of ordinariness. It brings pros and cons to such a neat relationship that one gets confused about the conclusions and certainly unsure about the idea of 'good old days'.

In those days, when teachers were almost nothing other than teachers, we had an unusual imagination of a college lecturer or university professor too. The teachers in colleges and universities were not too well off either, but they had better salaries than their counterparts in schools. These professors were almost like second or third fathers to their students. The sociocultural patriarchy of their mind or maybe just a sense of nobility attached to the act of patronising may be blamed for this. They also dressed up ordinarily. If they had to be classy, they wore something traditional such as a *band-gala* blazer. They were invariably seen carrying books in their arms. Their classes had pin-drop silence, as it was in schools. However, unlike schoolteachers, these professors knew that they were something; they did not think they were nothing. Hence, they did grocery shopping on the way back from colleges and universities, went home and watered plants, contributed to the household chores and also read and wrote for their own pleasure and fulfilment. They never failed to tune into radio stations such as BBC, Voice of America and All India Radio for abundant news updates. The people who hung out at tea shops, paan shops and other such places looked at them walking past and matched the time of their watches. These ordinary teachers were almost like walking clock, such terrific embodiments of punctuality. At times, they had students accompanying them from the market to their home, showing loyalty and carrying their baskets full of vegetables. But this labour of love was also accompanied by free lessons from the teachers. Neither did a favour nor did anyone forget to be grateful. This all happened when the teachers knew they were nothing in terms of socio-economic profile and something due to their ennobling work that made them the embodiment of values. One can say that these teachers were living in a time when nation-building was a prime goal in the national agenda. The planned economy perhaps had a bearing upon most of the salaried middle class, and teachers were not exceptions. Yet, such teachers were exceptional in executing the values of a nation. They taught both with equal ease and values of critical thinking and nation building at the same time. Somehow, it did not feel paradoxical. Instead, value of critical thinking aided and enhanced the value of nation building.

Such was the play of something and nothing in the image of the teachers in the days when teaching was truly a 'noble profession' in the eyes of everyone associated with it. Where parents failed, teachers were looked to for alternatives. Things changed pretty fast, with some educational commissions recommending a facelift in the salary profiles of teachers in schools as well as colleges. Rajdoot or Hero Honda motorcycles replaced bicycles. The kitchen garden was given away to a gardener to care for. Grocery shopping was given up for someone else from the family to do, or a student was assigned to this and other chores for no free lesson in return. Teachers started getting empowered in the milieu of empowerment across what was called the third world. It was during this heyday of empowerment that the nothingness of teachers began to disappear fast. Salary had already increased, and the teachers had started joining the consumer crowd. If a little improvement in salary can do such wonders, what was the harm in going for more? Many good teachers began to spend less time in schools and colleges. In fact, it is better to say that the workplace was reduced to a space for hanging out, socialising and humouring oneself. The staff room, common room and teachers' lounges became the real workplace. Teachers exchanged notes about the impact of empowerment, largely about the ways of monetary gain. After all, the children of these teachers were growing up; the demands at home had become louder. It was no longer only silent housewives who whimpered about their needs to be fulfilled. An army of youth on the home front of these teachers expected better than before. Out of necessity as well as with an idea of extra income, many teachers gracefully began to shift their gears. The courtyards, verandahs and living rooms of their houses turned into tuition centres. Early in the morning, at about 5 or 6 AM, the teacher appeared in dhoti, pyjamas or lungi and sat in the wooden chair leaning over the simpleton's table. In a truly traditional manner, the *brahma muhurta* was usefully spent in giving tuitions so that it all looked pretty pious. Students rode their bicycles, jingling the bell on the handle, and parked them against the walls of the teacher's house.

In dimly lit spaces, these tuition classes brought about enlightenment for students who paid from ₹50 to ₹100 per hour. These teachers used to write the details of every chemical formula, laws of physics, twists of calculus and coordinate geometry and rules of grammar on papers with sheaves of paper underneath layered with carbon papers in between the sheets, marked indelibly with illuminated boldness. The classes continued right up to an hour before the teacher had to start getting ready for the classes in schools or colleges. Throughout the tuition class, the teacher delivered similar lessons to four to five groups of students. In each group, some ten to fifteen students attentively received the lessons. Throughout the tuition classes to various groups, the teacher consumed a couple of cups of tea and maybe a plate of peeled and chopped papaya or guava. The mathematics teacher invariably started taking a pinch of tobacco in the middle of the lessons, as though it were essential grist to the mathematical mind. The dust of tobacco used to waft in the space, making every student sniff and sneeze helplessly, and thus all tiny mathematical minds will be opened to solve the mathematics sums. In colleges and schools, the teachers wrote formulas as quietly as possible, without even casting a glance at the pitiable creatures taking notes almost like stenographers. If anyone from the note-taking lot asked for a little explanation, the teacher asked them sombrely to make an effort to understand. What did those folks, who were supposedly the teachers of a supposedly inferior science, meaning social sciences or literature, do? They talked in the class, if they really turned up, and if they turned up in time, they really talked about almost everything not necessarily related to what they were supposed to teach. The ones who were supposed to teach classical literature and, even worse, poetry almost became melodramatic characters from those stories and poems. The diligent note-taking lot of students could hardly fathom what to take and what to leave. Everything turned hilarious, and almost every student attended these classes for the pleasure of the performance by the teacher. The backbenchers did not miss a chance to chuckle aloud, crack jokes and, at times, play so many pranks that the melodramatic teachers had to walk out in protest. But even these melodramatic teachers had students lined up for privately paid lessons in their homes. They dictated notes that described Dorothy falling in love, Caesar shouting out the message and Achilles finally falling down. Those who taught grammar made the language look like mathematics, full of formulas and vocabulary without meanings. Everything had to be eventually mugged up, from science and mathematics to social sciences, language and literature. But in this whole business, the teachers and professors metamorphosed into 'something' of 'some' clear value with 'some' obvious identifications. The nothingness of being just a teacher began to shrink in size and significance. Hence, it multiplied, as many of those teachers who gave privately paid tuitions also became the faculty members of rivalling coaching centres where they went to teach classes in the evening for a couple of hours. It was mostly after the coaching classes that they went to buy vegetables with some of the most loyal students, who probably received more benefits than merely the lessons imparted in the coaching. There is a little more to the story of the teachers becoming something. Many of these teachers also indulged in other odd endeavours. For example, they engaged in small-scale real estate businesses. They purchased land here and there in villages and cities. They built up apartments and rented them out. Some of them actually built students' lodges, where the students lived on rent. The tenant-students also joined in the morning tuition classes given by the same teachers, alias the landlords. Some were far more farsighted and, hence, they had small shops constructed on the land that they purchased at strategic locations suitable to become marketplaces. Sometimes they purchased many ready-to-move in shops to ensure the future of their own growing boys. For daughters, they just had to amass wealth for dowry. Many of them kept in touch with their villages where they gave their lands for farming on contract. They collected harvest from the contract farmers and sold it in the market. So, the teachers were now farmers in absentia too.

And why not? After all, everyone has a right to prosper, and so do teachers of schools and colleges. It is supposedly intrinsic to 'skill' that it ought to be capitalised. If a teacher has the skill of selling his or her knowledge of chemistry, it is because, as they say, skill ought to be utilised to serve material needs. Knowledge is power, if you have the skills to sell it well. Students of business management may have learnt this lesson. That is how the whole world is, a world of business and of people who can do business. This is the world in which it is perfect to say 'mind your own business'. Perhaps, more than a reprimand, it is meant as a suggestion to do your business well. So, teachers, be they in school, colleges or universities, are doing it. Once again, why not? The world of business already has schools rivaling in showing off, charging capitation fees apart from all the other amounts that parents have to pay for the many activities that schools do in order to provide what they call 'holistic' growth of children. It is certainly holistic growth of the schools, the shop owners, the board members and, lastly, if at all, of children. Someone may feel like shouting, 'Stop it!' 'It sounds so condescending and cynical,' many participants in schools and colleges may retort. So, let us turn to the other monsters that kill the appreciable ordinariness of the teachers. It is more pronounced in universities. The so-called scholars, who at times repent that they have to teach, play moves and countermoves against one another. One wonders why. Why do these teachers in universities behave like lawyers or bureaucrats? There is a strange struggle for power, recognition and fame. All tiny egos are ready to snatch from the other whatever they perceive as valuable. At times, one wonders whether it is a workplace in school, college or university or some kind of chessboard set with artificially intelligent pawns who make self-propelled moves. Every ordinary teacher is nearly dying to become a teacher-in-charge or head of the department or dean or principal or vice chancellor. It seems teaching is a state of sadness if one is only a teacher. I saw a video of a teacher who became head of the department in one of the premier universities in India. The video showed him saying that this was the day for which he worked so hard. Not only this, we usually see such videos on Facebook: teachers sharing the news such as 'Today I am blessed to become head of the department' or something of that kind. A large pool of colleagues and students very dutifully congratulate the teacher on his or her so-called progress. If they become a dean or, god forbid, a vice chancellor, there is much congratulatory hue and cry. On such occasions, it looks like nuisances are normal in academics. In another context, the renowned astrophysicist-cosmologist Jayant Narlikar[3] had observed such tendencies of scholars who are also teachers in the universities. The idea of an ivory tower assumes a paradoxical nature when a simple thing such as the position of an educational-institutional administrator acquires such prominence in the scheme of reckoning.

This establishes that most teachers always felt bad being ordinary scholar-teachers. They felt they were wasted as nothing as long as they only had to teach or research. We have read allegations that teachers work so hard to become vice chancellor. Some of them maintain very close and strategic contact with the leadership of various political regimes. They write, if they can, things which make them suitable candidates. It is even better if they do not write and they show sufficient loyalty by other means, such as, by attending their parties, accepting invitations to write speeches and speaking on their behalf when required. Many of these potential candidates for the 'high' job also shape up university campus politics, brainwashing groups of students and mobilising fellow teachers. In various provincial universities, it was noted that many vice chancellors were candidates with police charge sheets against them. At best, political regimes like to appoint bureaucrats for such important jobs or the teachers who have shown their credentials as adequately thick-skinned bureaucrats. Teachers are also happy to accept positions that are a notch lower such as proctor or member of important committees. It begins to show that activities of intellectual growth such as designing course curricula, teaching, advising students on the issues of research and writing are done perfunctorily. The real milestone is an administrative post. In other words, the goal that an ordinary teacher may celebrate is 'to become something' against 'be nothing other than an ordinary teacher'.

This is the larger situation in which most teachers operate. The dream of an ideal vocation is met with frustrating moves and counter-moves in the power game in the precincts known for teaching and research. Many teachers, particularly in universities, also say that they are not supposed to be teachers; instead, they are supposed to be scholars. Such is the comedy of errors in which anyone aspiring to be an ordinary teacher detached from power play finds it difficult to breathe freely. It is almost a professional hazard if one says blissfully, 'I am nothing, just a teacher.'

Notes

1. Kafka's diary has attracted many scholars for close readings. It is indeed a gold mine of meanings that can aid in understanding the trial and tribulations of growing up as well as the intricate details of the time and space in industrial society. See Franz Kafka, *Diaries of Franz Kafka (1910–1913)*, ed. Max Brod (London: Secker and Warbur, 1948).
2. The educational philosophy of Rabindranath Tagore was central in most of the institutional practices that he founded and espoused at Shanti Niketan, Sri Niketan and Visva-Bharati university. One of the lectures among many that Tagore delivered was on schools. See Rabindranath Tagore, *Personality: Lectures Delivered in America* (London: Macmillan, 1918), accessed 19 February 2021, http://www.gyanpedia.in/Portals/0/Toys%20from%20Trash/Resources/books/readings/03.pdf.
3. Though Jayant Narlikar was primarily concerned with the question of science in Indian traditions and narrated the whole trajectory of scientific tradition without getting lost in the maze of citations, he also had interesting observations on universities in India. For more, see Jayant V. Narlikar, *The Scientific Edge: The Indian Scientist from Vedic to Modern Times* (Delhi: Penguin Books, 2003).

12

Not the Owls of Minerva: Teachers in Higher Education!

Teaching is the profession of this author and, hence, one may perhaps expect some sympathetic articulations. What follows now may, however, disappoint. Tell me, when is one not at odds with one's job to which one is committed? As it is in general (job dissatisfaction), so is it in particular (in the academic profession). It is, by and large, safe to say that higher education is a big scam for various reasons. There is ample justification for it to be like a scam, and many of these justifications may appear in the guise of explanations. But just because a thief happens to present a good explanation, thievery cannot be fully justified. Any justification would make a thief into a scoundrel, and I try to dissuade such explanatory justification since I do not aspire to be seen as a scoundrel.

For a long time, schoolteachers have been seen pejoratively. Many sociologists of education, educationists and education researchers have empirically or otherwise established the systemic failure in quality education in various schools. In that national saga of systemic failure and assessment of educational policy and administration, teachers appear as helpless agents, if not always consciously vile. No wonder then that many schoolteachers that we meet, particularly in government schools, seem to have developed a sense of apathy towards the job. Under administrative instructions, they have accepted becoming more of a file-maintaining clerical staff member than simply a pedagogue. Another sense of apathy that prevails upon a large number of teachers in government as well as many privately run schools is with regard to ritualistic events with technical names such as in-service training programmes, teachers' workshops and so on. There is a mammoth service industry that develops modules and conducts such programmes for government as well as private schools. The majority of teachers attend them to fulfil the 'official' requirements. We get to hear hilarious accounts of such training programmes from teachers. They do many other things such as running errands on WhatsApp through the phone while attending such 'funny', unproductive programmes! In informal and friendly banter, rather than serious technical research, teachers generously relate that such training programmes are unrealistic and unrelated to the 'expectations' that they have to deal with in their schools.

Yet sociologists and educational researchers perceive them pejoratively as the schoolteachers responsible for the anomalies in government or non-government schools. If we browse through the reams of writing on this subject, fraught with technicalities and abbreviations in so-called research reports, we get an ominous idea that all ills are in school education. The doctors who diagnose the ailments of school education sit in the ivory towers of the universities or education research organisations. These diagnoses suffer from metropolitan prejudices against the teachers across the length and breadth of India. The researchers from big cities, bred in educational and training privileges, pass judgements on teachers. Many of these diagnoses are commissioned by government-aided regulatory bodies or funding agencies of various kinds. These doctors never turn the critical stethoscope towards themselves; we seldom get to know the pulse rate of these doctors, alias the educational researchers, sociologists or educationists.

We hardly get to see what ails higher education in colleges and universities. Whenever these sociologists of education have to reflect on the anomalies in the institutions of higher education, they invariably restrict their attention to structural problems, state interventions, hostile administration and a seemingly villainous vice chancellor. Seldom do we hear an analysis that accuses the scholar-teachers in universities and colleges of being accomplices in the scam of higher education. Thereby, the owls of Minerva are never suspected. We persist with the idea that Minerva, the Roman goddess, an equivalent of the Greek virgin goddess of wisdom Athena, presides over the mindset of our academics. Closer home, it is perhaps a taken-for-granted idea that the most authentic worshippers of Saraswati, the goddess of knowledge, live in the institutes of higher education, the varsity. To complicate the matter, on the auspicious occasion of *Vasant Panchami* (the fifth day in the month of Vasant, approximately in February, according to the lunar calendar), many Hindu academics may also be seen worshipping Saraswati, by reciting a hymn that we used to hear in schools:

> Ya kundendutusharhardhawla ya shubhravastravrita / ya vinavardandmanditkara ya shwetpadmasana
>
> (Salutation to Goddess Saraswati, pure white as jasmine, calm as the moon, bright as snow, shining as a garland of pearls. O goddess! Protect me and remove my ignorance).[1]

Paradoxically though, such hymns are lost in thin air just after the performance of the ritual. Therefore, Saraswati Puja allegedly is merely performing cultural politics in schools and universities. Many scholars have a penchant to deliver critical analyses about this through the lens of religion and politics. We can instead spot the absences (educational value) through the presence (ritualism). Hence, we can note that neither Athena nor Minerva nor even Saraswati is around in higher education institutions. There may only be a large number of flocking owls, hooting relentlessly in the language that only expert owls can understand. This owl does no good to us. It is self-congratulatory since one has always heard of the nobleness associated with academics. One of them in our respective family network must have spoken very highly of the teaching profession in general; when we come to sociology, we get a proper discussion on the commendable nature of a vocation, distinguishable from a profession. In the vocation of teaching, those who are willing to learn can feel passion, the calling. One teaches with a sense of philosophical profundity attached to the value-loaded idea of vocation. Within teaching, if you have in mind the highest institutions of education, such as a university, you certainly have unavoidable awe. The professors seem to be the new prophets in our modern, secular, liberal imagination. They are presumably supposed to strengthen, maintain and perpetuate the fine relation between teaching and doing, devising courses and pedagogy, lecturing and researching. They are supposed to profess possibilities, theorise and empirically prove an idea true. In the same breath, they are supposed to take concrete steps towards it. What is a world, best so long as imagined, worst when realised? The truth of the dreamt world ought to be checked in reality. For, the devil lies in the details of the truth. Even the good dreams appear nightmarish when judged in real time and space with full consciousness. Teachers, who are researchers and scholars at once, are at their best in such noble institutions. Though it is true that there is an assumed nobility, there is also always a dark shadow beneath a lamp. One can debate about the quality of the shadow and the strength of the lamplight. One can also go on saying a few good things about the functional importance of owls. After all, they are from the family of the same bird that is the vehicle of the Hindu goddess of prosperity, Lakshmi, worshipped during Diwali, the festival of light (and sound and smoke of crackers). For Indian academics, the owl of Minerva has been replaced by the owl of Lakshmi, since they generally yearn for wealth and prosperity like any other humans. Exceptions are few and far between. Wealth is indeed beautiful. It could enable many initiatives that could help bring about the necessary changes in many people's lives. But the wealth desired by noble academics does to them what it does to anyone else. It makes people greedier, seeking for more wealth. What kind of wealth is this? Perhaps, it is a wealth that makes the rich stupendously poor. Our academics suffer from severe intellectual poverty and enormous worldly riches. They suffer from expertise that gets them to the events of success of a mundane as well as spectacular kind—so much so that they have awards instituted for them that they can buy from one of those award-giving business organisations. Academic pursuit is all about curriculum vitae (CV).

After all, how do these academics stay in currency? They do so by building up an impressive CV. The simple piece of paper or the Microsoft Word file that contains all the details of what one has done since the beginning of enlightening education becomes the premise for a spectacle. Everything contained in this document fetches brownie points. They are focused like Arjun in the Mahabharata who could not see anything other than the target, the wooden bird's eye. These academics seldom see anything—no student, no colleague, no friends, no partners, no solidarity, no relationships, no empathy. They see nothing that can be part of the Cartesian sensuous body.

The philosopher René Descartes,[2] known as a founding figure of modern philosophy, formulated the body–mind divide in philosophical reasoning. It is almost an accomplished Cartesian cogito—a pure, singular and pristine intellect. Descartes referred to this pure intellect with a singular pronoun 'I'. When this 'I' thought, Descartes believed, everything else existed. Moreover, 'I' thought, therefore, 'I' existed. It all sounds heavy, like the heaviness of that light concept that Descartes hyper-emphasised: 'I', the pure intellect, good reason, almost like God. 'The pronoun 'I' is the easiest for a child starting to learn the rules of English grammar. The first-person pronoun 'I' comes so lightly that this is perhaps the first thing everyone frequently refers to. 'I say this, I think so, I mean, I want, I hate, I love and I do not know anything.' 'I' is the most ordinary, taken-for-granted pronoun since it is the most heard, most referred to, most spoken. Such a pleasant, ordinary and precariously light 'I' metamorphoses into that gigantic, beastly creature in Franz Kafka's *The Metamorphosis*. This is the 'I' of the academics, as far as the single-minded pursuit of CV mindset is concerned. However, one may like to add some more adjectives to an academic's 'I'. It is not so innocuous as it seems. The use of the pronoun 'I' does not serve a mere intellectual purpose. It is instead in the service of various other forces, determiners, authorities and objectives. The Kafkaesque 'I' is doing more than just striving to survive any fateful incident. The academic 'I' has been perpetually in rat race for this-or-that webinar during the pandemic. There are so many 'I's participating in so many webinars that someone joked that the number of webinars during the pandemic outnumbered the Covid-positive cases!

The academic 'I' has been by and large in the service of the CV. In general, we meet various senior professors who have a few books to their credit, celebrated for giving a new spin to the way sociologists engage with social questions. Many of them are genuinely stalwarts of premier universities. The celebrated professors have the habit of updating their CVs almost every evening when they return to their residence. Every invited lecture they deliver will be diligently entered with all due details in the CV. Any professor would love to accept invitations to such reputed lectures, and they feel unhappiness if they are not invited. Likewise, any panel discussion, seminar or gathering of professional significance that academics appear in and, of course, every single thing they write is presented in this piece of paper with an enormous sense of religious duty. It is no longer simple documentation of what one does as part of academic practices. It is certainly not about the vocation, in which a teacher is also a researcher, writer and scholar at once.

Vocation demands performance in calling, that is, doing without showing off. In the absence of vocation, we are inundated by academic orchestration with an explicit objective of CV building. In such a vocation, one may do so much and everything so equally enriching that one may not record them fully well. I have also seen some rare academics who find it challenging to present updated CVs. They may be considered unable to make one, and this may be instantly mistaken as skill deficiency, as the skill-teaching industry has popularised. But they are the folks genuinely dedicated to their vocation. They would not be able to decide which one was important, a two-hour-long interaction with a student or an hour-long inaugural speech of a seminar that they deliver without much fuss. Since they would not be able to put the research work they do to prepare for class lectures in the CV, their research would not be counted; but if one researches for a funding organisation, that would be counted. In other words, time spent in a coolie job of academic slavery would be more valuable than the time spent in an interactive exploration of knowledge. There is a structure in favour of those who are not in the vocation of teaching and learning, which cannot be blamed on any villain or demon from somewhere else. One cannot say that it is due to economic liberalisation and the competitive zeal of academics just like any other trader in the market. The senior professors who are in the business of updating CVs were not even born in the 1980s or 1990s and cannot be said to suffer from the mindset in India after economic liberalisation and digitalisation. The senior professors were the champions of nation-building post Independence. Such grandeur in their biographical background is, paradoxically, juxtaposed with such banality as CV building. Blaming forces from outside for everything anomalous in academia is profoundly misplaced intellectual logic, often heard in academic deliberations. Such reasoning should be kept in a safe closet. Many senior professors were born in the 1950s, had seen the process of nation-building in Independent India and shared the dream of the famous metaphorical 'midnight's children'. They were teachers who had age-old lectures on old, pale sheets of papers, which they read out in class lectures. They were the teachers who never took questions from students after the lectures. Notoriously punctual, they did not allow the students to enter the class if they came at 10:01 AM instead of 10:00 AM. They were truly protestant in their belief in the adage that time and tide wait for none.[3] Those punctual teachers waited for none of us and, instead, spent all the time in serving their objective of enriching their CVs. Yet they resorted to sermons on morality and ethics whenever they had to lighten their sense of guilt. They were genuinely too fastidious to be of any interest and expected every student to become so. All those stars in the academic horizons of post-Independence society had a strong fear of post-retirement life, a sense of ignominy. They were unsure whether they will enjoy the invitations for delivering lectures and whether their work will be still relevant, though they tried very hard with a strong CV at their disposal. On the whole, the academic stars of yesteryears fear resting in peace, death and something that folks may have valued traditionally, *vanaprastha*, a journey of renunciation. They want an easy death, which they assume, comes if they stay in demand—the flow and currency in the business of academics. They envisage the end of their existence with the same height of egoism that enshrines their CVs.

To reiterate, with exceptions few and far between, this is how teachers in higher education institutes were and still are. The younger academics practise this pursuit of CV with more aggression, following in the footsteps of the prototype of the successful CV professors of the glorious past. The declaration is that we are not teachers, but we are scholars instead. As scholars, we are not saddled with the arduous task of conversing with students, delivering so-called exciting and inspiring lectures in the class and wasting all our time in these academic chores. The profession, mind it, has chores and drudgery. What makes an impressive CV is more important than these chores. So, it is not surprising that many younger academics have taken to easy ways to 'somehow' manage the classes, lectures and other essentials associated with the teaching life. A 40-minute class lecture with fifty

PowerPoint (PPT) slides is a ubiquitous reality. Each PPT slide may be text-heavy with text copied and pasted from various books. The teacher teaching with these powerful (PowerPoint slides) visuals becomes the ringmaster of an awry circus. Either the teacher reads out from those slides or asks each student to take turns in reading them out. Punching in a few pauses and a line of observation and pointing out possible questions for the examination constitute the class lecture. Ordinary lectures that could excite the inquisitiveness of young minds and catapult them to a terrain of enquiry is more or less a forgotten experience. Even students do not seem to want such lectures. They want, and they are served, class lectures with pointers on PowerPoint slides. It is useful for writing answers in the examination, which is the ultimate goal for both the teachers and students. It is an inglorious arrangement in which the academics of today are left with plenty of time to work towards the most coveted thing—CVs. These practices have created a professional orbit of ordinariness that runs counter to the vocational orbit of ordinariness. In the professionalised, standardised, institutionalised ordinariness of academia today, none of those other ordinary experiences of teaching and learning that shaped our humanitarian praxis are in sight. We in academia have become professional owls without vocational joy and vision.

With these owls, the very ordinary meaning of the vocation of teaching ceases to exist. Ordinarily, teaching is all about interactions and conversations in repose, also known as debates and lectures. The beauty of the phenomenon called a meeting of minds happens in such discussions, inside and outside the classroom. Since there is no meeting of the minds, despite many rounds of the meetings of the research supervisor and students, most academic peers comment on the papers and research proposals of young scholars in the most idiotic fashion. Commenting discussants and academic reviewers, the so-called anonymous or known referees of the papers in the academic journals, tend to vend their own expertise. They do not comment on others' works; they tend to comment on their own area of interest and achievements, flaunting their knowledge. If they have a chance, they leave the young scholars, the paper writers, in the lurch. In the end, they say that these students are the worst and unwilling to learn from the teachers. The very same teachers formulate various workshops, promising that these workshops will inculcate the skills of writing research proposals, papers and so on. After they fail to do the basic, ordinary and, hence, beautiful job of a teacher, they pretend to be prophetic in the workshops they plan and conduct. This is truly hilarious. Quality time spent with these students could make no difference, but a day or two spent in a workshop will be miraculous. If this is not a scam, what else could it be!

There are various orbits of ordinariness associated with the world of academics, of which we easily witness—professional and vocational. It is entirely up to us to make a choice, even though Karl Marx told us long ago, 'Men make their own history, but they do not make it as they please; they do not make it under self-selected circumstances, but under circumstances existing already, given and transmitted from the past.'[4] Since no word is the last word on human endeavour, why shall we be confined to Marx when we imagine a better world for ourselves?

Notes

1. Though anyone who attended school in India may recall this hymn, for an easy reference, see the same at: 'Saraswati Vandana,' Drik Panchang, accessed on 19 February 2021, https://www.drikpanchang.com/lyrics/vandana/goddesses/saraswati/saraswati-ya-kundendu-vandana.html.
2. René Descartes was much reviled in modern philosophy for such binary formulations ever since Gilbert Ryle pointed out the fallacy. A quick reference to Ryle's philosophical trajectory and interventions is in this fairly condensed essay available at *Stanford Encyclopedia of Philosophy*, s.v. 'Gilbert Ryle,' accessed on 19 February 2021, https://plato.stanford.edu/entries/ryle/.

    This was well articulated with a perspective in history of philosophy in Bertrand Russell, *History of Western Philosophy* (London: George Allen and Unwin Limited, 1946).
3. Anyone familiar with classical social science texts can instantly recall the famous work of Max Weber in which he recounted many such ideas to strengthen the proposed relation between rise of capitalism and the Protestant faith. It underlines the relationship of various denominations of Christianity and eventually the significance of Protestantism in the

growth of modern thinking. Perhaps one can develop a few research questions based on the proximity of practices and prosperity of academics with values that originate in Christianity. For more details of what Weber had to say, see Max Weber, *The Protestant Ethic and the Spirit of Capitalism* (New York: Charles Scribner's Sons, 1958).

4. A quick access to Marxist literature is a click away, rather than a library away, so see Karl Marx, 'The Eighteenth Brumaire of Louis Bonaparte,' Marxist, accessed on 10 January 2021, https://www.marxists.org/archive/marx/works/1852/18th-brumaire/ch01.htm.

13

Mundane Divinity, Rigid Religiosity and Everything Trivial

For an illustrative beginning, the popular work that we will refer to is the first film in Satyajit Ray's Apu trilogy in Bengali, titled *Pather Panchali* (Song of the Road, 1955). The film showed us a family coming to the city of Benaras (now officially Varanasi) from a village in Bengal. It is an escape from the deprivation in the village where the family had lost a daughter. In Benaras, the young boy Apu frolics on the banks of the holy river, Ganga. He sees a microcosm of the cosmos there. On one bank, there are wrestlers practising bodybuilding. On another, there is a queue of devotees taking a dip before going to the temple, and on yet another, dead bodies are being cremated. Everything looks like a part of a large canvas—actions of daily life, monkeying monkeys, gutsy goats, cluttered cattle and humming humans. The teenage boy sees the city in the mundane activities of sacred life while meandering, munching chickpeas, shouting out the names of the stray dogs, whistling and meeting strangers. When religious spaces were a little less defined, humans grew up in them. Thus, they outgrew rigid religiosity so that they could merge with the mundane divine.

The anomalies that unfold in the terrain of ordinary religiosity cannot, however, be ignored. After all, we do see human-generated dirt and filth in the precincts of sites of sacred significance. If you go on counting, umpteen aspects of life join in the ordinary picture of a sacred universe. And unlike all such instances of rigid religiosity, we also come across markers of fluid faith in the domain of the ordinary. In the same spirit as Apu's, we must traverse the larger terrain of mundane divinity.

Not too long ago, we used to find some unmanned temples here and there, mostly in small towns or peri-urban settlements of metropolises. The priest would appear in the mornings and evenings to do the routine rituals. The temples were not the private property. They were imagined to be abodes of divinity above considerations such as inclusion and exclusion, purity and pollution. The gods and goddesses in the temples needed officiating priests at the time of waking, eating, sleeping and so on. Many of us who have grown up in small towns may recall this. Like we thronged temples, so we visited shrines or mazars, some big and some small. Even there, in certain hours, there would be fewer guarding eyes. No security guard watched for potential threats, and sacred spaces were seldom threatened. As a visitor, one felt at ease. As children, we felt our sense of freedom unleashed even in sacred places such as mazars and mandirs. And how was our sense of freedom affirmed in such places? Before I reveal that, I must sound an alert: do not jump the gun on a judgement just because we are so-called responsible adults now! Try to understand our experiences that hid gems of ideas and profound nuggets of wisdom.

So, we felt ourselves free since we could do very trivial things such as stealthily taking away a fistful of the goodies offered at the mandir and mazar by the more serious devotees. At mazars, the devotees used to offer a range of mouth-watering stuff—sugar-coated peanuts, shredded sweet bread, dry fruits and such delicacies. Maybe they appeared exciting since it was an unpredictable range. Getting the delicacies the way we wanted required us to be like one of the insiders or a thief from the perspective of a vigilante. From Friday afternoon till evening, there would be a queue of devotees at the mazar, each paying visits to thank the buried saint or to ask for new favours. In either cases, the devotee had to make offerings and promise to make more such visits with more goodies in the future. The atmosphere, filled with all kinds of *itr*, the locally manufactured scents, was a festivity of infinite charm. Besides, every now and then, an entirely new lot of children flocked there, each new face looking at the other in wonder! Exchanges of furtive glances and occasional smiles made the matter intimate. There were times when the guarding priests would catch the mischief of the children and shoo them away. The children would oblige by disappearing for a few hours. After all, there is some significance in the authority of an institution. It is better to respect that despite the perpetual plan to plunder the goodies. Our association with places of sacred significance did not spare Hindu temples. Some of us never understood why we were more known for stealing slippers. The slippers were entirely useless since we often used to forget to wear our own slippers on the way back from such important places. We were more excited about other things, and slippers rarely figured in our scheme of important things. Women were the best devotees in the mandir; they made far better offerings—wet rice with jaggery, sprouted groundnut with *misri* (candy sugar or rock sugar), *batasa* (sugar meringues or sugar drops) and *peda* (a doughy sweet dish made of thickened milk). Some of us would be steadfastly watchful about the offerings, and as soon as the devotee bade farewell to the god, we would oblige the gods by offering our service of consuming the offerings. Every time we wiped out the offerings we, ensured that some leftovers were left for the ants and mice, other service providers for the gods. Children and beasts were thus united in making the frozen gods and goddesses alive. We ate on behalf of the divine, and we felt divine thereby. Once in a while, the priest would stay on and collect the offerings as well as the coins that some women offered the gods. But the priest was too mortal to control the army of divinity. It was impossible for the outnumbered priest to successfully guard the divinity. One priest could seldom withstand so many children. We also managed to take away some of the coins hidden in the flower petals and leaves next to the feet of the statues or the Shiva linga.

Why do I narrate all this? It is not just to indulge in a nostalgic recollection but to revisit a beautiful idea conceived by Rabindranath Tagore, famously known as the religion of man.[1] Fondly called Gurudev, Tagore made his experience more central to his discussion on religion and avoided taking the arcane route of philosophical reasoning. As a result, he gave us a more profound philosophy than the drab rumination of philosophers, known as the religion of man. Tagore's idea was precisely about the way we experience religion in ordinary life. What stimulated his ideas? The Upanishads! That is right, but he was also inspired by the songs of the *Bauls*,[2] which he heard in the suburbs and the countryside. Bauls were mystic minstrels or bardic singers who roamed about singing devotional songs. There was a significant period in the history of South Asia, particularly in colonial Bengal during the 19th and 20th century, identified with the Bauls.

They brought about a syncretic temperament in faith and devotion by mixing elements from Sufism and Hinduism. Such songs of cultural subversion sought for the union of mortals with the divine.[3] Against this backdrop, Tagore emphasised relations, experience and faith. As a religious person, how does one relate to the rest of the world? Is it a relation of superior to inferior or is it by all means a relation of things in love? Some of these questions are far more potent than the attempt to answer them. But Tagore helps us answer them, and we begin to see those answers very much in our ordinary lives. For a person of religion, there is no distinction between mortal and immortal or mundane and divine! This is, of course, disastrous for the organised religions of the world, which operate with the idea of superiority of all those who believe. Many organised religions put down or, if they are too generous, put aside the non-believers. The religion that Tagore speaks of, looking at the ordinary folks around, does not distinguish between believer and non-believer. There is no proselytising zeal in it. Hence, it is far more liberating than any political ideology. This liberation comes from the uniqueness of relation that is central to Tagore's religion. This is not the idea of relations that sociologists teach students in the classrooms. Tagore's idea of relations helps humans to see the divine and the divine in humans. This relation thrives on the free play between mortal and immortal, children and the buried saint at a mazar, playmates and the divinity in a mandir. This is so until big toys occupy the centre of our conscience. These sleek toys are manufactured in such a way that there is rarely a relationship between the natural elements and humans. Playing with building blocks is pleasurable. Carom and chess are fun too. There is an established significance of toys, sports and healthy recreation. A word of caution is, however, necessary. This is not only because of the sports it creates in which humans grow away from the surroundings. The possession of such toys evokes a sense of invincible supremacy. We come across children who are more interested in getting a new toy as a present every week. They are more inclined to the joy of receiving a present, which leads them to feel good about possessing the toy rather than playing with it.

In the history of organised religions all over the world, gods have also undergone a great deal of transition.[4] The most significant one is about the way we, the humans of faith, relate to our places of worship and our gods and goddesses. At each corner of such places of worship, there is a security camera breathing down our necks; at every turn, there is a metal detector to weed out the metallic emotions towards gods, goddesses and saints. There are other ways of regulating the devotees: men in one queue and women in the other, the rich in one row and the poor in the other, and such awful segregation rules the bureaucratic management of the sacred. Everything that seems merely a practical, harmless arrangement speaks loudly about how we have meticulously eroded the possibility of us crossing the boundaries of minds. The sociocultural possibilities with the places of worship are fast succumbing, or have already succumbed, to the regime of the extraordinary.

Not just boys and girls, youths and elders, in relation with the sacred and the mundane, even our religious songs have not been spared. Many of us from cities, towns and even villages can vividly recall the beautiful sound of religious evocation. On wintry mornings, when everything seemed sleepy, we heard those sounds without fail. A temple, near or far, played the *choupai* (couplets) from the *Ramcharitmanas* or it played the songs of Kavi Pradeep,[5] which spoke of the magic of religious concerns in ordinary everyday life, saying,

> *Dusro ka dukhra door karne wale tere dukh dur karenge Ram*
> (Those who care for others, Ram cares for them)

The song in the nasal voice of Kavi Pradeep reverberates in our memory, without any need for technical citation. There is another one by Pradeep that sounded more like a prophesy to many of us who hummed along as we heard it in those good old days:

> *Dekh tere sansar ki halat kya ho gayi bhagwan, kitna badal gaya insan*[6]
> (What has become of your world, o lord, see how humans have changed).

We not only heard these sounds of faith but also got inspired in our imagination of the world. We forged friendships and relationships under these sonic inspirations. Our ordinary lives earned aesthetics from such songs, and our religiosity became fluid. On this note, we shall see what became of some religious notes that enchanted our ordinary religious feelings.

The playback singer Mukesh from Bollywood sang a choupai (quatrain) of Tulsidas's *Ramcharitmanas* along with an orchestra that included the famous singer Vani Jairam. Among other things, they sang the choupai from the episode of *Ramcharitmanas* called 'Bal Kand':[7]

> *Bhaye prakat kripala dindayala kausalya hitkari / harsit mahtari muni man hari adbhut rup bichari / lochan abhirama tanu ghansyama nij aayudh bhuji chari / bhushan manmala nayan bisala, sobha sindhu kharari*
>
> (Thus arose the lord, with mercy and compassion to the suffering, before a gladdened mother Kausalya; thus appeared the lord in the heart of sages, as they ruminated on his divine splendour; thus was the resplendence of the lord, his winsome eyes, dusky body, with four ornate hands)

Tulsidas's depiction of the newborn Ram and the scenario come alive in Mukesh's rendition. The distant sound of the song was very close to us. There was a lived ordinariness about all such songs, which became endangered after sudden tumultuous events in the 1990s. Paranoia determined our perceptions. These songs did not enchant us into believing in the innocence of our religions anymore. We were thoroughly disenchanted about anything that seemed even slightly enchanting. Our sacred canopy was shattered into unrelated fragments.

In the age of suspicion, everything trivial and mundane that the sacred spaces allowed us is deeply sacrilegious. Now if you sit in *dhyan* or *sajda*, you may have an apprehension that your belongings may be stolen away or that your footwear that you left outside may disappear. You fear that you may be groped in the crowd of worshippers. We are paranoid for various genuine reasons, ingeniously enhanced by the system in place. How do we overcome such anxieties, fear, apprehensions and paranoia? Bad things happen, but a strong perception of bad things plagues us far more than real incidents. In this paranoia, our songs and call for prayers do not persuade us to a disarmed surrender, let alone enchant us into belief. Instead, we stay alert about the pros and cons. We are fearful or unsure about the motive behind such religious calls. The sacred is the source of paranoid perception, paradoxically. After various fateful incidents in the history of religion all over the world, many unfortunate damages to tradition were taken for granted. The aesthetic ordinariness of faith dwindled. Meanings of everyday bhajans changed. Customary calls to the faithful began to trigger existential anxiety. A regime of paranoia and religious polarity debilitated the ordinary charm of religiosity. Wishfully, let us wish that this is not the end of mundane divinity in the face of rigid religiosity. Hopefully, let us hope that our ordinary playfulness—love and relationships with gods and goddesses—springs back according to the logic of ordinariness elucidated in this essay. Thoughtfully, let us think that there cannot be a full stop in the history of humanity.

Notes

1. It is one of the most relevant texts from the rich anthology of writings credited to Rabindranath Tagore. Originally a series of lectures delivered at Oxford University in the 1930s, the essay has resurfaced in several analyses in social sciences, much like other writings of Tagore. See Rabindranath Tagore, *The Religion of Man* (Delhi: Rupa, 2005).
2. Baul songs figure as intangible heritage in the UNESCO list. See, for more, 'Baul songs,' Intangible Cultural Heritage, UNESCO, accessed on 19 February 2021, https://ich.unesco.org/en/RL/baul-songs-00107.
3. In this regard, it is worth taking note of a fascinating reading of Tagore's relation with the Bauls and the idea of religiosity and subversion that Martha Nussbaum dwelt upon. In one of her lectures, she aids in seeing both the limits and possibilities of Tagore's songs. See Martha C. Nussbaum, 'Rabindranath Tagore: Subversive Songs for a Transcultural "Religion of Humanity", *Acta Musicologica* 84, no. 2 (2012): 147–159.
4. Among many well-researched works along this line, a couple of significant contributions are Karen Armstrong, *A History of God: From Abraham to the Present* (London: Vintage Books, 1999) and Karen Armstrong, *Fields of Blood: Religion and the History of Violence* (London: Vintage, 2015).
5. Available for a leisurely audience at 9431885 MK, 'Dusro ka Dukhda,' YouTube video, 21 September 2010, https://www.youtube.com/watch?v=t2Paz57Lkpg.

6. This was actually a song from a 1954 film titled *Nastik* directed by I.S. Johar. The song is picturised in the turbulent time of the partition of India and highlights the degrading interface of religion and politics. The song is available here: Gaane Naye Purane 'Dekh Tere Sansar ki Haalat,' YouTube video, 30 November 2017, accessed on 19 February 2021, https://www.youtube.com/watch?v=uL0Q1oTK0qo.
7. One can hear them out even now, say for example on YouTube: Hindu Mantras, 'Ram Charit Manas,' YouTube video, 26 May 2013, accessed on 19 February 2021, https://www.youtube.com/watch/h8jIWpDVIDU.

14

Ordinary Gandhi in the Time of Extraordinary Gau-Raksha

If it matters, this chapter shall start with a disclaimer that there is a dependence on how Gandhi, the Bapu, saw it all. Meanwhile, Gandhi's way of seeing is logically convincing for us today. It is with the prejudice that such a position is far more relevant in a time when the vengeful idea of 'an eye for an eye' is the norm. The ordinariness of Gandhian positions seems to be at loggerheads with the extraordinary concept of cow protection.

We have often heard a dictum in Hindi: '*Majboori ka naam Mahatma Gandhi*' (Mahatma Gandhi means weakness). The common-sense discourse held that everything Gandhi said was a sign of an unrealistic, utopian dream and the escape of a weak person, perhaps during Gandhi's time as well. A scholar of medieval literature and one of the wisest literary critics, Purushottam Agrawal,[1] tried telling us otherwise. He helped us see that '*majbooti ka naam Mahatma Gandhi*' (Mahatma Gandhi means strength). No one can deny the strength that is prevalent in the Gandhian practice of pragmatism. One ought to remember, however, that there is a sociocultural idiosyncrasy in what could be proposed as Gandhi's pragmatism. Gandhi's interest was not at all to merely wax eloquent about burning topics or loosely vend self-fulfilling prophesies or bask in the glory of iconoclasm. He was unlike the literati, celebrities, glitterati and Twitterati. On innumerable occasions, Gandhi disclosed his shyness, almost fear, of such glamorous positions. Uncomfortable with the platitudes showered on him, Gandhi intended to appear more in proximity with the ordinary. He steered clear of the spectacles, chaos, pretence and theatrics that pervade sociopolitical lives. He said what he lived through and experienced. He proposed what he meditated upon and realised. He propounded what emerged from his sustained dialogues with self and others. This all duly embeds Gandhi's pragmatism in the socio-moral vision of an experimental traditional ethos and the praxis of his own life. This shows in his deeds, words and his engagement with self and issues of the world at large. His pragmatic glance of scrutiny turns inward and outward at once without discrimination. The uncanny nature and scope of his pragmatism invite more systematic examination. Even in the most intimate of his writings, such as in his autobiography, Gandhi reminds us, 'I simply want to tell the story of my numerous experiments with truth, and as my life consists of nothing but those experiments, it is true that the story will take the shape of an autobiography'.[2] Thus, the autobiography was aptly titled *An Autobiography or the Story of My Experiments with Truth*. The documentation of personal trysts with the truth acquired the significance of a soul-searching exercise. Gandhi did not do it with a sense of self-righteousness or to promote a brand of guru-ness that is the logic in the merchandise of spirituality. His objective was not to sermonise as a moral preacher. Indeed, he articulates discomfort with the epithet of 'Mahatma' while narrating these tales. Instead, he narrates his life story with unique rationalism that admits the inevitability of human vulnerability. In his own words:

> Far be it from me to claim any degree of perfection for these experiments. I claim for them nothing more than does a scientist who, though he conducts his experiments with the utmost accuracy, forethoughts and minuteness, never claims any finality about his conclusions, but keeps an open mind regarding them.[3]

This sense of rationalism based on self-introspection prevails in Gandhi's pragmatics. It is a unique kind of scientific thinking in which process is more crucial than final judgement; the persuasive appeal of a proposition is more important than the infallibility of conclusions. Such is the methodological orientation in Gandhian pragmatism that it solicits that 'the seeker after truth should be humbler than dust'. The dust, invariably crushed by feet, shall be heavier than those who want to know. That is how it has been in various religious-philosophical traditions. Gandhi cites the dialogue between Vashishtha and Visvamitra, the Upanishads and even Christianity and Islam to underline the importance of humility in recounting the propositions based on self-realisation.

Gandhi's pragmatic scheme tends to integrate various issues that were bones of contention in his time as well as now. Be it the idea of *Sanatani* Hindu (broadly, a Hindu who observes traditional practices), untouchability, *nai Talim* (a practise-based system of education that Gandhi espoused), issues of equality and discrimination or various aspects of communal tension, Gandhi spoke of them through his experiences and experiments and in interaction with many interlocutors. One such issue that stirred passion among Indians, then as well as now, is the protection of cows. Gandhian pragmatism unspooled a curious stance. He held the cow to be of utmost significance for the Hindus. Cows are, as they were, more socially important than for any religious ritual reasons. This is fairly ordinary, for we have witnessed the relationship between livestock and humans. Life is socioculturally woven around cows, buffaloes, goats, dogs, cats and so on. Anything seemingly religious is only to adorn and substantiate this relationship. In fact, Gandhi lamented that Hindus have not given due respect to the cow, which he calls the 'giver of plenty'.[4] His own words about cows are: 'Not only did she give milk, but she also made agriculture possible. The cow is a poem of pity. One reads pity in the gentle animal. She is the mother to millions of Indian mankind.'[5] There is a meaningful mix of utilitarian and moral importance in Gandhi's evocation of cows. Respect for cows means adherence to innocence, pity, piety and protection for the socially weak and helpless. Given such objectives and associations with cows, Gandhi says, 'To carry cow protection at the point of sword is a contradiction in terms'.[6] Interestingly, this is placed under the larger rubric of Hinduism that is characterised by an evolved stage of acceptance and tolerance. Answering a vital question, 'Why I am a Hindu', Gandhi clarifies that a faith is to be lived and not to be exclusively propagated with proselytising zeal. Similarly, the relationship with the cow is a lived relationship rather than a preached one. Gandhi understands Hinduism as he lives it and envisages it to be in an India of his time. The ability to have a critical departure from dogmas is what makes Gandhi attracted to Hinduism. In this spirit, he supports the idea of *varnashrama* for the clarity of roles and duties.

However, it does not mean that Brahmins are absolved from bodily labour or the Sudra is prevented from acquiring knowledge. Nor does varnashrama mean a proscription of inter-dining or even intermarriage. Instead, both inter-dining and intermarriage, along with the division of labour without exclusive privilege, could make Hinduism an evolved religion. This also meant adequate freedom to choose one's calling in life, without fear of class and caste prejudices attached to them. This broader experience of Hinduism allows Gandhi to underline cow worship as apotheosis. Though Gandhi sounds idealistic, there is a tint of self-criticism towards the way Hindus treat cows. He sets a revealing series of probing questions in his own words:

> How we bleed her to take the last drop of milk from her, how we starve her to emaciation, how we ill-treat the calves, how we deprive them of their portion of milk, how cruelly we treat the oxen, how we castrate them, how we beat them, how we overload them. If they had speech, they would bear witness to our crimes against them which would stagger the world. By every act of cruelty to our cattle, we disown God and Hinduism.[7]

The pitiability of cows is more vivid in every act of protecting them. Gandhi painstakingly showed in the *Hind Swaraj* (1938)[8] that our cow protection societies are, in fact, cow-killing societies. Gandhi shows that some of the effort of protecting the cows, such as *pinjarapoles* (enclosed animal shelters) in the centre of the cities, is geared towards further exploitation of them. The business and cultural elites support such arrangements that make the cows available for more disrespectful treatment. Gandhi places the orchestration of cow protection alongside the other prevalent evils of Hindu society such as social inequality. Just like hollow symbolism is anathema to Hinduism, so is untouchability and the ostentatious protection of cows. Gandhi found it paradoxical that a religion that worships cows countenances the cruel treatment of human beings. Respect for cows and fellow humans go together for Gandhi. Hence, he would decry any act of violence in the name of the protection of cows. He holds the communal distrust between Hindus and Muslims at the core of the contention about cows. Any riot or vengeful act against Muslims has not protected a single cow.

Instead, they have, Gandhi says, 'stiffened the backs of the Musalmans and resulted in more slaughter'. This is possible to see through Gandhi's pragmatism that the mob lynching of alleged beef-eaters or cow-traffickers is purely anti-cow and anti-Hinduism. Gandhi enables through a pragmatic reasoning a critical understanding that such violent acts seldom save any cow and that they serve some other vested interests. Gandhi notes, 'As a Musalman friend writes, beef-eating which is merely permissible in Islam will become a duty, if compulsion is resorted to by Hindus'.[9]

Since this is a rationalist, practise-based pragmatism, Gandhi engages with a couple of critical issues pertaining to cows. He admits a commonly heard idea that cow slaughter was a Vedic rite and the Brahmins ate beef. He recalls the Sanskrit texts from his childhood memory that informed him about such ideas. He finds it, however, difficult to accept, saying:

> Hinduism does not rest on the authority of one book or one prophet; nor does it possesses a common creed—like the Kalma of Islam—acceptable to all. That renders a common definition of Hinduism a bit difficult, but therein lies strength also. For, it is this special feature that has given to Hinduism its inclusive and assimilative character and made its gradual, silent evolution possible. Go to any Hindu child and he would tell you that cow protection is the supreme duty of every Hindu and that anyone who does not believe in it hardly deserves the name of a Hindu.[10]

As is evident, Gandhi presents a different version of Hinduism in which a believer's mundane sentiments matter more than classical texts or priestcraft. Likewise, he critically revisits Islamic injunctions to emphasise that the Musalmans have no religious obligation to slaughter a cow.

> The Koran, so far as I have been able to understand it, declares it to be a sin to take the life of any living being without cause. I want to develop the capacity to convince the Musalmans that to kill the cow is practically to kill their fellow countrymen and friends—the Hindus. The Koran says that there can be no heaven for one who sheds the blood of an innocent neighbour.[11]

Having said that, Gandhi returns to the idea of a freedom-based choice for Musalmans, rather than a coercion-based prohibition, for, coercion and violence only endanger the Hindu way of protecting and persuading. In a radically different tone, therefore, Gandhi notes, 'Fullest recognition of freedom to the Muslims to slaughter cows is indispensable for communal harmony, and is the only way of saving the cow'.[12] This was the pretext for generating an appeal to the Hindus to participate in the Khilafat Movement. Gandhi aspired to convey this message to the Muslims that the Hindus respect their cause and can come with them to protect Islam. By doing so, the Hindus would obtain the protection of the cows. 'Not by killing or quarrelling with the Musalmans, to save the cows, the Hindus shall die in the support of the Khilafat.'[13]

Through one particular issue of cow protection, this discussion aids in understanding the nature, scope and merit of Gandhian pragmatism. The latter appears iconic since it is informed by traditions, yet not chained to dogmas and mores. In the pragmatic scheme of Gandhi, there is a possibility to criticise the decline of Hindus and yet see the evolutionary zenith in cow worshipping. This is unique pragmatism aimed at bringing about the much-needed trust surplus across communities so that each community could care for the other. Gandhi's pragmatic rationalism rules out any way forward in the act of violence, including contemporary unrest about the cow. There could be many disagreements with Gandhi on the details of his propositions. However, it is hard to disagree with his broader pragmatic vision about an India in which communities could live with each other with due emotional and socio-religious vision.

Notes

1. A popular scholar such as Purushottam Agrawal embodies such insightful edges that one ought to cruise through this website for diverse contributions, from books, articles to conversations and lectures. See Purushottam Agrawal, accessed on 19 February 2021, https://www.purushottamagrawal.com.
2. See M. K. Gandhi, *An Autobiography or The Story of My Experiments with Truth* (Ahmedabad: Navajivan Trust, 1960), xii.

3. Gandhi, *An Autobiography*, xiii.
4. M.K. Gandhi, *Hindu Dharma* (New Delhi: Orient Paperback, 1991), 5.
5. Gandhi, *Hindu Dharma*, 7.
6. Gandhi, *Hindu Dharma*, 10.
7. M. K. Gandhi, *Selected Writings*, ed. and introduction Ronald Duncan (New York: Dover Publications Inc., 2005), 176.
8. M. K. Gandhi, *Hind Swaraj or Indian Home Rule* (Ahmedabad: Navajivan Trust, 1938).
9. M. K. Gandhi, *The Way to Communal Harmony*, compiled and ed. U.R. Rao (Ahmedabad: Navajivan Trust, 1963), 88.
10. Gandhi, Hindu *Dharma*, 120–121.
11. Gandhi, *The Way to Communal Harmony*, 88.
12. Gandhi, *The Way to Communal Harmony*, 90.
13. Gandhi, *The Way to Communal Harmony*, 90.

Cacophony of Celebration?

Illustration artist: Sajal Roy, Dhaka, Bangladesh

15

Awry October, Fury of Festivity and Destruction of Virtues

October is a beautiful month in the mind of schoolgoing children and also for some of us who keep our childhood awake even though the regime of adulthood is at odds with it. In the climatic sense, this is so since there is a decline of summer and the gentle knock of winter during this time in the northern part of India. October is a month of festivals. It is a month when the temperament of the weather begins to change in the northern part of the subcontinent and becomes more predictable in other parts. Except for some unpredictable cyclones or a shorter version of monsoon, things are more or less settled. Many flowers that await the arrival of winter begin to bud and bloom. Early morning in October, there is a divinity attached to an ordinary site: the bed of *parijata* flowers, known as *harshringar* or *shiuli* in Bengal. It is also known as the night jasmine, botanical name *Nyctanthes arbortristis*. Wherever there is a tender tree of the night jasmine, there is a thick sheet of flowers underneath. We also know them as coral jasmine when we want to make the flower sound more intriguing. Taking a walk in the morning, one chances upon the inviting night jasmine flowers laid out on the way. It has a truly disarming ordinariness, fragrant and yet frivolous, spectacular and yet mundane, simple and sweet. Around this time, some new birds, mostly migratory during winter, begin to show up too. The birds visiting this part of the planet are welcomed by the fragrance of flowers, stable post-monsoon greenery and relatively easy-going humans.

No wonder that this is the month in which we witness the celebration of the absolute mother, the great goddess Durga, the nurturer of all, who turned ferocious to slay demonic obstacles. The devotees who read the *Durga Saptsati* for the ten days during the period of the Puja may be familiar with a specific part called '*Devi Aparadha Kshamapana*

Stotram', a verse in Sanskrit which begs for pardon from the goddess for any wrongs a devotee may have committed in the process of worshipping. The verse is revealing as it says:

> *Na mantram no yantram tadapi cha na jane stutimaho / Na chavhanam dhyanam tadapi cha na jane stutikathah / Na Jane mudraste tadapi cha na jane vilapanam / Param jane matastvadanusaranam kleshaharanam*
>
> (O Mother! Neither I know any incantation nor I have any mystical talisman. I don't know any hymn either. I have no idea how to invoke you or how to meditate on you … But one thing I know for certain that seeking shelter under your protection, and following your order, is definitely going to end all afflictions.)[1]

Curiously, throughout this stotra, there is a refrain that is reminiscent of an axiom. It says, '*Kuputro jayet kwachidapi kumata na bhavti*'[2] (There may be bad sons, but there are no bad mothers). By way of begging for forgiveness, the worshipper reveals an ultimate truth. One is ignorant about how to really invoke, worship and celebrate. Moreover, since there could be bad worshippers, rather than bad mothers or nurturers, one expects a kind exemption. Perhaps, this sums up what the participants of festive October end up doing.

This is the month of many possibilities, new turns and unfolding stories. Some old mythologies reappear against the backdrop of new times with new meanings. Some old motifs from the realms of art and culture are recycled for new context. Some reveries bygone resurface in family banter: 'You remember? That year during the puja it so happened…' The never-ending threads from memory compel us to relive happiness and sorrow both. We are persuaded to participate in the festivities disclosing the occultness of October, the attraction of cultural hustle and bustle and the manifold joy of receiving novel components for our memories. Even in the simplest of ethnological monographs, the occult is not innocuous as it entails layers of ordinariness. An occult ceremony gives us occasions to make our choices despite the blinding affects, and we will see that as we proceed.

Though the lunar calendar may change the dates and sometimes some of these festivities may fall in the last part of September or early part of November, it is mostly October that assumes centrality as the month with larger share of festivities. Just to add to the intrigue of October, there are also newly found insects that begin to swarm in and out of our living spaces. Agrarian societies promoted the festive practice of burning hay in order to control the burgeoning insects. One wonders what we control now that insects are endangered creatures. All our fireworks (including bursting crackers) are perhaps meant to endanger ourselves today. After pushing the insects out of human civilisation altogether, we persist with fireworks to choke our lungs to slow demise. The perpetuity of our love for burning (hay or harvest remains) and bursting (crackers) is paradoxical in the face of our claims to have accomplished an information society connected through the Internet. Everyone is informed, and yet, everyone is forgetful about the consequences of the mindless pleasure. Let us not become one of those 'progressive' schools that teach kids not to burst crackers and indulge in producing poisonous smoke outside their glorious precincts. Children learn about the values of living with organic relations with nature inside the school. As soon as the bell rings to announce the end of the day in school, children leave the lessons behind or recount them in front of the uncles and aunts only to impress them. Thus their contributions, along with that of their grown-up peers, to the awry-October continues. Let us talk about the festivity that adds to the package of October.

Among many festivities, big and small, there will be the ten-day festival of Durga Puja, then Dussehra, followed by Laxmi Puja and Diwali. A large chunk of time is spent in the usual rut, commercialised rituals and glitzy, obscene displays of wealth and possessions. There is the predictable sight of folks dressing up, turning up, eating away and leaving the remains behind, so to say. Pandal hopping, to see and to be seen, is ubiquitous during Durga Puja. One wonders who is the performer—the artists singing and playing the instruments in the orchestra in those pandals or the feisty audience reveling in the tune of the festival. Who is the real performer in such an important cultural event that invites us to rediscover our youthfulness no matter what our age is? The pandal organisers, designers and programme managers secretively, or quite explicitly, slip in the mix of religion and politics. It seems natural since religion, culture and politics can seldom be totally separated from one another in everyday life. Many of us who flock to the puja place seemingly with a sense of devotion for the great mother goddess also join in the seamlessly colourful fusion of culture and politics. All kinds of Ramlila would also be underway in many places. Some Ramlilas are star-studded; not only yesteryear television artists show up in cameo roles but also the political leadership lines up to show, see and be seen. We may have seen several performances of Ramlilas[3] in small towns, villages and even in the peripheries of metropolises. The performances brought to us a sense of ordinary aesthetics pertaining to the enactment of the roles from the epic Ramayana. The actors looked like ordinary folks, draped in rugged costumes and fairly simple on the whole. With changing times, some of these performances assumed a larger-than-life outlook. Ironically, there are spectacular performances of Ramlila, which was originally known for its ordinary aesthetics. It is not surprising to see the actor essaying the character of Ram with a tattoo on his bulging biceps, Sita with a Botoxed face and Ravana nearly a monster with whom no humans can connect. Then there are those performances of Ramlila in which all the lead actors look famished, tired and skeletal. They still do a far better job because they maintain the truthful appearance of human actors. Hence, the mythological characters look more credibly associated with human lives. The Ram of such a Ramlila may be as vulnerable as Ravana who looks like the fellow next door. Let alone tattoos, with no biceps to flaunt, no glamour to relish and no smart props to play with, these are the Ramlilas that attract credibility to occult October. Leaders who play second fiddle in the political drama drop by and make special announcements, or they simply go and touch the feet of the actors playing Ram, Sita, Laxman and Hanuman. The politicians who never bother about providing a square meal to the poor do *arti* (a way to show devotion by greeting with the sacred fire) of the poverty-stricken, jobless, ordinary actors. It is a beautiful sight, truly, since we are never free from the context in which we watch a mythological drama. The texts and contexts of the performance lead us to the day when the monsters, devils and demons of our imagination are slain. The effigies of the demons Ravana, Kumbhkarna and other kith and kin are quite ornate, crafty and winsome. Only the brother named Vibhishan, who betrayed the demons by becoming an ally of the god, is not represented. All such demons and demi-demons stand tall, fastened by hooks, on the grounds of various parks and public spaces on the day of Dussehra. The arrows of Ram may not be as efficient as that of a specially invited cabinet minister or prime minister or anyone from the who's who of politics. They shoot flaming arrows at the effigies that embody the bodies of demons, which go up in flames with a burst of crackers. Magnificent sentiment, malicious intent. Year after year, we repeat the logical error of setting the demons on fire. The narrators of the story, though, made it very clear that there is a specific site in the anatomy of the demon where the prana, the essence of life, is secretly stored. It is no wonder then that the demon never dies in a true sense. It is only a festive illusion.

Thus comes this all-too-pervasive festival of light, Diwali, when darkness dawns upon this part of the earth. Originally, the idea was to illuminate our household and neighbourhood so that our darkness is dispelled and we are awakened to the light. This pertains to the age-old wisdom in Sankrit, the famous adage '*tamso ma jyotirgamaya*' (take me from the darkness to the light). We can easily recall this nugget of wisdom from our memory without any technical citation and understand the importance of rising in the illumination. But then, the logic of science helps us to understand that too much light around us may disturb our sleep, or worse, make us sleepless. If we do not sleep, how do we awaken? If this sounds too literal, let us restrict ourselves to the symbolism: too much light makes the awakening of the soul difficult! The massive illumination outside does not make much difference to our inner psyche. We all light so many lamps, candles and decorative electrical strings of colourful light. This is to celebrate the return of Ram to his kingdom after completing the ordeal of exile and the struggle with destiny. Unfortunately, this was only a small pause in the ordeal, as the various versions of the Ramlila inform us. This is followed by Ram's action on a complaint about the chastity of a washerman's wife. Ram had to do something about the questioned chastity of his own wife, Sita, who had stayed in Lanka, and then only could he be righteous enough to pass a verdict on the case of the washerman's wife. In many Ramlila performances, the countercurrents of the story unfold.

We helplessly witness the rise of manifold demons in us. The abundance of light around us becomes a veritable wildfire, burning insects of all kinds and not only dogs and cats but also humans and cattle. So many crackers are burst around us that we cannot hear our choking lungs, burning eyes and numbing senses. The light around us conjures a picture of an inferno, the mythical hellfire, a calamity beyond human control since any apex body of law cannot stop it. Only a Dante, the Italian poet of many centuries ago, can helplessly show a divine comedy in which the inferno was far removed from its counterpart, paradise. A good soul persevered to get away from inferno to reach paradise. We are perhaps not so lucky. We harbour the inferno, mistaking it for paradise, because Ram's Ayodhya exiled Sita. That was the complaint of Khattar Kaka in Hari Mohan Jha's literary work. Both Ravana's Lanka and Ram's Ayodhya turned out to be inhospitable for Janaki, literally the daughter of Janak, another name of Sita. Be that as it may. We are, for sure, condemned enough to be complacent about our inferno. We put on all the lights, only to hide the deep darkness. We burst all the crackers only to drown the sighs of sorrow. We join in any euphoria, including that of festivity, only to conceal our misery. A permanently clogged road a day or two before Diwali must make everyone wonder about our monetary power. Everyone seems to be out to buy silver, gold, appliances or, if nothing else, a spoon. For Dhanteras, customary buying is like habitually swallowing a pill that the doctor has advised you to take to control your blood pressure. If one is done with the buying, one needs to exchange packaged gifts with kith and kin, friends and clients, bosses and masters. Exchange of gifts sounds pretty sweet, but one cannot afford such generous sweetness in the time of diabetes. So many boxes of sweets make the rounds, and if one is up-to-date, then boxes of chocolates, cookies and dry fruits are even more desirable. Would relationships be jeopardised if one does not indulge in this give and take? No one would like to take a risk since relationships are most tenuous when ordinariness is tossed out of the frame of mind. One has to abide by what is in vogue. Else, there is always a chance of losing an opportunity. It is like losing a friend because one could not remember his or her birthday and could not wish on time and certainly could not buy an appropriate gift.

Just imagine the difficulty in friendship amongst the elderly folks if we stick to the format of wishing on birthdays and giving away gifts in time. In old age, when you are likely to be amnesiac, suffering from dementia or simply forgetful, you may be inclined to friendship without exchanges of gifts or accuracy of memory in reciprocating. Elderly folks perhaps operate with a different logic of friendship and festivities, without much fanfare. Due to their own reasons, they try to keep their October as simple as possible. Yet there could be bliss in that simplicity. In the light of this wisdom too, the October festivities ought to be taken seriously, like all similarly important occasions. We truly need to figure out the so-called good deeds that we ought to be doing in order to prevent the feeling of being prisoners of our inferno.

The agrarian logic of lighting small fires to ward off the multiplying pests no longer applies. What applies is the showing off of mistaken opulence. Just like there may be colour television sets beaming entertainment news even though basic amenities are lacking, there is a mistaken idea of opulence. Mere possession of income and the ability to buy things for festivities does not amount to sufficiency. Yet, there is so much happiness that one can put on a flood of LED lights, burst all kinds of crackers and consider in our minds the perceived demons of darkness decimated. We seldom enquire whether we can really decimate demonic darkness in entirety. It is truly an October gone awry; it is truly a fury of festivity that inculcates the value of nuisance in our children. The destruction of virtues knows no class or caste divide. More or less everyone is complicit in the crime of destruction of the future. This is the destruction of the ordinary values associated with the occult of October. When a Gond, from the Gond community in Chhattisgarh, celebrates Dewari, an equivalent of Diwali, they perform and communicate to one another the virtues of the old days. Some LED lights may have entered their world too. An excitement about buying the joys of the festival could be detected as well. But one thing is crystal clear: they defy the logic of market and consumption interfering with their festivity. Girls and elderly women burst into endless singing on Dewari evening. They go around the neighbourhood, extending their good wishes without carrying any packet of gifts, and get thanked in turn by the hosts. One need not be romantic about any assumed purity and authenticity of the tribe. Yet no one can be oblivious to the cultural enchantment the Gonds engender on the occasion of Dewari. They maintain the ordinary, human and simpler occultness of October, the human-friendly charm and enchantment of festivity, intact. But, how can one learn from the practices of a tribal community when one is so sure about what our education has done? In the wake of aggressively affirmed cultural superiority, and the month of October gone awry, we have nearly become indifferent to the ordinary bounties that the month of festivity offers.

Notes

1. The quote in Sanskrit as well as translation are taken from an online source where the authorship for translation is not specified. See 'Devi Aparadha Kshamapana Stotram,' Bhakti Sadhana (blog), accessed on 19 February 2021, https://bhaktisadhana.wordpress.com/2015/12/02/देव्यपराधक्षमापन-स्तोत्/.
2. See 'Devi Aparadha Kshamapana Stotram,' Bhakti Sadhana.
3. It is worth pointing out that there is a range of fairly well-researched monographs on the varieties and workings of Ramlilas in India. A reputed work is Philip Lutgendorf, *The Life of a Text: Performing the Ramcaritmanas of Tulsidas* (Berkeley: University of California Press, 1989). Besides, a contextualisation of Ramlila in the wake of globalisation was accomplished in Nita Kumar, 'The Ramlila Project: Indian Identities in an age of Globalization', in *Cultural Change and Persistence: New Perspectives on Development*, eds. W. Asher and John Heffron (London: Springer, 2010), 147–167.

16

No Ram in the Rant

Imran Khan, the prime minister of Pakistan, initiated the avowed process of reopening the thousand-year-old Jagannath temple in Sialkot. He said that the Prophet advocates respect for the religions of other communities. Then he also visited Kartarpur, free from bureaucratic hassles. Though commentators of all hues may be duly sceptical about such moves of political leadership, there is a discursive value in such instances. The idea of a South Asia based on fluid faith rather than rigid religion is truly coveted. To reiterate a point (discussed in other chapters in this book too), fluid faith allows us as faithful people to be ordinary. On the contrary, rigid religion tries to take away ordinariness while making us ignorant and available for manipulation. If it is an article of faith, you may be playful. If it is a religious matter, you have to be careful. In spite of the spectre of organised religions all over the world, there is a yearning for the ordinary life for the faithful.

One is, however, mindful of such a generous interpretation of an unusual event in Pakistan. There are chances of abusive comments online and on social networking sites. Due to heightened tensions between India and Pakistan in recent times, the likelihood of being subjected to ranting rhetoric about religion and politics is more. But it is difficult to totally ignore the specificity of the opening of the temple in question. This heritage temple in Sialkot was shut since the Partition. The presiding deity in the temple is Bhagwan Jagannath, literally meaning the god of the universe, a variant of Bhagwan Vishnu who is the nurturer of the universe according to religious canon. The saffron aura of the god disarms any hostility. Saffron itself is a beautiful colour. Mythologies add to the tranquillity associated with saffron; it is in histories of hostility that a colour such as saffron acquires various interpretations. History has kept saffron on the boil and turned an otherwise beautiful colour into a bloody red, so to say.[1] Like any other colour, saffron has a long story too. But the dominant version is what becomes the basis for further perception. The prevalent notion of saffron is, unfortunately, a triumph of spectacle over the ordinary aesthetics of colours. This is, to reiterate, extraordinary religion conquering ordinary faith.

The extraordinary exuberance of emotions rides on the back of folk faith. When 'rant' replaces 'chant' and the wisdom worth chanting disappears from the public, the social pathology grows stronger. Chanting is usually an inward journey in traditional Hindu practices. On the bank of a river, after an early morning bath, devotees sit quietly facing the rising sun and chant. They may do so at home at dawn and dusk. You may recall the face of your mother who chanted with her still face, rhythmic heartbeats and symphonic breathing. There was no sign of aggression, militancy or cacophony. There was no drawing of lines between insider and outsider, this world or that world, this community and that creed. The act of chanting is an act of defiance of any boundary; it is instead about making everything one. It is in oneness that a person lives in the act of chanting, without divide and distinction. It is a sublime religious performance done in quietude. Eyelids humbly drop and the heart joins the symphony of stillness. Thus begins an inner spiritual journey. Many of us have felt this even while doing other things in our ordinary lives. Say, for example, while reading a book, we undergo a quasi-chanting experience. Psychologists have pointed out the meditational value of reading. But the poets have shown us that there is a similar submersion when one does something of one's liking. One can once again invoke the logic Mahatma Gandhi applied to cleaning latrines. He requested that he, along with other coinhabitants in Phoenix, South Africa, and later in Sabarmati ashram in India contribute labour and clean latrines. One can read many reasons into the Gandhian act of cleaning, including freedom from caste-based distribution of work, celebration of human labour and even the evolution of finer aspects of humanity in sanitation work. Some elderly folks count beads while chanting; some others use the markings on the fingers. The faces of the chanters beam beatific smiles that can probably unite the whole of humanity. Chanting, in short, is a promising evocation of the strength of humanism—so ordinary and so resplendent, an act in the fold of fluid faith.

Ranting, on the other hand, is not. It is not an act to unite the whole of humanity. It is certainly not for going beyond oneself and forging relationships with the unknown. The images of the ranting crowd making violent noises do not suggest any possible transcendence. Instead, such images evoke fear of the Other. Gods can seldom sit comfortably in terrified hearts filled with hostility. Devotion demands a surrender that is not available to those on the warpath vending warcries. The rants are forceful, violent and exclusionary. They instantly reinforce divides, deepen them furthermore and make the differences look nearly invincible for humanity. In the soundscape of contemporary India, such rantings divide and defeat the promises that Bhagwan Ram himself may have chanted in any version of the Ramayana. Ram is a purushottam in *karuna* (compassion), but he has, unfortunately, been reduced to a spectacle of political conquest. Everything about which Ram himself is apologetic in the epic is actually central to the act of ranting. Such rants depict an undesirable image of the god of whom Ram is an avatar: Vishnu, the celebrated nurturer of the universe. There is seldom a sense of nurturing in the rants that invoke Ram, an incarnation of Vishnu. Instead, one hears a grudging vengeance in them.

Amidst such rants, one wonders about the reality of Ram. Born and brought up in the socio-religious environs of India, one inherits various imaginations of Ram. Scholars of Hindi literature and poetic epics from the saint-tradition have informed us about at least two varieties, Sagun Ram and Nirgun Ram; one is qualified with images and characteristics, whereas, the other is without any identifiable tangibility. Both versions of Ram enamoured Hindus for a very long time. The romance with Ram brings to us the chants by great saints such as Raidas, Guru Nanak, Tulsidas, Valmiki and Kabir. If one goes on adding to the poetic romance with Ram in modern Hindi poetry, the chanting becomes even more mesmerising.

The name 'Ram', thereby, begins to signify far more profound pluralism than what one can hear in any jingoistic rant. Tulsidas's romance with Ram made him elucidate many insightful interactions of characters in *Ramcharitmanas*. In interactions within the epic, stories about Ram assumed a polyphonic significance. There was the prince Ram who was ready to keep his father's word. There were many other equally significant facets of the character of Ram. Many of the devotees of Ram thus recount several images of Ram. Let us think of Sabri's Ram. Sabri was an elderly tribal woman devoted to Ram. She had a chance meeting with Ram, and, to greet him, she offered him berries that she had meticulously collected in the jungle. She tasted them to ensure that Ram gets to eat the best of berries. Ram crossed social boundaries as he relished eating the already-tasted, *jootha,* berries. Ordinary devotees usually point out a profound lesson in this interaction of the god with a devotee, here Sabri: Ram defies all boundaries for love. Moreover, an unforgettable and beautiful part of the epic poem is known as '*Kevat-samvad*', the dialogue between Ram and a boatman named Kevat. The latter, a Mallah (hereditary profession of sailors placed lower in the social hierarchy in caste-based social division), makes it clear that he expects something in return for his service of ferrying Ram across the river in his boat. Ram agrees to pay whatever he can. Kevat puts forward an intriguing condition by suggesting that it has to be service in return for service, rather than any other kind of payment. According to Kevat, he and Ram do similar jobs of ferrying folks across. Kevat takes people from one bank to another of the river, whereas, Ram takes them from one world to another. Kevat demands that Ram should return his favour by ferrying him from this world to another. It is through this deep intimacy with Ram that many such characters find importance in Tulsidas's epic.

A more polychromatic Ram with diverse emotions unfolds if we turn to the 8th-century poet Bhavabhuti's *Uttar Ramcharit* and the 5th-century poet Kalidas's *Raghuvamsam*. Rama is seen in emotional shades that cast an enchantment of ordinariness. In Bhavabhuti, Ram is an embodiment of love for Sita, and, in Kalidas, he sheds tears in deep melancholia. Touching upon the idea behind Ram, Veena Das translates a verse from Raghuvamsam thus:

> Suddenly Rama was with tears much as the moon is
> that rains down the hail
> For fear of scandal,

by him, she was banished
from home
the daughter of Videha
(who) from the heart, could not be expelled[2]

Many such interactive instances demonstrate Ram as an emblem of plural value orientation, emotions and actions. Therefore, *Ramkatha* was so dear to Mahatma Gandhi who envisaged the stitching together of Indian faiths with the name of Ram. As the annals of India show, Ramkatha was also a valuable practice for the Congress party members of the good old days.

Humanism around Ram is becoming a fast-disappearing genre of socio-spiritual quests. It was this humanism that spontaneously allowed even a subversive discussion such as that of Khattar Kaka in Hari Mohan Jha's modern Maithili literary work.[3] One expects the opening of the heritage temple in Sialkot to be more than a gimmick or an act under pressure.

What will happen in Pakistan, too, will be no different. One remembers the terrible murder of the renowned qawwali singer Amjad Sabri when he was on the way to give a performance to mark the holy month of Ramadan. There had already been a popular opinion in Pakistan against the musician and qawwali singers. A hardcore fundamentalist character in a critically acclaimed Pakistani film *Khuda Ke Liye* (For the Sake of Allah, 2007) expresses this opinion. In the film, the character is responsible for brainwashing Muslim youth into Islamic fundamentalism and militancy. He makes a condescending remark about the world-famous qawwali singer Nusrat Fateh Ali Khan. It seems anyone who likes to perceive Islam in the context of everyday life or Sufism would be deemed a heretic. If this is so, it is not surprising that there is an atmosphere of intolerance to art and aesthetics in general. If art turns a critical glance towards the sociopolitical anomaly, even the state machinery will break loose. A certain art installation presented a visual critique of the extrajudicial killings in Karachi lately, and the authorities swung into action to stop the exhibition. There are ample reasons to believe in a rant of very similar, or maybe worse, kind, already in effect in Pakistan. Pakistan may have jeopardised the ordinary aesthetics of religious life long ago.

Notes

1. One learns about it from a fascinating historical account in Sadan Jha, 'Challenges in the History of Colours: The Case of Saffron', *The Indian Economic and Social History Review* 51, no. 2 (2014): 199–229.
   Underpinning such a contextualised reading of colour is Michael Taussig, *What Colour Is the Sacred?* (Chicago: University of Chicago Press, 2009).

2. While addressing the famous Sanskritist Gary Tubb's scepticism about Ram's emotions, an anthropologist of ordinary lives Veena Das invited us to think why Ram means something more than what the mere utterance of the word connotes. See Veena Das, *Textures of the Ordinary: Doing Anthropology After Wittgenstein* (Delhi: Orient Blackswan, 2020, 329–330).
   Also see Gary Tubb, 'Baking Uma', in *Innovations and Turning Points: Towards a History of Kavya Literature*, ed. Yigal Bronner and David Shulman (New Delhi: Oxford University Press, 2014), 71–82.

3. This was cited in the other chapters too.

17

Blissful and Blasé: Tourism versus Pilgrimage

The serene silence of the mountain was suddenly ruptured by a flock of men and women blabbering nonstop. It was as jarring as the sudden yelp of a person stabbed from behind in the dead of night in some crime thrillers. Loudly and clearly, tourists had arrived—some not yet done munching on chips from plastic packets, others pouting with dehydrated lips for selfies and still others jumping around almost like a pack of monkeys. One of them was the embodiment of a walking, talking encyclopaedia. He never ceased to speak about some topic or other, ensuring that everyone in the pack receives his pearls of wisdom. Some girls, nicely wrapped in warm clothes, never stopped shrieking, 'Oh my God, this is so cold!' After exhausting their desire to see, be seen and show, they left, without taking back their leftovers, plastic wrappers, bottles and a whole lot of molecules in the surrounding.

We are playing double roles as citizens and consumers in a developmentalist world. Everything is determined according to a picture postcard imagination of a sleek world that we dream of inhabiting. Therefore, we tend to be blissful in being blasé. Most tourism packages we purchase cover destinations, privileged facilities, satisfactory journey and accommodation, right food and other such basics. At least, that is the way we calculate the efficacy of such packages. The packaged journeys are well planned, taking care of risk to such an extent that there is little uncertainty left. There is no chance of wandering, getting lost and meeting strangers and certainly no accidental mingling with communities that we pass by. The strangers we meet, if at all, are by and large like us, the same kind of folks with similar outfits, demeanour, likes and dislikes. In our fun voyages, we consume scenes, sights, services and even the presence of host communities in the surrounding. Only slightly different from foreigners who would like to click a photo of the natives at the drop of a hat, we are more interested in collecting snippets of an imagined, incredible India. Like everything else, tourism too suffers from economic determinism, excessive industrial interference, impoverished sociocultural imagination and, thereby, the birth of the vulgarity of a photographic gaze. We tour, for, we want to capture with a camera, a kind of conquest.

In the middle of all this, unsung stories await our reflection too. Let us reflect on two young girls who packed their tiny knapsack one evening without any plan and left for the mountain. Let us call them by imaginary names, Ida and Pingala. Originally, these words stand for the breath from the left and right nostrils respectively in the language of yoga, and the two girls were as smooth, ordinary and exquisitely free-flowing as Ida and Pingala. They had no phone or easy access to Google and, hence, they just landed at the New Delhi railway station one evening to find out that the next train to the nearest foothill of the Himalayas, Haridwar, is from the Old Delhi railway station. Not knowing what to do, they stepped out of the railway station and saw a tonga (literally, a horse-drawn carriage) going to the Old Delhi railway station. They hopped on and were soon off to reach the ticket counter where they asked for general compartment tickets for the train to Haridwar. Thoroughly unprepared as they were, they shoved themselves into a jam-packed general compartment of the train. As they pushed in, the crowd from inside pushed them out and, hence, they had to stand on the *paidaan*, the entrance of the compartment, clutching the hand bar. Co-commuters exchanged notes with them, and one of them also offered a bidi, the local leaf-rolled smoking tobacco. They got to see the world in a general compartment otherwise beyond their access. A situation that no urbane tourist would like to undergo unfolded with inherent irritation, people's negotiation and shared misery. Early morning, when dawn was yet to break, Ida and Pingala reached Haridwar, stepped out of the station and occupied seats on a shared minibus. Right at dawn, they were roaming about the streets of Rishikesh, hunting for an accommodation. None of the hotel rooms were available, so they started trying their luck in the ashrams, boarding for pilgrims, mendicants and wanderers. Unfortunately, someone from the ashram management told them that they would not find accommodation since both of them were girls. Failing to fathom the logic of rejection, they continued and eventually managed to convince one ashram owner of the clean, sacred motive of their visit and, hence, their eligibility to seek accommodation in an ashram. The owner of the ashram was a sadhu who let them in with a mysterious smile. In a properly ventilated room, austerely arranged with a simple bed on the floor, they rested. They fed themselves on the gruel that was on offer for food in the ashram. Then, they continued on the journey to unknown and uncertain destinations. For hours, they sat on the bank of the rivers with their feet dipped in and saw the world go by—the jingle of the bell, the calling out of names, the sound of conch shells blowing, the giggles of the schoolgoing children and, if nothing else, the gurgle of the river. Steeped in the music of the situation, they walked all the way to Neelkanth, a destination known for a Shiva temple and, on the way back, they thought of discovering a shortcut. Away from the main road, they were walking along the *pagdandi*, narrow pathways, across a jungle. They came across a signboard that informed them that the jungle was a part of the Rajaji National Park, a forest reserve known for wildlife including leopards. Ida slowed down, and so did Pingala, as they came across another board that prohibited going ahead in the direction in which they were walking. The board informed them that leopards could be sighted in that direction. Unaware of the route, they began to look for someone who could lend them a helping hand. It must have been just a few minutes, though it felt like ages, before they came across a man, seemingly a forest guard. He promised to lead them out, but before that he wanted to drink the tea that he was making on a bonfire. Be it generosity or usual compassion, the guard offered them the smoky-tasting tea. But it was the most replenishing potion at the moment. After consuming tea, bantering about life as a guard in a jungle and sharing the journey of the wandering girls, they managed to find a shortcut to Rishikesh. When Ida and Pingala returned to their urban home in Delhi, everyone asked for the details of the journey. They had fascinating stories to tell. But the friends demanded to be shown the photographs. They had none!

Ida and Pingala's journey of free-flowing breaths is rare. Instead, other kinds of journeys, mostly of tourists, dominate our understanding.

It is in such touristy journeys that self-certifying photographs become the inevitable consequence. A common scene at the sites of tourism: a man clicking a picture on a cellular phone or an easy-to-handle digital camera of a woman against the background of scenery! We see the woman posing for the shot doing everything necessary for looking pretty through the lens. An incredibly sweet smile pouting to fake a kiss for the camera and orchestration of love for the place become part of the scheme. The reflection of the sunlight strikes the dark goggles worn by her and returns to the gaze of the camera. A sense of being blasé surfaces from the bliss of being ignorant about the surroundings and its lively details and the space that invites silence. The scene and its complexity could be breathtaking, turning the cameras and cacophony of tourists silent, if and only if they are allowed time and space. The images of tourists visiting the places, clicking photographs and freezing themselves in the otherwise volatile frame of time ignites a critical imagination. One remembers the Cartesian formula of 'Cogito, Ergo Sum' (I think, therefore, I am) and feels the necessity to reframe it for a touring man and woman: I pose; therefore, I am! No one knows how followers of the philosopher René Descartes would react to this manipulation of the original formulation. The posing, to be framed in the shifting frame, be it by a man or a woman, is geared towards, as it is popularly called, capturing the moment. It may sound innocuous, look pleasant, hint at romance and seem to be a non-issue. Getting photographed in a location against a backdrop, however, is akin to the idea of conquering the unconquerable. The subject of the photograph seems to fail in dealing with the awe of the ambience, the magnificence of the mundane and the enchantment of the ordinary. That sense of failure underpins aggressive photography, so to say. After all, everyone usually says, 'Let us "capture" the scene'. It can be safely said in other words that they seek to imprison the wilderness in a frame. Evidently, as tourists, we fail to cope with the affective power of ordinary places and people, culture and cuisine, dialogue and details. Perhaps, therefore, a camera, or consumption in general, plays an important role.

In contemporary India, this seems a common dream in the eyes of the great demos, basically the consumer-citizens, youthful or aged. This is a dream to see good roads like pathways to dreamworlds, fast trains like exclusive carriers for the impatient class, unhindered supply of energy, communication driven by cutting-edge technology, employment opportunities for the literate masses and so on. To dream of prosperity and seek for the fundamentals of comfortable existence is fairly legitimate, as legitimate as imagining a god or a whole pantheon of gods under the aegis of a religious doctrine. Practices of tourism are under the ambit of a quasi-religiosity mixed with developmental dreams. We salivate over the dream conveniences at home and in the world. The history of religions, however, offers us umpteen examples of religiously guided dreaming that created mythologies, inspiring philosophy, art, aesthetics, cultural and civilisational progress. But then, in the same breath, religious dreaming also underpinned 'blind faith', reducing the dreamers in several cases into 'passive appendages' of the 'active fetishes'. A fetish is as good as god. We surrender to both the same way, the way we are helplessly hooked to our smartphones that never fail to challenge our individual smartness. Dreams have metamorphosed into mass hysteria. In short, religiously determined dreaming has also decimated the human agency to think critically and debate about the implications of religious faiths. Hence, sociologists of religions have largely looked at religious dreaming and mythological manoeuvrings with due scepticism.

In this regard, the photographic gaze reveals a deeper malaise: seeking to freeze the moment without arriving at a harmonious relationship with the place that we visit. This is what unsettles the narrow economic imagination of tourism and enables us to take a critical look at the ways in which tourists (dis)engage with the places they visit. This is the note on which tourists become conquerors of the world with cameras in their hands and money in their cards, very much akin to the German dramatist and playwright Goethe's *Faust*. *Faust*, arguably, is the best tragedy of development;[1] the latter seems to unleash dark and hidden energies, like Faust did. The tourism industry contributes to revenues, a key parameter of judging development, while they arguably slay sociocultural sensibilities. All our privileges, riches and resources turn out to be props of a Faustian developer. The implications of this development works against us, yet we have defined them, or industry has, as 'fun'.

However, the scholar Diana Eck[2] offers us the notion of the sacred geography of India. This suggests that a large number of people moves around paying tributes to gods and goddesses, ancestors and prophets. By doing so, they unwittingly curate a geography of cultural contacts that may not be fully appropriated in the cartography of state, market and industry. This geography is distinguishable from that of the powers that be. One of the earliest Indian sociologists writing about the sadhus of India, G. S. Ghurye,[3] underlined the functions of the mendicants. This is, of course, being pointed out since social scientists have lately distanced themselves from anything like the sacred or sadhus. As a matter of fact, the folks who contributed to innovative thinking in poetry and art have been never detached from the wandering monks, unknown saints and such characters. Tagore's association with the wandering Baul singers is just one such example.[4]

Many of us perhaps still remember that, ordinarily, touring meant pilgrimage. There was no other notion of tourism for ordinary people. Even those from the upper middle class who decided to go on a quiet retreat never lost sight of the places of religious significance around their destinations. Pilgrimages too entailed travelling far and wide, temporarily dislocating oneself from familiar zones to unfamiliar. But the pilgrims do not exhibit the same tendencies as the tourists guided by tourism industry! Or are we expecting too much from contemporary pilgrims equipped with phones that are no less smart? Let us think of the conventional pilgrims who leave such connecting devices behind even in the age of round-the-clock virtual connectedness. A particular kind of consciousness underpins sacred geography, which requires pilgrims to witness the divine, the spiritual and the essential in all the places they visit. However, the idea of sacred geography is not necessarily to glorify the pilgrimage mode of tourism. This is also not to romanticise an imagined 'ancien regime' of existence. There may be inherent issues, duly debatable, within the modes of tourism, for which mythology and history are invoked more often than not. We know anthropologically that the sacred is never free from the spectrally present profane. A good number of Hindu pilgrims, alias tourists, buy tour packages to go across the Indian ocean, looking for the Ram Setu (the bridge that the army of Ram created in the Ramayana).

The buyers explore what is sold as the Sita Trail in Sri Lanka, and they come back happily with a cache of photographs to tell their kith and kin, 'We saw where Sita was kidnapped and kept!' Really! The tourist-pilgrims usually abandon any scepticism upon return. The awareness of the profane reaffirms people's belief in the sacred and, thus, people seek for the sacred. Hence, it is immensely vital to guess that Eck's sacred geography perhaps had the shadow of profanity deeply buried somewhere. It is evident in contemporary India for sure as we track down the garbage littered by the pilgrims on the way to all the sites of religious significance. When we encounter many deeply clogged and quasi-dead rivers, deemed sacred in the Hindu worldview, we get a clear idea of the profane lurking alongside the sacred. It acquires more velocity when tourism is structured through the gaze of the camera that captures 'all good things' to be shared on social networking sites or saved as visual memorabilia.

Let us look at an exemplary situation to vindicate what is being criticised. As a hub of educational institutes, Dehradun, also known as Dronagram after the guru Dronacharya in the Mahabharata, is situated in the foothills of the Himalaya, abutting the Rajaji National forest and feeding on the flowing Ganga in the vicinity. To make it more fulsome, the mighty height of Mussoorie overlooks the fertile plain of Dehradun. The scene turns far more mesmerising when night descends in the valley, conjuring a mystical charm of twinkling dots. This seems a perfect place for a camera-clad tourist to flock to and stay for a day or so and move onto climbing the uphill terrain. Indeed, the Google-aided map, or most typical tourism guidebooks, with paper too glossy to be credible, entices everybody to become a tourist—to climb up, join in the milling crowds of the Mall Road at Mussoorie and pose for a photograph against the background of reminders of human existence dotting the plains or move towards Kempty Falls to stand next to the fierce, feisty fall of the magnificent Kempty and get photographs clicked. Amid the crescendo of the jubilant crowd, the swish and swoosh, gush and gurgle of the fall are drowned out. Nobody would ever think that the Kempty has been terribly tampered with, miserably manhandled and 'beautifully bracketed' only to make it convenient for tourists to have their photographs clicked.

Many such sites have designated spots for photo shoots. Intoxicated by the illusive swagger, do tourists imagine the miseries of a waterfall in the mountains? We perhaps think that it is a job for the expert—ecologist, scientist or a maverick social anthropologist who intends to write a polemical essay on the tourists' behaviour. Hence, we perpetuate dirt and endanger such places without thinking that they too have a life of their own. We suffocate them with our litter, our noise and our reckless behaviour, and we objectify them as mere sources of our sensations, devoid of sensuous pleasure. This is not very different from what we do with many fellow humans, pets or objects that we buy in the market; we approach everything with the same attitude of a proud consumer. We do not listen to whispering *Cheer* (pine), crooning *Devdar* (cedar), singing silver oaks (known with various names in the Kumaon and Garhwal regions) and spontaneously blooming, innumerable little flowers in the soothing company of moist grass. We are mostly prisoners of the unbridled cacophony of our voices, which we carry from our place of origin to everywhere we go. We go to Dhanaulti, a sleepy hamlet, yet another hill station perched a little above Mussoorie, and we encounter mist. The thick, velvety and milky cloud engulfs us in the evening. We, however, remain what we are—noisy, careless, pleasure-craving consumers. No, we do not get any mystical message even though the whispering pines deliver them to us; the crooning Devdars and the clouds adrift with open arms to embrace and kiss us on our forehead do not enchant us. We do not wish to open our minds and hearts to receive such unsaid messages and interpret and ponder upon them to work out a philosophy of our own lives. Alas! We miss a chance to be an amateur philosopher, a poet, a storyteller, a monk and a mystic—an ordinary man and a woman! We remain an amateur tourist, with a camera as a weapon in our hand and the restlessness of our troubled existence under the veneer of our beautiful bodies.

At this point, let us turn to the schools and schooling in the foothills of the Himalayas. A long list of so-called elite schools appears on the webpages in the territory of Dehradun. Some of them, needless to name, have a long, glorious past, where the children of the Indians, powerful and elite, studied. The advertisements of these schools, as if an omnipresence replacing that of the divine, resemble that of five-star hotels. They flash the facilities in the school, including the racecourse with the best breed of horses and the swimming pools with sparkling clean, blue water, in addition to the state-of-the-art facilities for education, the high-profile faculty members and a luxurious boarding facility. Of course, there is a mention of the educational facility, seeming to suggest that only a 'good facility' makes for 'good education'. Any middle-class parent would perhaps drool over the opportunity to send his/her ward to one of these schools by paying high capitation fees. The advertisements on billboards along the streets display the 'cool faces' of young kids in their best uniforms. Young models promoting the schools! By all means, these schools try to distinguish themselves, their students and their teachers from others, as if their educational vision can have nothing in common with others. However, in the spectacle and grandeur, a sceptical mind may not fail to read a possible 'vacuum of vision'. Dehradun and Mussoorie, put together, seem to be the paradise of educational dream merchants as well as affluent dreamer-parents. They, indeed, contribute to the dreams of a development-worshipping India. Children from upper-middle-class families are educated in these so-called elite schools. Almost in continuum with the logic of tourists, these students remain largely learner-tourists. Their engagement with the environment of the region remains abysmal. The lack of curricular design for a constructive and longitudinal interface between the students and the local community and environment is evident in many ways. However, one needs to penetrate into the thick walls of these schools to find empirical evidences other than the evident arrogance of teachers and students in these schools. At most, elite schools perform window dressing to show off their environmental concerns, to conveniently add to their annual day functions or the colourful school prospectus. In sum, there is a kind of civil society tourism that the schools perpetuate.

Amid this, however, there are schools run by the state government without much to advertise. According to contemporary logic, one advertises specialities, distinctions and achievements. 'No advertisement', following the common sense of development, means 'no distinction'. Children from the vicinity trek up and down the hills to these underfunded schools. No exclusive yoga or pranayama can do the wonders these children will attain unwittingly due to the way they spontaneously engage in everyday life. They need no exclusive window dressing event to show off their engagement with the environment. They simply live it without putting it on exhibition. They know, even if not by name, the distinct aroma of herbs and flowers. They know the places where serpents might dwell. They know the turns in the hills that may be haunted. Their sense of belongingness is an essential component in their learning and growing process. This is conspicuous by its absence in the schools where learners are tourists in some sense.

To conclude, it is worth recapitulating an instance stuck like a shard of glass in my memory. One New Year's Eve, a place in the Kumaon region of Uttarakhand named Kausani was bathed in the silver light of the full moon. Everything seemed quiet in this small hill station surrounded by thick pine groves on one side and the Himalayan peaks on the other. It was this serenity of Kausani that compelled M. K. Gandhi to reschedule his trip and stay there longer than planned to finish writing his treatise on the Gita. The ashram named after Gandhi in Kausani still stands as a testimonial. That evening in Kausani, the humans had retired for the night and dogs had stopped barking. The peaks, Trishul, Nanda Devi, Neelkanth and others, were romancing in the alchemic magic of moonlight and the quiet night. Nothing but the whispers of the pine trees and the gentle beats of the heart was audible. A sudden burst of carnivalesque noise rose from one of the resorts nearby. Some tourists were celebrating New Year's Eve; it conveyed nothing but the vileness and violence of urbanity. One could not hear till late the symphony of silence, the secret messages of the Himalayan peaks, the songs of moonlight in praise of the mountain and the hymns of the saintly pines whispered in all humility. Instead, one had to hear the mindless razzmatazz of the visiting tourists and perhaps the helpless sighs of the local residents. Without much effort, one can imagine the tourists clicking photographs of each other while dancing to the tunes of the disc jockey around the bonfire in the safe confines of the resort. One can guess that they must have come across a package tour offered by one of the agencies. It must have benefitted the service industry, the hotel industry, some of the local residents employed in them and so on. It must have also given an adrenaline rush to the visiting tourists. However, it destroyed the sanctity of the place! Perhaps the debates on sustainable development have to acknowledge the unsustainability of it in the face of daily assaults on the significance of the places. Perhaps one also needs to ask whether our dreams of development, without educational consciousness, disable our cognitive and spiritual abilities—so much so that everything blasé becomes blissful!

Notes

1. It is worth recalling a masterpiece where the parallel between Goethe's drama *Faust* and sociopolitical developments in historical trajectory was one of the central features. See Marshall Berman, *All That is Solid Melts into Air: The Experience of Modernity* (London: Verso, 1983).
2. For more along this line, despite the irritating level of oversimplification, see Diana Eck, *India: A Sacred Geography* (New York: Three Rivers Press, 2012).
3. This is certainly a rare work by a sociologist. See G. S. Ghurye, *Indian Sadhus* (Bombay: Popular Book Depot, 1953).
4. This was pointed out in other chapters in this book too.

18

Models without Roles!

The proposition of models without roles is souring, particularly since we still believe in the idea of role models. Reading history piecemeal or mugging up general knowledge has led to this. Then, we did not find these role models bombarding us with impressions. They did not labour hard to convince us of their eligibility. Did Bhagat Singh come to advertise himself to us ever? Those role models were occupied with their envisioned roles. Unlike today's role models, they were not the constructions of various public relation (PR) agencies, in circulation and demand through calculated orchestration. Since we invariably find out that the role model is indeed only a model, it is painful. There is an abundance of shared doubts about the roles these models play and, thus, they seldom evoke favourable sentiments. At worst, we get disillusioned to such an extent that cynicism overcomes our mind. It is in that situation of cynicism that we tend to explore an altogether different idea of role models. A cinematic representation of a well-known star who has had ups and downs in his life creates a role model. It only reaffirms the difficulty in finding a role model in contemporary India.

The idea is not to imitate the elitist reviews of popular melodramatic cinemas that appear in newspapers and periodicals after every Friday release. We already overstuffed ourselves on the blockbuster *Sanju* (2019), to the extent of suffering a bout of indigestion. While many said that it was a whitewashed biopic of the actor Sanjay Dutt, many of us also enjoyed watching yet another cinematic treat from the master of melodrama in contemporary Hindi cinema, Rajkumar Hirani. Rejecting or glorifying the film is not the intent behind the unpleasant expression 'models without roles'. There is absolutely little doubt that Sunil Dutt, an actor who took the plunge into political and social life headlong, was a much more suitable model with explicit roles and a better subject for a fair biopic than the junior Dutt. Even if there is no biopic on Sunil Dutt because the story of his life may not serve the same tangy spices as that of others, he is an undisputable role model given the virtues of his social actions. Hence, it is needless to vilify *Sanju* on that count.

Instead, a question can be posed about our unrequited hunger for a role model despite too many Twitterati posing as one. The hunger shall remain despite platters in front of us full of bizarre food items, since we also seem to be terribly confused about the idea of a role model today. We are closer to a catharsis of fakery; it will not be surprising if, one day, the whole nation becomes crazy followers of a fake model based on a fake social media profile! Just imagine the hilarity of that possible pathology, in which every follower is surfing the pages related to a fake model on Twitter, Instagram, Facebook and such platforms. The followers will only enable the person (or group) hiding behind such a fake profile to enact a variety of possible roles. They could be a number of sinister roles, misinforming the followers and misrepresenting ideas and individuals. We have heard of such accounts related to some fake names as well as some real names. In spite of disclaimers of all kinds, the web surfers do visit those pages and consume the memes, placards and messages. A good number of constructions of models floating around us make us suspicious and gullible. We are trapped in the personalities and ideas on the internet—the sublime and the ridiculous, the glorified and the suspicious. In between fake and fictional, we have also an array of overly dramatised constructs passing off as role models or, better to say, models without roles!

Perhaps the idea of role models underwent some Kafkaesque transformation after liberalisation or, if that is a convenient marker only for social scientists, post-Y2K (or the turn of the millennium). Children in schools, neophytes in colleges and semi-skilled professionals in the liberal market of employment zeroed in on names that were far from logically justified. While some of the seniors, teachers or scholarly types, emphasised one category, the dreamers of a new Indian order of sociopolitical reality had something else in mind. The new gods emerged while the old ones were either refashioned or cast away altogether. The journey is very aptly summed up in the transformation of a Mahatma into a mere glitzy brand or a Babasaheb into a mere weapon of militant identity politics. The transformation also witnessed some of the old ones in a new avatar; historical icons resurfaced with novel look and purpose. Many such newly packaged icons were diminished into yet another stakeholder in power politics too. Some well-known diplomats, public intellectuals and social activists joined in the list. There is no need to waste time in naming and shaming them all. The idea is to understand the ordinary reasons why some of them took centre stage in our quotidian life and how they fell down.

Indeed, if there is a role, it is only to obscure the crystal-clear truth that we are too blinded by the glitz and glamour to see our real role models. The difference between a celebrity and a newspaper vendor is that the newspaper vendor does not have an industry to which he can sell his performance. His role, so well performed, is performed in ignominy, and so, he is not counted as our model even once. Not just him, many of our house helps, without whom we can seldom imagine the smooth functioning of the household, are far more suitable candidates. It is only during the extraordinary crisis that was the lockdown in 2020 that we suddenly realised how our everyday, ordinary life depended on unsung role models such as our house helps. More often than not, we are oblivious to the roles that they perform without due respect. Even worse, we tend to reciprocate to them with a meagre bonus payment on occasions and consider our job done. We do so without any ethical hiccup since these unsung heroes would not start a campaign to expose our apathy. They do not make news like some well-known actresses and models of the glamour industry do on their Instagram or Twitter profile.

As if this is any less, we begin to crave a biopic on a former Miss Universe who also became a successful film actress or on an alumnus of an engineering institute who began to write popular English novels due to the help provided by Microsoft Word to correct grammar and vocabulary. In spite of critics writing him off as an insignificant novelist, his novels are so widely read that he has now become a spokesperson on burning topics in television chat shows. Likewise, we yearn for a glorious narrative on a fairly young cricketer who became a star by hitting several boundaries and sixers in T20 matches. All such narratives may make it to popular cinema and may earn gross revenues. But it is doubtful whether they deliver anything more than models without substantial sociocultural roles. Teachers, sportspersons, cultural performers and many others do not even figure in the larger pool of models with significant roles. So many unknown heroes are setting examples with their struggles, but their names and biographies are hardly recorded. They do not fit the Page 3 tableaux in newspapers and television. Except when they are given a token mention on the occasion of award ceremonies, they remain by and large unrecognised by us. Even after felicitation, if there is one, they do not register their presence. We want a glamorous, at times scandalous, man or woman for a role model, apparently. Is it not questionable that some film stars and models are deemed the epitome of women's empowerment in India? It is just like saying that women are better off in India since Pratibha Patil was the honourable president in recent times. Stomach churning in disgust, one turns over the pages of newspapers every morning to see numerous women struggling to find the basic minimum safety and respect that is due to them. If there must be biopics, such struggling women should be made the subject. A list should be made of many such unsung folks who have been in the sociocultural battlefield and been marked by the violence against them. Our national media hesitates to report about them; our visual culture, including popular cinemas, fails to see them; our popular novelists are oblivious to them; and, of course, we have little interest in even being curious about them. The glamour industry constructs, the new and old media circulates and wannabe citizens actively consume and reproduce: a variety of models without roles. On the other hand, millions of models playing significant roles in society and polity remain largely under-reported, far away from the glitz and blitz, silently working and struggling with rationales worthy of human pursuit. The real role models do not sell, whereas, the glamorous models without any roles whatsoever, do.

Before such a cynical take overcomes us, we shall resort to nostalgia of the trail of ordinary heroes as our role models. The walls of our government schools showed the mass-produced images of historical icons such as Tagore, Gandhi, Nehru, Ambedkar, Azad and Vivekananda among others. We also saw Kabir, Nanak, Raidas, Surdas,

Paramhamsa and others. We saw them alongside the mythological figures, exuding warmth and wisdom. They created a visual abundance around us from where we could choose anyone as our models. We had the luxury to eject history from the visual mythology and, hence, the models were immune to the intricacies of everyday life. In short, we created our role models out of the icons from history and mythology. If it seemed too abstract, we deemed our school headmaster, class teacher or the favourite teacher of our favourite subjects our role models. The teachers did not have glamour; they only commanded respect. We adored them next to our parents, who were equally concrete role models. If parents were not so available, there was always an avuncular uncle out there, visiting us once in a while and presenting to us enchanting tales of the world they roamed. They were very ordinary folks of flesh and blood. They felt pleasure and pain, hunger and thirst, and yet mouthed and enacted values. We had no difficulty in ennobling them as our role-bound models, since they were doing rather than only preaching, living their life with values rather than merely advertising and pontificating. These role-bound-models reflected more commitment to the chosen roles in their biographies than their personal prejudices and privileges. This was despite the fact that we witnessed their failures and vulnerability, their obsessions and weaknesses. They appeared to be truly real role models, intimate and afar at once. As we grew up, we began to chisel our role models out of the fictional characters. They were not there in the concrete sense and yet always lumbering about. If we deemed Feluda or Byomkesh Bakshi as role models, we had no hesitation in appointing Harry Potter in that position either. We may not have forgotten the days when we fancied a Mulla Nasruddin as a role model. We aspired to follow in Mulla's footsteps and be witty and wise like him. Even modern literary constructs attract our following if we heed them. In this vein, it is sufficient to recall a character from modern Maithili literature, mentioned in other chapters in this book, Khattar Kaka, who uncannily embodies critical thinking despite exhibiting the stereotypical features of an ordinary person. The character makes for an all-time relevant role model. If we go further back in time, we can hail a poet from Karnataka, Akka Mahadevi, as a role model for giving us the unusual terrain of the sensuous and critical idea of devotion as she celebrated her love for Shiva.

They all shared one common trait: there was no glamour industry or PR agency working for them. Yet, they seemed to be models with roles, evoking adoration and inspiring our minds. Perhaps this was why we imbibed the idea of appreciating the aesthetics of the ordinary.

19

Our Ordinary Amitabh Bachchan: Politics, Prejudice and Pride

Like the teeming billions of India, I am one of the crazy fans of Amitabh Bachchan, the actor whom we know through characters that he essayed on the silver screen from the glorious decade of the 1970s onwards. I loved him as an actor and, hence, I have a strong hatred towards his pride, prejudice and politics. This may also be because emotion is seldom monochromatic.[1] We have read debates about it in psychoanalysis. This is particularly so when we read emotions in mythology. The common-sense idea that love colours our perception, and so does hatred, ought to be questioned. Love and hatred are seldom separable. I, hereby, examine my strong love coupled with strong hatred for the actor and the associated modern mythology that dominates the cinephilic India of our times.

Everyone, ever since the 1970s, has a share in the larger-than-life modern mythology related to Bachchan. The way he rose to renown in popular Hindi cinema is nothing less than heroic. Despite having a father of such literary eminence, Harivansh Rai Bachchan, he did not have an easy way in. Romance and tragedy kings, as some of his predecessors were called, ruled the roost. Many interviews available online inform us about the lack of receptivity for the actor that Bachchan aspired to become. The credit for making a fine actor out of him goes to a master of Hindi cinema classics, Hrishikesh Mukherjee. Mukherjee belonged to the league of one of the most prominent icons of Hindi cinema industry, Bimal Roy. It all showed in Mukherjee's fine art of filmmaking with perfect assembly of acting, sequences, songs and emotions in addition to many other aspects such as costumes, light, camera work and a huge part of post-production. Bachchan, who had literally gone unnoticed in *Saat Hindustani*, somersaulted to a tiny yet significant share of fame with Mukherjee's *Anand*. It would not have been so easy had it not been for the fine balance that Mukherjee created in *Anand*, and that made way for Bachchan to shine along with the ever-shining Rajesh Khanna. The intense character of a staunch believer in modern biomedicine, fondly addressed in the film as *Babu Moshai* (the Bengali version of gentleman), was appropriate for the visibly beleaguered Bachchan in the dramatic narrative of *Anand*. Further, as if Hrishikesh Mukherjee was not yet done, he tried repeating the magic minus the romance king Rajesh Khanna in *Mili*, which starred Jaya Bhaduri, then an admirer of Bachchan. The latter was to continue the look of an intensely stoic character who did not like anything related to frolicking life. Obviously, *Mili* did not do as well as *Anand*, despite the best of performances by Jaya Bhaduri, Ashok Kumar and Bachchan. The latter then had directors who were godsends, adept at cinematic dramas in which the intense, unhappy and deeply troubled look of Bachchan fitted well. Features underlined as negative for the lanky actor turned out to be positive.

This was the opportunity to avenge! Vijay, the angry young man, was no longer a man of letters like the believer in biomedicine, the Babu Moshai of *Anand*. Prakash Mehra's *Zanjeer* and Yash Chopra's *Deewar* had Bachchan playing a police inspector and a porter-turned-gangster respectively. The changing nature of the characters, which made Bachchan eligible for these roles, is noteworthy. One should also not lose sight of magnanimous actors such as Ajit who played the villain, Pran a Pathan friend and Jaya Bhaduri a cherubic street girl in Mehra's *Zanjeer*. The nature and effects of the full drama allowed Bachchan's character to turn heroic. It also appeared in popular Hindi cinema and India when disillusionment with nation-building was high, and the anger and frustration of the youth were palpable.[2]

On the other hand, Yash Chopra was a newly trained master who had already had a mix of success and failure at two kinds of genres, romance and vengeance. While Chopra tasted the sweetness of success with *Dhool Ka Phool*, a story of troubled romance, his equally meaningful work, *Dharmputra*, based on a novel by well-known modern Hindi novelist Acharya Chatursen, did not do so well. *Dharmputra* was a beautiful work about the troubled romance of a Muslim couple, a Muslim boy growing up into a Hindu fascist and the catharsis in the end.[3] *Deewar* was a relatively clean brush for Chopra as the tale of vengeance for a social wrong. Now, Vijay, played by Bachchan, was the central character for all practical purposes. Every dialogue he mouthed became iconic statements. The writer duo Salim (Khan)–Jawed (Akhtar) were wise and insightful. From the script of the film, it is evident that the writers were well aware of the historical-political milieu in which they were narrativising the tale of Vijay. Hence, the dialogues aptly divulge the sentiments of an angry India, such as, *'Pehle us admi ka sign le ke aao jisne mere haath pe ye likh diya tha, mera baap chor hai'* (I will be the culprit but first you hold that man culpable who declared my father a thief). Then there was no turning back, and obviously, there was no turning right then. It was all left or centre. The filmography of Bachchan says it all.[4]

The point is not to repackage and deliver an exhaustive list of films and write another story of felicity. It is to underline the fact that an actor who came out of nowhere (non-cinema background) inched nearer to many of us by doing such varied characters. The point is that many of us who grew up in the 1980s feel a personal connection to the actor who became our voice. Through Bachchan's triumph, we developed our own narrative of anger, love, hatred and vengeance. Each of us, growing up in the late 1970s and 1980s, identified with the characters that Bachchan enlivened for us. The youth emulated not only his hairstyle, look and demeanour but also the stance, perspective and words of the characters that he did in those films. In the middle of our celebration of the rising star or even the star already risen, we forgot one simple lesson. Amitabh Bachchan was always a director's actor. One can safely say by revisiting his filmography that he was never an independent actor. With bad directors, sordid scripts and imbalanced assemblage of various aspects of cinema, Bachchan did badly. If you do not believe that, just look with some interest at the long list of his flop films. By watching a few of them, you can easily figure out how poorly he performed as an actor. True, some from the list of bad films also look like good works, once again due to the skills of the filmmaker rather than that of the actor we are celebrating. Yet, we loved him, so much so that we began to believe in the cinema magazines calling him superstar. Why not, after all, he gave an unequivocal and solid voice to our sentiments when the liberal democracy of India had gone awry!

But we had started looking at Bachchan through the sheen and shine of diligently manufactured glamour. It happens with any industry; a commodity is emphasised for its values. The industry of cinema is not far behind. The only difference is that it glamourises not only its product, the commodity called cinema, but also the cast. Glamour for our actors and actresses is, thus, an appendage to the commodity of cinema. Bachchan's predecessors benefitted from this. So did Bachchan, but a little more than his due because he became the patriarch of an industry who could relentlessly reinvent himself. With every turn and twist in time, we saw Bachchan in a new avatar, and the industry injected a new lease of life into the glamour meant for him. However, we, the people of India, had ceased to look at Bachchan from the perspective that we looked at him in the beginning of a veritable *Bachchan-nama*. He was no longer our man, even though he continued with the anger of youth despite his grey hair. We no longer sung along with him, we did not join him in fistfights with the villains and we had nothing of him to emulate the way we did back then. When Bachchan began to be addressed more as Big B, we had stopped identifying with him. Our Jay-Vijay was an ordinary man, a tall figure with small wants who wanted to die in his mother's arms or, for a change, in the arms of his bum chum in *Sholay*.

Perhaps, we started to see the changes long ago when he jumped into the electoral-political fray and defeated veteran politician, Hemvati Nandan Bahuguna, the former chief minister of Uttar Pradesh, in Allahabad (now Prayagraj) in 1984. It is said that Bachchan nearly killed Bahuguna's political career in that election. We were amazed, if not thoroughly shocked, when he came to be known as an aide to Rajiv Gandhi steadily rising to power. Then began the prolonged whodunnit of the Bofors scam, leading to worse. Bachchan, dramatically called it quits, due to strange reasons muffled in intriguing emotions. If his entry into politics amused the ordinary folks, the exit certainly enhanced doubts that spread like Chinese whispers. This, indeed, applied to Bachchan's short stint in politics, and then another innings in the cinema ensued. The man who came with a rebellious character in a film literally meaning revolution, *Inquilaab*, and then a peppy character in *Shahenshah* teaching harsh lessons to the corrupt folks fell from the high pedestal in our personal mythologies of him. This was truly the undoing of our hero who had run away from the demands of politics according to the people's popular perception, even though we were not sure of the facts and fiction. This was the same hero for whom many from his vast fandom observed fast and prayed day and night when he was fatally injured during the shooting of the film *Coolie*. We never wished our hero an untimely death. Yet we could not turn blind to the fact that in public life, he fell in our eyes. It all began to get murkier, with facts mixing with our fiction. We saw him hanging out with the powerful elite in Uttar Pradesh and joining the business board of Sahara Shree Subrata Roy along with others of his ilk. Amitabh Bachchan bagging awards conferred upon him by the Mulayam Singh Yadav government did not contribute positively to his popular public image either. Everything related to him was adding to the negative emotions that we had already developed in our personal narratives related to him.

At last, our fallen hero appeared in the plush hall at Rashtrapati Bhavan to receive the glorious Dadasaheb Phalke Award. The timing is noticeable, when the whole nation is raising queries in various ways, through peaceful protest or just by critical conversation, about the fundamental issue of citizenship. In agreement or otherwise, the man who did many characters with which we identified, never cared to respond to the political pulse of the people. Perhaps, this is what he considered appropriate. But political aloofness is not the equivalent of political neutrality. The actor who commanded our emotional pulse had nothing to say when we were beleaguered. It all only provoked us to apply some strong adjectives to him, not appropriate to mention in formal writing. Thus, as he rose to the proud moment when he received the Phalke Award, I, as a disgruntled and dissatisfied fan of Amitabh Bachchan, asked: What should a hero do these days in India, accept an award or return it? I do not know the answer yet, and perhaps I would hate to find out.

Notes

1. This was a focus in the discussion in other chapters in this book too.
2. An easy way to interpretatively connect the national scenario with the emergence of the angry young man is possible by referring to a host of writings, including Vinay Lal, *Deewar: The Footpath, The City and The Angry Young Man* (New Delhi: Harper Collins, 2010).
3. This was discussed in Chapter One of this book.
4. There are many hagiographic, chronicled compilations of Bachchan's filmography. One such work, awarded and complimented, is by Bhawana Somaaya, *Amitabh Bachchan: The Legend* (Macmillan India, 1999).

20

Gandhi, Nehru and the Politics of Extraordinary Names

There was a university campus that had no names for the various roads inside it for many decades since its inception. Recently, they were named, with the name on a billboard at the mouth of each road. When students and teachers walked on those unnamed roads, they used to describe each road fully well, referring to memories associated with the roads. Friends curated memories about those unnamed walkways, unnamed landmarks. They told each other stories about who met under which tree along which road and where they began to fight and decided to break up. Unnamed roads were recognised through the personal narratives of the passers-by. Microhistories and microgeographies were intertwined with nameless roadways. Anyone could say, the way a cinema actor said in a popular film song, *wahin jahan koi aata jata nahin* (let us meet at the same road, the same lane, where no one comes)! Now, with a clear name for each road, we have only a list of names for the whole university campus. It is all official now. Nobody tinkers with official names. Letters will not reach or will take longer than necessary if the officially designated name is not mentioned on the envelope. Registration of property is unimaginable without sticking to the given names. We do not think of those roads through personal narratives any more.

If a university is a microcosm of the universe, the naming of the roads and consequent disability to describe them reflects the malaise of our time. That is, it is only the name that matters, not the character. Be it places or people, these naming tactics make our lives easy and imagination poor. This gives us convenience at the price of personal relationships with people and places. Every now and then, there is something about a place being named, rather, renamed, into something else. Allahabad, or Ilahabad as people called it, Faizabad and many places were renamed. Curiously though, the names 'Prayag' and 'Ayodhya' were already cultural nomenclature. So was the case with Bombay becoming Mumbai. But the cultural nomenclature replacing the official one diminishes the freedom one feels with the unofficial, informal names. In a stroke, such an intimate name turns out to be a bone of contention and, thus, the process of impersonalising the cultural nomenclature ensues. That is the side effect of name politics, which follows the logic of changing an ordinary name into an extraordinary one. That is the template of name politics, which does not allow a place and people to operate with the names with which they can associate. The moment an ordinary name is given an official, bureaucratic and political spin of any kind, it becomes a turf for warring groups.

It is not like this has never happened before. Historically, big names are sullied for some imagined mileage in the present. There need not be a serious rationale. However, all the mud-slinging thrives on a common premise that emphasises the spectacular value of the names of historical characters. Something like this happened with the names of characters from our beautiful mythologies too. A divine figure from mythology acquired political and historical hues. Seldom do we realise that when we utter the word associated with gods these days, we indeed subscribe to a large corpus of historical encounters associated with it. Ethnologists, missionaries and colonial administrators had to zero in on exact words for gods in the colonies and, more importantly, preachers had to find appropriate words for their gods to convince the folks who spoke vernacular languages.[1] In this way, many gods become more than what we usually think they are. Continuing with this line of thinking, we can understand that the most brutal was the extraordinary deification of our dearest Hanuman, the mischievous monkey god. He had enormous inherent power about which 'he had to be reminded' because he was cursed in his childhood by the sages for subverting the order of things with his extraordinary power. Such sweet arrangements in the mythological tales were so that these characters could be relatable for common people. Being ordinary and yet with inherent levels of unseen ordinary power made Hanuman an endearing character. Hence, people find Hanuman relatable, so much so that children can playfully become a character like Hanuman and walk around stomping their feet and doing all sorts of mischief. We never thought that someone is slinging mud on Hanuman or Ram when we saw an actor play these characters in a *bahurupiya* performance, a tradition in which ordinary actors disguise themselves and appear in public as various characters. Those characters were spectacular, but not the way some of our historical names have been made out to be. We could make some unusual additions to Mahadev, the famous Shiva or Rudra, depending on our personal interests, and yet we were not accused of any sacrilege. We did not ask the disguised person, a bahurupiya, about the authenticity of the role they performed. Rather than conducting an enquiry about the costumes and make-up match, we reverentially beheld the goddess Kali in bahurupiyas performing the role of the goddess. In the guise of gods and goddesses, they took artistic and creative liberty as they responded to the audience's questions. We just enjoyed seeing them in various forms. Playful associations with the divine were perfectly fine in that ordinary cultural trope.

People hurl mud, coloured powders and balloons on each other during the celebration of Holi in various parts of India. There are seldom any serious repercussions. Really? The morning after Holi, we read reports about someone attacking and brutalising another person due to unsolicited throwing of colours or mud used in the celebration of the festival. I am sure in those cases, too, the offended person presumes his name to be too big to be available for the riffraff. Commoners cannot enjoy the freedom to be playful with the big names. These days we hear of various defamation cases against any criticism of the people who have big names. Potential contenders in the politics of big names enjoy this privilege. However, it varies according to the level of power. The ruling party will be intolerant of the criticism of 'big' names of their party, while those not in power will take it lying low, awaiting their ascendance to power. Lately, unsubstantiated and condescending remarks, memes and captions about various names on social media acquire such velocity that they reverberate across the nation. Jawaharlal Nehru, Mohandas Karamchand Gandhi, B. R. Ambedkar and others have been subject to misinformation. All such instances hurt sentiments, offend social groups and become a source of perpetual anxiety. Provocative messages circulated on chatting apps about different communities and various ethnic groups often become bones of contention. Needless to say, there is the problem of the medium and the message. But then, it has something to do with the reception and the value orientation also. It looks like each community or group of followers has become an excessively vulnerable sentimental island. Due to a low degree of self-understanding, one gets easily offended. This is how those going through turbulent adolescence behave. Our communities seem to have a pathologically prolonged adolescence, just refusing to overcome the emotional and psychological fragility. To look at it in another way, this emotional and psychological fragility is sustained by the politics of big names, overly fattened pride and thick prejudices. Not only historically and mythologically significant characters, it also includes the names of roads, trains, cities, caste and creeds and so on. Paradoxically, this unsurpassable seriousness is about something that was declared nearly immaterial in our modern civilisation. One of the most important modern bards, Shakespeare, asked what is in a name. You may call a rose a marigold, but it would still give you the same fragrance! You may call yourself X, but you would still be what you are in the eyes of your folks and yourself. You may call Mahatma Gandhi names, but his name would still be synonymous with the enormity of compassion, love and commitment to praxis such as Satyagraha and Swaraj. There is absolutely no other meaning of any word that we would use for Bapu. He is so much in the corpus of ordinary imagination. Everything about him has become folklore, flowing freely across the boundaries of caste and creed. We would always mean, by any metaphor or epithet, the same Gandhi we love and the same Gandhi with whom we may have serious disagreements on various issues. Imagine how those so-called Gandhians would have reacted to the ordinariness of Gandhi that is being discussed here. They would have been up in arms, just like some so-called Ambedkarites these days. Likewise, some Marxists thought themselves to be the embodiment of Marxian knowledge and exhibited intolerance to any alternative reading of Marx. The so-called true Marxists had to dutifully resort to the well-known divide between young, sentimentalist, romantic communism and the mature, scientific theorist of capitalism, which elsewhere Althusser[2] has characterised as an epistemological break in Marx. Anyone experimentally engaging with Marx beyond such a divide was declared by staunch Marxists as merely an insignificant passer-by. Marx, a thinker of ordinary lives, has been forcefully made into an extraordinary entity immunised to any intellectual adventure except by that of the vanguard Marxists. Perhaps, this is a human tendency common to both scholars and youth.

Beyond extraordinary names, there is an enchanting ordinariness about the characters, the diverse embodiments of intellect and emotions, behind the names. They are available in our everyday life for our playful engagement. Similarly, beyond whatever names we have earned, we ought to be available to our friends, our kids, our students and our teachers for all kinds of mischievous activities. A friend taking the liberty to laugh at you is not a curse. It is a blessing for which one should work hard in ordinary life. In another context, Rajkumar Hirani, a popular Hindi filmmaker, tried to do the same with Mahatma Gandhi, fondly called Bapu, in the film *Lage Raho Munna Bhai* (Keep at it, Munna Bhai, 2006). Historians and Gandhians had problems with it. How could you make Gandhi the butt of ridicule? How could you make the character of Gandhi say that all his statues should be demolished? In the same spirit, Jahnu Barua, the Assamese filmmaker, played with our emotions for Gandhi in the provocative film *Maine Gandhi Ko Nahi Mara* (I did not kill Gandhi, 2005). One must congratulate these filmmakers for committing much-needed sacrilege, so to say. The cinematic narratives built relationships between ordinary folks and historically significant icons such that the names were endearingly imbued with emotions. After all, Nehru was 'Chacha Nehru', an avuncular figure that invites relationships; so why do children not enact skits about the historical chacha? After all, Mahatma Gandhi was a bapu, more formally called the Father of the Nation; so why should we not take liberty with our Bapu? The filmmakers have brought these extraordinary names to the plane of the ordinary because the possibility was already created by these personalities. If we are scared of being playful with them today, it only reveals the problem with the regimes of power, conditioning of the mind and boundaries set around us. This is fairly new degeneration. Perhaps, we want to follow the divide between the sacred and the profane, originally a biblical idea. We have always played with the sacred in the most profane manner, and we have elaborate rituals sacralising our profane activities too. In our engagements with gods, goddesses, historical figures and elderly folks, we create our own stories. Creativity does not subscribe to the simplistic binaries of sacred and profane.

Shakespeare may have revelled, and so did his 'star-crossed' characters Juliet and Romeo in the famous drama of love and hatred, saying, 'What's in a name? That which we call a rose by any other name would smell as sweet!'[3] It is by rendering the big names meaningless that Juliet declares the vengeance of the warring families (of hers and that of her lover, Romeo) futile. The two are re-baptised into lovers rather than the members of their respective families. Even if we do not call love by that name, it will still feel like and connote love only. It takes two characters to be star-crossed and yet cling on to see beyond the order of the things, beyond the status quo of names and established norms. The adverse consequences or bad luck notwithstanding, they blissfully endure the tragedy of drama.

Ordinarily, people are star-crossed, seeing beyond the seen and facing the consequences. They do not stop despite the apprehension about good or bad luck. But another simultaneous practice is to surrender to the status quo, crying in bad faith, unwilling to own up to actions and consequences.[4] Hence, folks have, unfortunately, reduced everything into some or other name, despite the cultural practice of having a nickname. Among Bengalis, the name to address an individual informally and intimately is called *dak naam*. Strange names without much meaning emerged. We have heard a wide range of pet names such as Chintu, Pintu, Binni, Minni, Tunna, Jhunna and so on. These nicknames tend to be so much more important than the official names inscribed on school certificates that folks become more accustomed to the nicknames. One can recall people not responding to their formal, official name because they were more used to hearing their informal pet names. It means the ordinary practice of names is in favour of taking names lightly. This is despite the various problems one faces due to mistaken names. There are issues concerning names in South India. The surname, first name and family name put together in one person's name, unlike the simplicity of pet names, creates hilarious confusion. The name of the place, family and ancestor is inherent to the name of an individual and, hence, reducing it to a pet name amounts to misrecognition. For example, which part of this name should be used to call out the person—Hirunindravur Srinivasachari Thothadhri? It has also led to goofing up names, such as Ramesh Subramanian being called Ramesh Submarine Man! Lately, parents have become so conscious about giving a unique name to children that they frame strange names by joining one half of the names of both parents. For example, a daughter of Ramesh and Maya is named Ramaya. If this is still fine, let us think of this name. Parents are Abhishek and Meera, so the daughter was named Abhimeera! Naming to pronounce the uniqueness of a child has manifested all kinds of interesting conclusions.

Perhaps, this is where the seriousness of names wins over ordinary playfulness. We cite official reasons such as documents, passports, Aadhar card or PAN card for naming us correctly. We need the name correctly spelt on the certification of matriculation exams and higher education, for it is directly related to the scrutiny that precedes any employment. One can go on listing the pragmatics behind clinically clear record-keeping without which our official identification may land in doubts. Hence, we wish away the ordinary practices associated with our calling name, and we sacrifice a great deal of lightness about our names. The burden of names is more suitable for power than for people.

Notes

1. In a philosophically polished deliberation, Veena Das discussed the choices for the vernacular equivalent of God for the Christian liturgy in India to follow. See Veena Das, *Textures of Ordinary: Anthropology After Wittgenstein* (Delhi: Orient BlackSwan, 2020).
2. For a quick glance through the contributions of Althusser, see *Stanford Encyclopedia of Philosophy*, s.v. 'Louis Althusser,' accessed on 20 February 2021, https://plato.stanford.edu/entries/althusser/.
3. Quoted from Act-II, Scene-II of Shakespeare's play 'Romeo and Juliet'. See William Shakespeare, 'The Tragedy of Romeo and Juliet,' ed. Barbara

A. Mowat and Paul Werstine (Folger Shakespeare Library), accessed on 20 February 2021, https://shakespeare.folger.edu/downloads/pdf/romeo-and-juliet_PDF_FolgerShakespeare.pdf.

4. This is more or less like Jean-Paul Sartre characterised bad faith; for a quick glance, *Stanford Encyclopedia of Philosophy*, s.v. 'Jean-Paul Sartre,' accessed on 20 February 2021, https://plato.stanford.edu/entries/sartre/.

21

Vernacular Cannibalism: When a Big Language Monster Eats Up Smaller Ones

There is a good variety of ordinary languages in India. Sir George Grierson in the twelve-volume *Linguistic Survey of India* (1903–1923)[1] had identified only 179 languages and 544 dialects. The numbers, however, varied across documentation. From the Census in colonial India onwards, the calculation and categories underwent transformation. The Census, thus, has attracted critical scholarly attention.[2] In post-Independent India, mother tongues, the languages spoken by communities and social groups, were also identified. An analysis of the census data in 2018 informed about 19,500 languages and dialects spoken as mother tongues.[3] The statistical accuracy or critical debate on the categories of calculation and Census politics is not so much an issue here. The idea is to admit that vernacular languages have been the fulcrums of linguistic identities from time immemorial, recognised as such in colonial and post-colonial India too. Recognised or otherwise, these languages create a trope of cultural dynamics that we ought to understand. Folks in various cultural contexts speak these ordinary languages, invariably known as folk languages or vernacular or subaltern languages. But there is always a discreet hierarchy of languages that comes to determine our linguistic preferences, amply evident in our everyday usage, popular cultural texts and cinema inter alia. The hierarchy of languages ennobles one language over others, creating a space for linguistic pride and prejudices. This is when one or some languages acquire extraordinary values and 'other' languages either mimic or get swallowed by the supreme one.[4] The seemingly extraordinary language effectively tears apart other languages, chews them up and swallows them forever. Educated observers, however, may call it a process of modernisation, national integration, unity in diversity or, even worse, the progress of a language.

Recently, a group of scholars at the Indian Institute of Advanced Study (IIAS)[5] in Shimla, India, were complaining about the supremacy of English-speaking liberal scholars. As a reaction, they aspired to compete as Hindi-speaking scholars. In the competition, all they had to do was to mimic their English-speaking counterparts and practise strategic inclusion and exclusion. Even worse, they thought they could say anything in Hindi and that would be unique scholarship in Hindi. Evidently, Hindi folks were reacting desperately to the dominance of English. The matter gets more intriguing when we notice Maithili-speaking scholars concretising the dream of making Maithili as esteemed as Hindi. The politics of the Maithili language public sphere in the wake of the emergence of Hindi as a national language has been an area of enquiry for some scholars.[6] Hindi poets have had no hesitation in following the styles and codes of the counterparts such as Maithili, Bhojpuri and Awadhi or even Urdu and Persian. They tend to encompass other languages within Hindi even now. Urbane Maithili-speaking people speak Maithili that invariably sounds like Hindi, a case of Hindi-ised Maithili. This Hindi-ised Maithili is profusely loaded with vocabulary, linguistic styles and codes. Yet there is a perpetual outcry for Maithili distinction heard amongst the Maithili-speaking folks. The paradox is truly telling since, for all practical purposes, the contemporary Maithili of the urbanised vernacular speakers is hardly distinguishable from Hindi. Likewise, there are many language communities inclined to speak their respective languages but follow the sociocultural codes of Hindi. But then, our concern should not be only Hindi. It is a larger apprehension of the submission of languages to a superior one. In some cases, the superior one is Hindi; in another, it may be English, French, Italian, Japanese, Korean and so on. The intriguing question is: what determines the superiority of one language over another? In the same vein as in the rest of the book, we obliquely turn to the idea of ordinariness, in this case of the languages, while asking as to what diminishes their charm among the folks who speak them. Far from theoretical or archival data-based analyses by scholars as is available elsewhere, here we seek to rummage through the memory of the ordinary vernacular languages.

This chapter is to remind us of a concealed case, a critical condition that enhances the status of one language over the other. Removed from the romance with the vernacular, there is a veritable act of 'vernacular cannibalism' performed in the frame of cultural politics. One vernacular code of communication, ennobled as a national language, can prevail upon another one, which may be, however, dear to folk speakers. Many languages in North India succumbed to this ominous phenomenon. Some other languages have been successful in the struggle, undergoing, however, an equally vengeful process of 'language-cultural' nationalism. A person who speaks their regional language would not care whether others speak that language or not and would go on exuding excessive pride and prejudice. One can minimise the sense of judgement inherent in this example or other such examples of language-community relations in the following part of this chapter by thinking of equally appropriate exceptions. This means that there must be plenty of Bengali-speaking folks who care for the non-Bengali-speaking people in their midst. If such a disclaimer does not have a calming effect, one can make it even safer by placing the idea of Bengali–non-Bengali dynamics in a more historically sound instance of cultural-political mobilisation along language in Bangladesh.[7] The divide of language-based community identification was so strong that it led to diverse consequences inside Bangladesh. At another level, the hilarity of it was manifest in a famous television show produced in Pakistan named *Loose Talk*,[8] in which the renowned actor Moin Akhtar in the character of a Bangladeshi cricketer was interviewed by the journalist Anwar Maqsood.

To return to the case of hierarchy of vernaculars, it is pertinent to recall the impact of Hindi on other languages. Hindi hegemony and the logic of the modern nation state irreparably damaged the group of languages known today as Bihari. The name 'Bihari' though means nothing without taking note of the diversity within. Maithili, Bhojpuri and Magahi, just to name a few languages, cannot be lumped into one. Even Angika, which many feel is a variant of Maithili, is distinguishable. Likewise, Awadhi could be deemed qualitatively more fluid than the strictly organised Hindi. But who cares if the Hindi of Bhopal sounds more pronounced than Chhattisgarhi?

For the sake of intellectual convenience, let me focus on the case of one language, Maithili, broadly spoken in north-eastern Bihar and the Madhesh region of Nepal. This will be useful to conjure a mythology out of the history of vernacular language, particularly with reference to Maithili, and, meanwhile, perpetuate the provocative idea of vernacular cannibalism. In the typical practice of cannibalism, after a war, the victor eats the meat of the vanquished. Such a practice was usually associated with a primitive society and ancient kingship in the anthropological narratives produced by missionaries and ethnologists of a bygone time. By eating the meat of the vanquished, it is believed that the victor consumes their power. In other words, the victor internalises the essence of the defeated and deceased. This is more or less like the phenomenon of the marginal being co-opted by the central, the periphery swallowed by the core or the vernacular adjusted in the mainstream. Like in the mythological acts of primitive societies, there is a potential performance of language cannibalism in the domain of the vernacular. Needless to say, vernacular language cannibalism is not as spectacularly macabre as the anthropologists' imagination of cannibalism of the primitives. More precisely, it is akin to a cordial contest between the vernacular languages in which the vanquished dissolves into the victor. In vernacular language cannibalism, the victor and victim, the winner and loser, become somewhat one; the contestation of languages thus gets more complex. A possible language hierarchy arises, in which the farther removed a language is from people, the better it is placed.

To begin with, let me turn to a pertinent part of my biographical narrative. As a child, I encountered a language puzzle about Maithili, my mother tongue, and Hindi, the language spoken in formal spaces such as schools, colleges and marketplaces. A strange fuzziness marked our choice of language, gradually disappearing to establish the significant superiority of one language, that is, Hindi. In a small town named Darbhanga, in the early 1980s, folks had a distinct language attitude. If we addressed anyone in the marketplace or neighbourhood in Hindi, we were met with strange glances.

In a sweeping conclusion, the Hindi-speaking person was deemed an outsider to the Maithili-speaking folks in these small towns. We had to constantly juggle between Maithili with linguistic insiders and Hindi with others. The 'Hindi other' appeared to consist of two types of folks. One type was the Maithili-speaking folks who had either migrated to industrial cities of what was then Bihar and is now Jharkhand, such as Ranchi, Dhanbad, Chaibasa, Jamshedpur and so on. The other type was of those who were travelling across Bihar due to transferable professions. The 'Hindi others' were more adept at switching languages and shifting accents. But, back home, they were always reminded of the distinction of Maithili. In short, the Maithili folks in small towns and villages did not take it well when they heard someone speak to them in Hindi. They expected, however, that government officials such as the police or block divisional officers would speak in Hindi. Even more interesting, when a trader from the Bhojpuri-speaking part of Bihar came to the Maithili-speaking region, he was greeted as 'another', not entirely 'other' but different. While buying bangles from the Bhojpuri-speaking trader, the womenfolk in the villages in Mithila would hilariously mimic him. It was a sweet sight of vernacular languages meeting, like strangers willing to embrace each other. Neither felt threatened, and both poked fun at each other. The *Maithiliwala*s said that these Bhojpuri folks sound funny and uncouth; the *Bhojpuriwala*s believed that the Maithili folks always sounded famished and beggarly. But neither wished any Hindi-speaking person to prevail. Likewise, on various festive occasions, bahurupiya performers came from Rajasthan to perform in various parts of Bihar. Those actors had an uncanny ability to switch to the language of their audience. They always appeared like performers from among the audience. The bahurupiyas spoke Rajasthani language amongst themselves, though. This vernacular drama was commonly found all the way across the Ganga basin, from the erstwhile Banaras to Ilahabad, officially renamed into Varanasi and Prayagraj respectively, lately. The relation between Bhojpuri and Awadhi brought about a similar situation of 'another-ness', rather than 'other-ness'. Distinguishable strangers ever ready to exchange cordial notes created a sense of difference and yet connectedness.

Without any threat of superior or inferior, they merged into each other on several occasions in ordinary practices. This remained so long as one language did not become an extraordinary entity. The cultural histories of vernacular languages shall be read through such confusions of sound around the ordinary folk. Historians harping on clarity may not be comfortable with the confusions of sound or perpetually intersecting speech marks. They may present to us a clear delineation, the extraordinary character of a language at the price of a diffusive geography of languages. That is fine in one sense but does not exhaust the volume of the history of ordinary vernacular sounds.

Returning to the case of Maithili, one can decipher its dynamic relationships with 'another' languages, despite the Maithili-speaking community emphasising the distinction of Maithili among the Maithili folk. This distinction is what began to appear as the extraordinariness of Maithili. However, this distinction had come with a price. There was a dominant version of Maithili, chaste and reflective of the cultural pride and prejudices of the elites. Many scholars have elsewhere observed that it was the Maithili of the *Shrotriya* Brahman,[9] roughly from the northern part of Mithila, namely Madhubani and Darbhanga. The impact of this predominant dialect was seen in Saharsa and Purnia as well, for one rarely heard proposition is that Purnia was the oldest hub of Maithili-speaking Brahmins. This was a pundit's version of Maithili, which relied heavily on the styles and codes and even vocabulary resonant with Sanskrit. Many Maithili festivities, including Vidyapati Mahotsav in the towns, sat well within the framework of Maithili elites. These festivities underlined the significance of the language and rich literature since medieval times. Indeed, the preference to write in Maithili was revolutionary since it was a people's language and not central to orthodox philosophical discourses. In fact, Mandan Mishra, the Mimamsa scholar, engaged in a philosophical duel with Adi Shankara, the propounder of the Advaita philosophy, in Sanskrit, not in Maithili. This was in the 8th century, and the scholarly/intellectual importance of Sanskrit did not diminish even after folk Maithili became the pivot of the pride and prejudice of the cultural elites.[10] There is a popular saying in the village of Mahishi (in Saharsa district) where Mandan Mishra lived. Apparently, when Adi Shankara was hunting for the abode of Mandan Mishra, he came across villagers who said to him in Sanskrit, and from then on, everyone says this:

> Swatah pramanam, partah pramanam, hirangana yatra, girogiranti shishyopashishyairapih, giymaan mavehi tan, mandan mishra dhaamah.[11]

The shloka still reverberates in the memory of ordinary folks, including the author of this book. The saying meant, in translation, where even parrots indulge in discussion on the Vedas, karmas, eternity, divinity and other such philosophical concerns, that is the abode of Mandan Mishra.

The language puzzle in posterity in the case of Sanskrit hegemony is noteworthy.[12] The renowned medieval Maithili poet Vidyapati turned to the vernacular language of ordinary folks to the dismay of his literary contemporaries who persisted with Sanskrit. Maithili was juxtaposed with Sanskrit, which was then predominant. The interface of the Maithili spoken by the common people and the Sanskrit of Maithili elites hints at the evolution of a particular variety of the language in the history of Maithili literature. Anyone reading ancient Maithili poetry may encounter a Sanskritised version of Maithili. This encounter of languages produces the intrigue that summons an anthropological unraveling. This largely Sanskritised Maithili occupied the space of learned, priestly and upwardly mobile upper-caste groups. However, there was another Maithili that refused to be in the clutches of the elite. This was a fluid tongue that did not care for the distinction of chaste and rustic, authentic being pure and influenced being polluted. This version of Maithili is often heard in the song culture of women from both upper and lower castes in the linguistic region of Mithila. The rustic Maithili encompasses a large swathe of linguistic geography, which the Maithili elites would scornfully call southern Mithila.[13]

This distinction of chaste and rustic is usually explained euphemistically as literary Maithili and folk Maithili. Jayakant Mishra, a historian of Maithili literature, classified even folk Maithili under the larger umbrella of literary Maithili.[14] Curiously, folk Maithili is co-opted without underlining the uneasy relationship between the chaste and the rustic, northern and southern, cultural elites and the rest.

Language intrigue vis-à-vis Maithili is fraught with the acts of co-opting, erasing, decimating and many verbs that can replace the human act of cannibalism. If it was cannibalised by the Maithili elites in history, it was also subject to similar linguistic violence in its encounter with Hindi. Likewise, one can note how Bhojpuri suffered its own fate when the popular Bhojpuri culture industry, through cinema and music, began to determine the way the language ought to be spoken. If it was state and national politics in one case, it was popular industry in the case of Bhojpuri.

One should also make a quick note of what happened to Hindi. The latter went through dramatic transformations in the language politics in modern India. The cultural elitism of northern India transformed it into a language of the upper caste and upper class. The State aided this drama by creating an official vocabulary in Hindi, including hilarious words such as *Loh-path-gamini* for train and *dhumra-dandika* for cigarette. This was a romance of State, language politics, Hindi and Sanskrit and politics of roots and authenticity that shaped up a linguistic hegemony of India. An acclaimed scholar Alok Rai[15] proposed to see this transformation as an offshoot of communal majoritarian politics. This was not the Hindi of the people, which appeared in glorious light in the history of the Hindi language and literature. This is reflected in the parliamentary politics of Hindi too, and, hence, Rai notes (in a response to the historian Shahid Amin's question), 'In the Constituent Assembly debates for instance, it is very clear that the Hindiwallah seeks to speak in the name of people who are out of power'.[15] Yet, Hindi also succumbed to the rising dominance of English and other European languages. It was a matter of embarrassment to read a magazine or novel in Hindi in public transport. Everyone wanted to flaunt the ability to read in English. As if the language game was still not complete, many educated parents aspired for their kids to learn other European languages in their schools. Hindi was left behind as a political language of some powerful elites, who themselves were not sure what to do with Hindi when they travelled abroad.

In this short synopsis of language politics, the brutalised and bruised languages are that of the ordinary folks. Most importantly, we began to forget the relations of the languages around us. The ordinary charm of languages connecting 'one with another' was replaced by a power relation of language characterised by relation of 'one with other'. Children forgot this basic idea, and so did teachers of the various languages, that languages connect through sounds. They are learnt through sounds too, no matter the distinctions in the rules of grammar and uniqueness of vocabulary. It is in the sound track of the languages that ordinary charm and potential connectedness emerge.

Notes

1. This digital archive has volumes of the Linguistic Survey of India. See George Abraham Grierson, *Linguistic Survey of India* (Calcutta: Office of the Superintendent of Government Printing, India, 1903–1928), accessed on 20 February 2021, https://dsal.uchicago.edu/books/lsi/.
2. One may recall a critical discussion in Bernard Cohn, 'The Census, Social Structure and Objectification in South Asia', in *An Anthropologist among the Historians and Other Essays*, ed. B. Cohn (New Delhi: Oxford University Press, 1987), 224–254. For an interesting reading on the categorisation of languages in the census documents in colonial India, see Asha Sarangi, 'Enumeration and the Linguistic Identity Formation in Colonial North India', *Studies in History* 25, no. 2 (2009): 197–227.
3. See Office of the Registrar General and Census Commissioner, India, 'Data on Language and Mother Tongue,' Census India, accessed on 20 February 2021, https://censusindia.gov.in/2011Census/Language_MTs.html.
4. A wonderful reading with sophisticated historical materials that enriches our understanding of the rise of national language is Francesca Orsini, *The Hindi Public Sphere 1920–1940: Language and Literature in the Age of Nationalism* (Delhi: Oxford University Press, 2009).
5. This observation emerged during June–July 2019 when the author of this book was on a short visit to IIAS, Shimla, and had an opportunity to attend the interactions with the in-house fellows, quite a few of them Hindi-speaking.
6. A fabulous account with more fascinating details is in Mithilesh K. Jha, *Language Politics and Public Sphere in North India: Making of the Maithili Movement* (Delhi: Oxford University Press, 2017). This was a well-researched step forward building on Paul R. Brass, *Language, Religion and Politics in North India* (Cambridge: Cambridge University Press, 1974).

7. This is dealt with as a primary hinge for the liberation war of Bangladesh. See A. F. Salahuddin Ahmed, *Bengali Nationalism and the Emergence of Bangladesh* (Dhaka: International Center for Bengal Studies & University Press Limited, 1994). Also see Ali Riaz, *Bangladesh: A Political History Since Independence* (London: Bloomsbury, 2016).
8. See this particular episode of Loose Talk, 'Moin Akhtar as a Bangladesh Cricket Team Player,' 8.08, 27 September 2017, accessed on 20 February 2021, https://www.youtube.com/watch?v=t0HBdDw_aa8.
9. In this regard, among others, the detailed work to refer to is Hetukar Jha, 'Understanding Caste through its Sources of Identity: An Account of Shrotriyas of Mithila,' *Sociological Bulletin* 23, no. 1 (March 1974): 93–98.
10. Perhaps, the power of Sanskrit persisted in spite of the decline in its relationship with statecraft. On the contesting arguments about death (and if that is too strong a term, let us say decline) of Sanskrit, one may feel inclined to critically revisit Kaviraj's response to Pollock. See Sudipta Kaviraj, 'The Sudden Death of Sanskrit Knowledge,' *Journal of Indian Philosophy* 33, no. 1 (February 2005): 119–142. And also see, Sheldon Pollock, 'The Death of Sanskrit,' *Comparative Studies in Society and History* 43, no. 2 (April 2001): 392–426.
11. This is entirely from the author's memory.
12. In another context, this issue has been elaborated upon with reference to more significant historical materials, in Sumathi Ramaswamy, 'Sanskrit for the Nation', *Modern Asian Studies* 33, no. 2, (May 1999): 339–381.
13. For more along this, see Richard Burghart, 'A Quarrel in the Language Family: Agency and Representations of Speech in Mithila,' *Modern Asian Studies* 27, no. 4 (October 1993): 761–804.
14. See Jayakant Mishra, *Maithili Sahityak Itihas* (Maithili) (Delhi: Sahitya Akademi, 1998).
15. A masterpiece of sorts is Alok Rai, *Hindi Nationalism: Tracts for the Time* (Delhi: Orient BlackSwan, 2001).
16. 'A Debate between Alok Rai and Shahid Amin Regarding Hindi,' Minds@UW, accessed on 20 February 2021, https://minds.wisconsin.edu/bitstream/handle/1793/18542/12AminRai.pdf?sequence=2.

22

Spectacles of Success and Failure

Anam Das, literally meaning a nameless slave, was a meticulous student who learnt all the tricks and formulas diligently and applied them to score so high in exams that he was awarded a gold medal in the convocation. Let us not specify the whereabouts of the convocation, since it could fit anywhere—in school, college or a university. The purpose is to celebrate the triumph and phenomenon, not the location. From then on, awards came to him the way yawns come to a lazy mind. He got awards for punctually appearing in the class, for writing a seminar paper, for winning the funds for research projects and for developing the course curriculum. He even got an award for doing yoga, eating mangoes and sleeping less! Whenever he failed to win an award, he returned home to remind himself of the tricks and formulas and he nearly won the lost award. He learnt the tricks of publishing, and he published papers in reputed journals. Then he published books with renowned presses, and then he was part of all the events of literati and glitterati. He created a buzz among Twitterati too. His book was declared a bestseller and felicitated with heard and unheard awards. Yet, he was unhappy. He became head of the department, then dean, then proctor, pro-vice chancellor, chancellor and finally governor. He craved for something more. His drive to become immortal was mortalising him endlessly. Spectacles of success gave him only a momentary kick, and even though he had a hangover, the high did not last. He died unhappy with an illustrious CV.

We live with profound ideas in our surroundings, and ironically, we practise profound vulgarity without any hiccups. One idea of success and failure came from M. K. Gandhi, the Mahatma, who suggested that satisfaction lies in the effort, not in the attainment. The full effort, inclusive of the process, means and enchanting details of the struggle, is itself full victory, irrespective of success and failure. Gandhi was not preaching moralistically. It again came from his own biographical experiences. How often do we heed our obsessive craving for success that almost turns into suicidal tendencies at the thought of failure? This is bound to happen since we have safely declared the thoughts of our predecessors as useless ruminations. Had we really explored ideas, we would have even come across a frightening reminder from one of the most dreadful thinkers since it is always a dread to spell his name correctly: Friedrich Nietzsche. He told us that success has always been the greatest liar! It lies about us, you, them and anyone who tends to get defined and determined by success. We tend to think that successful people have something inherently unique and the failed ones are essentially condemned. There was a reason why the suicide rate among Protestant Catholics was very high in the early 19th century. All those Protestant entrepreneurs who failed in business considered themselves unwanted by divine providence. This, in fact, became the premise for the German sociologist Max Weber's thesis. What was not noticed was that we tend to make spectacles out of our success and failure. Success and failure both are held up as extraordinary instances in the biography and history of humanity. Such exhibitions jeopardise our ordinary world.[1]

Take a quick glance at nationally reported phenomena of spectacles of success and failure in India. An annual spectacle pertaining to school as well as higher education is splashed in the news reports every year. Names may change and faces may be different, but year after year, it is the same story: a child scoring 'almost 100 per cent' (95 or 98 per cent) in the Board examinations. But then, the euphoric news reports are curiously juxtaposed with saddening information more or less every year: a child committing suicide in depression after failing in the exams. A report in the immediate aftermath of the announcement of the Board examination results in 2014 informed: 'Hours after the Board exam results were out, reports of half-a-dozen students attempting suicide surfaced from across the state (Madhya Pradesh) on Thursday.'[2]

The suicide reports were, needless to mention, juxtaposed with the reports of spectacular successes—95 per cent, 98 per cent and 99 per cent scores! Furthermore, to get a sense of consistency, a similar report in 2013 read: 'Three suicides by students were reported from different parts of the city (Chennai) as the results of the final exams of different classes began coming out.'[3] The numbers of students consulting psychiatrists have been burgeoning. Psychological counseling is a common practice to which most schools in India and even the CBSE subscribes.[4] The common sense is that it is 'stress' that nudges the students to take extreme adverse decisions. But the fact is that no spectacle is devoid of a tragic appendage, as Greek and Indic mythology remind us. This basic tenet helps to reason with the twofold malady: 'spectacularly' high score and 'spectacularly' successful attempt at suicide. The spectacles of success with high scores and, ironically enough, spectacular tragedy are sides of the same phenomenon. Overlapping the spectacle of high scores and tragic instances of depression and suicide is the news of high cut-off for admission in the undergraduate colleges of the University of Delhi. It means that only those students who obtained spectacularly high percentage in Board examinations would be allowed to study in colleges and universities that have spectacular branding. Only the highly successful will go to some reputed institutions. One should also think of the recent report on the phenomenal rise in suicides in India in the last few years. Psychologists hurriedly underline stress as a reason. A good fraction of suicides is by students, and a whopping number of farmers and businesspersons is included in the macabre statistics too. Is stress merely a psychological experience? No, it is social, and hence, one should see it as a little more than stress. It is the kind of value system that celebrates orchestrated supremacy of achievements in general, and shows of success make good stories for journalists who have terrible conceptual fogginess about the whole thing. Even spectacular failures, such as increasing rates of suicide, seem to be saleable items of information; hence, everyone waits till the item is fully ready with a cadaverous pile of dead bodies. The newsmakers and new consumers are both worshippers of the exhibitions.

 This is the rationality of success as eulogised by those who say a rising sun is to be saluted. But the setting sun or the midday sun could have equal significance in human aesthetics. The dominance of the rising sun, however, obliterates the possibility of appreciating the other varieties of the sun in popular perception. Staying on in the melancholia of the setting sun, reasoning with the values of basic minimum existence and rejoicing in the ordinary and mundane does not belong to the value orientation. Similarly, the dominant logic of success renders everything not greatly successful into secondary, inferior or, in the worst cases, failures. While the learners, along with their parents as well as teachers, succumb to this way of thinking, do we ever realise that the seemingly innocuous success may be a spectacle and a commodity that we unthinkingly consume? In this context, even a fulsome story from the Mahabharata gets skewed in popular discourse. Every child hears this from teachers and parents as an adage: Be like Arjun, focused and single-minded about your goals! When asked about the goal, every child is supposed to follow Arjun and say, 'I can see only the bird's eye.' The singularity of the object in sight here alludes to the focus of an individual on a chosen target.

The idea of being like Arjun, figuratively, means that one must be target-oriented, goal-seeking and career-centric. Let us have a quick reasoning with an instance of a parent aspiring for his/her child to get admission in a school, for example, named after Ramakrishna Paramhamsa, a saint after whom institutions of learning were established by Swami Vivekananda. The admission involves tough competition among the youngsters writing entrance examinations. At the end of the day, if we ask the parent of a selected child whether the child would aspire to become like Ramakrishna Paramhamsa or Swami Vivekananda, the answer is invariably in the negative. With some beating about the bush, the parents would admit the 'need to be pragmatic', opposing becoming like the saintly figures after whom the schools are named. The parent would in all possibility suggest that career is what the employment market defines or what a career counsellor suggests as per the aptitude of the children. In this scheme, the character of Arjun from the Mahabharata appears to be a model that can enable a child to aim at the bird's eye in the competitive examinations of various kinds in a veritable rite of passage.

What is the episode in the Mahabharata that places Arjun as an ideal for learners across generations? The very first section of the Mahabharata, the *Adi Parv* (the beginning), offers an episode impregnated with critical insights. In the prelude, Dronacharya, the ideal teacher, sheltered by the great guardian of the princes of the kingdom of Hastinapur, Bhishma, has embarked on teaching the scion-disciples, the Kauravas (sons of King Dhritarashtra) and the Pandavas (sons of King Pandu). Arjun is one of the princes, along with his other brothers and cousins. The episode underlines the political motives in the education policy of Dronacharya, the great scholar of *Dhanurveda* (art of archery). Thus, at the very outset of the education, Dronacharya seeks from his disciples a pledge that they would do him a favor at the end of the education. All the disciples religiously take the pledge. As the episode proceeds, the best disciple Arjun performs the pledged favour—punishing King Drupad who happened to have insulted Guru Drona in the past. However, way before that, we read about the evolving association between Arjun and the guru. The latter is immensely impressed with Arjun's diligence. One evening, Arjun is forced to eat his dinner in darkness when the lamp is blown out by a gust of wind. He stumbles upon the idea that 'practise is more important than (in)sight'. Hence, one can eat even without seeing one's hand, mouth or plate of food. He, thus, begins to practise archery during pitch-dark nights. Impressed by the meticulous practise of Arjun, the guru promises him the best knowledge and training: no one would equal the supremacy of Arjun's knowledge in Dhanurveda. It was this very promise that made Dronacharya deny Eklavya, an ambitious boy from a low-caste family dwelling in the forest, a chance to learn archery. Eklavya, however, watches from the bushes the princes' practises under the tutelage of the guru and learns the fine skills of archery. When the princes discover that Eklavya has learnt the best of the skills of archery, they report it to the guru. The guru, along with the princes, goes to find out the secret of Eklavya. The latter reveals that he practised under the virtual tutelage of Guru Dronacharya, watching his instructions stealthily from the bushes. Arjun, the best disciple of Dronacharya, reminds the guru that there was not supposed to be anybody comparable to him in archery. Thus, the guru asks Eklavya to sacrifice his thumb as fees for the lessons he had learnt clandestinely. Eklavya chops off his thumb, instrumental in the practise of archery and, thus, paves the way for Arjun to become an invincible, spectacularly successful archer.

At last, after the training in archery has come to a finish, the most significant aspect of this episode unfolds. The guru has arranged for a special test, a kind of final examination, for all the learners. An artificial wooden bird has been perched on the branch of a tree, camouflaged by the leaves. The guru summons all the disciples one by one and asks a set of questions to test their concentration, a matter of 'practise rather than insight'. Everybody fails during the questioning and is not allowed to release the arrow from the bow. The guru believes that nobody can hit the bird's eye without delivering the expected answers to his questions. Arjun arrives and answers the guru's questions, revealing the single-minded dedication of the great archer.

The guru asks, 'Do you see the tree, the bird, as well as me?' Arjun articulates firmly, 'My venerable teacher, I see nothing, but the eye of the bird.' To test the examinee further, the guru asks another question, 'Tell me how the bird looks in shape and size.' Arjun solemnly says, 'I know nothing of how it looks; I see nothing but the bird's eye alone.' The ecstatic guru commands him to release the arrow and Arjun successfully shoots the bird's eye off.

Every child learns the value of single-minded pursuit of skills to attain the similar kind of spectacular success. Hailing Arjun, however, is at the cost of valuable criticality of 'insights'. The Mahabharata makes it explicit by showing Arjun in a different light in the *Bhishma Parva* (the episode of the great battle), whereby, he needs a divine teacher's help, his insights, in the middle of the battlefield. The accomplished practise that won Arjun platitudes is nothing without 'insight'. The practise helps in what an insightful educationist named Paulo Freire called 'banking education'.[5] In this model of learning and teaching, critical reflections, holistic vision and humanistic insights are superseded by the method and techniques based on acquisition of skills through single-minded practices. But the larger purpose of education is not merely practice; it is insights and critical reasoning. In sum, the episode underlines the disability in the ability to see only the bird's eye. The storyteller of the Mahabharata is tacitly critical in his approach to the issue under consideration. Hence, the supreme archer Arjun is depicted as emotionally embarrassed and morally messed up on the battlefield of Kurukshetra. Unfortunately, most of our popular narratives, communicated through mass media and cinema, only emphasise the extraordinary ability to see, metaphorically, the bird's eye, at the price of the ordinary tendency of a learner to reason with plethora of things in the surroundings. Most popular cultural tales are about attaining spectacular success, be it in school or a television-based competition programme: a child has to be extraordinary to sustain a position in one of those varied television shows!

A very brief but significant mention of a couple of exemplary narratives from popular contemporary Hindi cinema could aid in finding the veritable pulse of the people. In *Taare Zameen Par* (Like Stars on Earth, dirs Aamir Khan, Amole Gupte, 2007), the protagonist, Ishan, a dyslexic child, performs badly in most subjects in the examination. He, however, turns out to be a triumphant victor by the end of the cinematic tale. The film, which earned rave reviews from critics and whopping commercial success, shows that Ishan is good at painting while not interested in other subjects. The schools, parents, teachers and the presiding rationality of success do not appreciate his abysmal performance. But then, the cinematic make-believe leads us to believe that efficiency in painting can transform an allegedly badly performing student into a handsomely performing one. Curiously enough, extracurricular activities such as painting and drawing are co-opted to vouch for the rationality of success in the cinematic tale. The film shows Ishan being celebrated by admirers as well as critics only upon his spectacular success in a painting competition. The probing question here is: what if Ishan did not do well in the examinations in spite of his spectacular paintings? What if he did not do well in the painting competition either? Why could he not be celebrated without being successful as per the dominant paradigm of schooling? Ironically enough, the cinematic narrative shows, quite regressively, that the alternative mode of education ought to be balanced with the dominant mainstream. This is despite the fact that the film laments the insensitivity of mainstream education. In yet another commercially successful film, *Three Idiots* (dir. Rajkumar Hirani, 2009), admired by all for a critique of the dominant rationality in the domain of education, we see that the protagonist Rancho succumbs to the idea of spectacular success. Ironically, this feat is premised upon a long-drawn critique of mainstream education and expectations thereof. The protagonist, along with a handful of peers, appears to be subversive of the status quo, the dominant rationality of success. They ridicule those who mindlessly, or rather single-mindedly, pursue success in the examinations and eye a so-called bright future in terms of successful employability. They present incisive critique of the idea of a bright future being defined by high-salary jobs. In other words, the film criticises the logic of advanced capitalism, which determines the character of the learning in the institutes of higher education. But then, in an unexpected irony, the protagonist is eventually a spectacularly successful professional. This is not to be mistaken for a mere cinematic device to shock and entertain. It is reflective of a deeper structural issue. The rise of the critics, or maybe fall, to the level of idealised spectacular success reveals our deeper crises: one can criticise the dominant notion of success, but one has to attain the same at some stage in life! Most popular criticisms of the dominant notion of success are primarily yet another way of telling 'rag-to-riches' tales and strengthening the rationality of spectacular success. It is also premised upon a seemingly innocuous, though duly debatable, idea of 'merit eventually wins'. However, our popular cinematic tales seldom question the determinant presence of the dominant rationality behind every spectacle of success. Nor do we question them in our everyday life. No matter how long the list of cinematic narratives we draw, the eventuality is the same: 'victory' of the 'victim'. In this triumph, the ordinary process of learning, thinking, imagining and experiencing succumb to the extraordinary notions of success and failures. Thus, we only shed crocodile's tears on the reports of suicide, considering them fateful results of stress. This is so since we continue to expect the victims of a value system to turn out to be victors without upsetting the values that are pernicious for ordinary life.

Notes

1. This is discussed elsewhere in the academic register. See Dev Nath Pathak, 'In Pursuit of the Spectacles of Success: Implications of Dominant Rationality in the Domain of Education,' *History and Sociology of South Asia* 9, no. 2 (2015): 126–145.
2. *Times of India*, 'Dejected over Board Exam Results, Five Attempt Suicide, One Dies,' 16 May 2014, accessed on 25 January 2021, http://www.

newindianexpress.com/cities/chennai/Stressed-over-exam-results-three-teens-commit-suicide/2013/05/09/article1581232.ece.

3. *New Indian Express*, 'Stressed over Exam Results, Three Teens Commit Suicide,' 9 May 2013, accessed on 25 January 2021, http://timesofindia.indiatimes.com/city/bhopal/Dejected-over-board-exam-results-five-attempt-suicide-one-dies/articleshow/35174550.cms.

4. CBSE (Central Board of Secondary Education), 'Understanding Stress: Common. Accessed. reactions,' accessed on 25 January 2021, http://www.cbse.nic.in/Helpline%202008.htm.

5. A well substantiated critique of banking model of education became popular with the masterpiece written by Paulo Freire, *Pedagogy of the Oppressed* (New York: Continuum, 1970).

Thou Shall Be There, Nonetheless

Illustration artist: Sajal Roy, Dhaka, Bangladesh

23

Ordinary Art and the Quest for Distorted Icons

In a time that is visibly against fluid artistic imagination, the iconography of Gandhi would be an easy bone of contention. How we see and imagine Gandhi determines what we can do with him. Some meaningful historians have given a provocative idea. There were at least six attempts to kill Mahatma Gandhi in his lifetime, of which the sixth one was successful. Far more important is an observation that there have been perhaps six hundred thousand billion or more attempts to kill Mahatma Gandhi after the sixth attempt that ceased his physical existence. First in those innumerable attempts to kill Gandhi after his assassination was when the dead body of the 'half-naked fakir'[1] was taken out in a huge procession with grand fanfare in Nehruvian India. The innumerable symbolic murders of the Mahatma, who sought to maintain a meaningful ordinariness, persists ever since he was given the splendid farewell. The meaning of his existence has been ridiculously transformed into inscrutable ironies. The man of practice and saint of experimental truth would have cried far more in pain than he did when the brutal bullet shot from the pistol triggered by Nathuram Godse hit him.

In everyday life as well as in universities, we have witnessed merciless Gandhi-bashing to such an extent that any professor reading and discussing Gandhi was looked down upon by the progressive left-liberal scholars. If one wished to be known as a good scholar, ironically enough, one had to be a Gandhi hater, to begin with and, thus, an eligible candidate to be a Marxist, feminist, progressive historian of the subaltern, thinker of Dalit plight or even a follower of right-wing politics. We heard some bright academics say about a professor who taught about Gandhi in a course on social thoughts in modern India, 'He is a good scholar and wonderful teacher, but not really good that he is a Gandhian!' Therefore, it is not surprising that killing the long-deceased Mahatma has been an everlasting fad. It is in that spirit of symbolic murder that Gandhi was reduced to a pair of spectacles on the banners of *Swachh Bharat Abhiyan*, as if the man called Mahatma had nothing other than his austere rimmed spectacles. Also known as Swachh Bharat Mission or Clean India Mission, this was an initiative of the Government of India started in 2014 for a country-wide cleanliness campaign, also aimed at the elimination of open defecation and waste management.[2] The government offices were instructed to conduct the campaign across India. It resulted into a series of orchestrated cleanliness drives, with everyone from the ranks and files having a photograph clicked while holding a broomstick. The machineries of government boast about the success of the campaign, yet a fact finding remains at large. The Abhiyan was disclaimed as a political sham by several critical readings, but the fact that it pretended to be premised on the values of cleanliness espoused and practised by Gandhi discloses the possibility of reducing him into propaganda. Therefore, the Mahatma may get easily displaced by anyone on the symbol of the *charkha* (spinning wheel). To maintain the perpetuity of metaphorically killing Gandhi or reducing him and his ideas into a political programme, a clinically clear iconography is needed, rather than artistic fluidity of imagination.

Thus, we felt a mild tremor about a famous sculpture of Gandhi made by a pioneer of modern sculpture in India, Ramkinkar Baij. A protégé of Nandalal Bose and an embodiment of the artistic ethos inculcated by Rabindranath Tagore at Shantiniketan, Baij experimented with the European aesthetics that we see in the works of Picasso and Rodin. The Gandhi sculpture situated at Gandhi Mandap garden atop Sarania Hill in Guwahati is an example of Baij's fine work, which has captured the essence of the figure. A masterpiece in modern Indian art, Baij's sculpture brought about an idea of an ordinary Gandhi of ordinary Indians. In 2017, a strange piece of information appeared in a few newspapers. Then a member of the Legislative Assembly (MLA) from Guwahati (East), Siddhartha Bhattacharya, said, as reported by the *Indian Express*:

Look at the statue. Look at the disproportionate hands and feet. They do not resemble those of the Mahatma in any manner. His face is distorted, as also the pair of glasses. That is why we have decided to dismantle it and place a new statue there.[3]

Clearly, the angst here is about the fact that Baij's Gandhi is not available for appropriation for political propaganda. It is an artist's Gandhi. How to kill such an ordinary Gandhi or the Gandhian spirit that remains alive with a low profile and heightened senses? It does not facilitate our murderous streaks, and hence, it is bad art!

It sparked an opportunity for us to rethink our relationship with art, to begin with. This is indeed an opportune moment in the history of post-Independence India that underlines the intricate relation between art and politics, aesthetic imagination and society. The issue stares us in the face even though we try to look away. Even though the bone of contention may be neutralised, we ought to understand the dispute on ordinary aesthetics in an artistic representation. Obviously, such aesthetics would not fit the sense of extraordinary aesthetics that guide political dispensations. For the power and cultural elite, art and aesthetics means works with pleasant affects. That is how most of the ruling class think of art and culture.[4] An artist, on the contrary, may not be necessarily guided by a frozen idea of 'beautiful'. The beauty of an artwork may lie in the discourse that it implies. This was so even in the nationalist deliberation on art that we read in the writings of the famous Sri Lankan Tamil art critic, Ananda Coomaraswamy.[5] For him, Indian art was beautiful because it led everyone to see the Indic essence that unfolds when you talk about that artwork. We may disagree with Coomaraswamy's nationalist perspective since academic readers have been intolerant of any such connotations, but we may not like to miss a chance to glimpse the basic idea, that is, artworks are discursive. The essence is meaningless, let alone beautiful, if it is not talked about. Hence, Coomaraswamy undertook a reflective reading of the old murals from well-known caves, vestiges of the past and ruins of temples and monasteries. None of those iconographic sculptors had visual clarity; in fact, even today, many sculpted works depict a headless or limbless Buddha at the sites known for such remains. We admire, ordinarily, the fluid artistic imagination in those old sculptures, murals and even in the traditional Kalighat painting, *pat-chitra* and Madhubani/Mithila painting. I have never heard anyone complaining about the smudged images of Sita-Ram, Radha-Krishna or Gauri-Shiva in the murals that womenfolk made on the walls inside as well as outside their houses in Maithili-speaking parts of Bihar and Nepal. Perhaps, now there will be complaints and, hence, there are already training workshops for the new artworks that could show the gods, goddesses, heroes and icons more clearly, determinately and discernibly. Our ordinary art is in danger. This serves well for those who want to abuse gods, goddesses, heroes and icons.

There has not been much controversy about Ambedkar statues except of desecration once in a while. But if one cruises around, every town big or small will have its own sculpted Babasaheb Ambedkar reminding the township of the imperative of working for the socially marginalised. Each of these statues across India vouch for the artistic liberty the unknown sculptors took to carve out the image of the historical icon. Somewhere the nose is twisted; somewhere size is dwarfed. There may be a statue with the rimmed glasses not fitting the face of the sculpted hero. The seekers of clinical clarity in sculptures may not appreciate it because they have forgotten about Paleolithic rock art that advanced into systematic sculpting. It is seldom about that elusive clarity; it is more about the expression of an artist and art's effectiveness in evoking sentiments. Such works always imply the beauty of ordinary imaginations and artistic expressions. Every work of art need not follow the modernism of Raja Ravi Varma with the colourful clarity of images that led to calendar art (chromolithograph). The historians of art may, however, suggest that even Varma's works of visual art had layered meanings, complicated metaphors and suggestive artistic practices that entailed the making of his art.[6]

It was in that spirit that the famous cartoonist R. K. Laxman conjured a hilarious image of the then prime minister, Indira Gandhi, with the pointed nose sticking out of her face. It was foolhardy of some loyalists to express dismay at the cartoonist's expressions. And why do we look into the historical artistic expressions alone? Revisit the umpteen statues of the monkey god Hanuman in temples across India. Do you not see the face of Dara Singh who immortalised the character of Hanuman more than once in popular cinematic and television productions? Or is it my own love for Dara Singh that colours my vision whenever I see a statue of Hanuman? But it was for sure that many statues of Santoshi Ma were modelled on the statue of the goddess we saw in the film named after the deity. Then, this ought to be leading us to be more democratic about the artistic representations of gods and goddesses, heroes and villains, victors and victims.

To return to the outcry about Baij's sculpture of Gandhi, a few points are noteworthy. First and foremost, we do not seem to appreciate a Gandhi-like Gandhi statue. Since Gandhi himself celebrated inconsistency, why do we expect consistency in the artistic representation of Gandhi? We can recall some diehard Gandhians feeling upset about the way Richard Attenborough depicted Gandhi too in that renowned film that won him an Academy Award. They thought there should have been more petals showered than what the film showed, whereas, there were other folks, mostly educated critics, who thought Attenborough made a hagiography of Gandhi. Neither party was willing to leave the artistic space to the filmmaker. We do not want to see Gandhi through Gandhi or through the artist who has reinterpreted Gandhi. We are seeking to see Gandhi through a matrix of contemporariness aptly described as 'Branding Gandhi' by William Mazzarella, a sociologist of consumerism.[7] This is very much in tune with the larger phenomenon of the changed scheme of aesthetic judgements. The cultural sociologists have been informing us with ample evidence from across the globe that we desire to see a consumable item in all our icons and iconic ideas. We want not just a national flag but an aggressive spectacle associated with the flag. We do not like an ordinary and organic relationship with diverse communities; we are happier with State-imposed rhetoric of unity in diversity even though a mob is ever ready to lynch a chosen few. We cannot appreciate an old photograph with sepia tint; we seek to have it photoshopped and cleansed of its silent historicity, and so on.

In this scheme of aesthetic judgement, perhaps what Mahatma Gandhi told his grandnephew Kanu Gandhi when he wanted to photograph him would be thought foolish. Along with many other conditions, Mahatma Gandhi said that he would never pose for the camera. Kanu Gandhi's photographs of Mahatma Gandhi are classical visuals with rich embedded historicity. Now, however, they are tinted and, of course, in none of them does the Mahatma bother to pose, smile and tilt his body for a better frame. He looks like everything that he personified: ordinary, mundane and hilarious at times. The new logic of aesthetics about Gandhi would ironically allow us to photoshop all those old photographs clicked by many visiting photo-journalists as well as native documenters. Else, they may not look good! Also, someone may say that they look distorted and not like Gandhi. This perhaps reveals an intricate relation between the new techno-mediated imagination of our icons and the sanitised imagination of developed India. This is the time when most officially circulated photographs of the leadership are suspected of having technically aided alterations. This is not merely studio-based professionalism in photographic practices. Such so called aesthetic alterations are done in abundance, everywhere, from a small cellular gadget in a running train to a big establishment of public relations and publicity agency. Not only in photography, it is also vivid in other fields of art. A muscular Mahatma is as normal as a gym-going actor with splendid biceps essaying the role of Ram in a recent televised series on the Ramayana. Even later editions of Amar Chitra Katha seem to have shifted gears in showing such icons as up-to-date. Hence, in our common sense, the best aesthetic articulation of the imageries comes not from the sculptors but from the technologists of the museum in London and Hong Kong—Madame Tussauds. Wax figures befit the sanitised developmental imagination of history, icons thereof and a nation named India. As if it were a climax, we had one of the latest sculptors of Mahatma Gandhi making news in the international media in 2015. Philip Jackson created the sculpture, inspired by a 1931 photograph of Gandhi, which was located and unveiled in the haloed space of Westminster Square in London. However, many began to whisper in social media that it was not the image of Gandhi in the sculpture, and that it was, instead, an image of Ben Kingsley, the actor who commendably essayed the role of Gandhi in the Oscar-winning biopic by Richard Attenborough. Everyone in India, as well as in the diaspora abroad, celebrated that Gandhi received a respectful space in the precincts of Westminster Abbey in proximity with the statues of other significant world leaders.

The ordinary art in masterpiece sculptures may soon be a thing of the past. The new regime of sculpting brings some the statues of historical icons with pomp and a gala show. The Statue of Equality with the sculpture of Ambedkar in Mumbai is supposed to bear that effect, and the Statue of Unity with the mammoth sculpture of Sardar Patel situated at Sardar Sarovar Dam in Gujarat has already accomplished the same. Each of these statues is supposed to proclaim that it is superlative, tallest, broadest, widest, largest and so on. They hold no meanings without such superlatives, and thus, the ordinary art is sacrificed. The statues are no longer related to the aesthetics of ordinariness. The heroes are far removed from 'we the people'. Heroes have thus been made victims of an awkwardly extraordinary imagination, and such is the fate of our gods too. The statue of Ram in Ayodhya, planned to be the biggest, is supposed to outdo the Statue of Liberty in New York. The state tourism department would like to set an example by putting up the statue of Ram on the banks of the river Sarayu. The Spring Temple Buddha in Henan, China, has already been notable in such a series of statues. Bhutan has its own great Buddha Dordenma near Thimpu, commemorating the sixtieth anniversary of the fourth king Jigme Singye Wangchuck. A worshipper cannot make eye contact with the extremely elevated bronze statue of Buddha. But, cleverly, the artists thought of placing over a thousand small-sized statues of Buddha underneath. These are more intimate and accessible to the ordinary worshippers. Likewise, there is a curious situation at Jakhoo hill, one of the highest points in Shimla. After an arduous climb up the hill, braving gangs of menacing monkeys, on the top, we meet an intimidating, gigantic statue of Hanuman that is over a hundred feet high. The statue almost overlooks the mall road below. Once again, ordinary folks can hardly even reach out to the feet of the statue, where a plaque says, 'Inaugurated by Abhishek Bachchan' (the film star son of the film star father Amitabh Bachchan). There is no possibility of forging a relationship with this spectacular statue, which, however, has crystal clear features, eyes and nose all in place (as some photographs show). Most visitors like to stand by the platform of the statue and click selfies. Such sculptures are perhaps needed for the photographic regime of our time. Only if one can tear oneself away from the extraordinary Hanuman statue, one can get around to an ordinary, mythologically significant temple that has only a footprint to be worshipped as the sign of Hanuman. There is a tiny statue of Hanuman too, with which one can make eye contact and almost enter into a devotional conversation. The humble and sublime footprint in that simple temple provides the ordinary worshippers solace and redemption of faith.

Perhaps this says it all. Our imagination, mode of imagining and ideologies attached with the act of imagining has undergone a dramatic change in the past few decades. A simple image of a charkha with Gandhi (spinning wheel associated with Gandhi's imagination of India) is too dull for visual consumption. Hence, an opportune replacement of Gandhi with contemporary stakeholders makes a sense despite the inherent paradox. Gandhi reduced to a pair of glasses on the hoarding of *Swachh Bharat Abhiyan* shall be deemed part of the reductionist visual regime too. Many evidences can be marshalled to underline the new regime of taste, aesthetic imagination and art consumption. This seeps into the way we imagine ourselves in India today. Accordingly, we wish to appropriate historical icons. We may not know everything about Swami Vivekananda, but he could be celebrated as the champion of national (Hindu) pride. We may not have the slightest inkling of the transformative politics inherent in the critique of the Hindu social structure that Ambedkar proposed, but there will be slogan shouting and mobilisation in his name. Many nationalists will quote a bit of Tagore here and a bit there, with confident ignorance of the antithesis of nationalism that Tagore not only articulated but embodied. This is indeed an interesting time in human history that compels us to consume the selective and palatable versions of the critical thinkers of modern India. Then, what the Bharatiya Janata Party (BJP) MLA Siddhartha Bhattacharya has been reported as saying is a reflection of the way we see things and the thing that we have become!

Notes

1. Famously, Winston Churchill employed this phrase to disparagingly refer to Mahatma Gandhi, which the latter deemed a compliment. See Peter Gonsalves, 'Half Naked Fakir: The Story of Gandhi's Personal Search for Sartorial Integrity,' accessed on 26 January 2021, https://www.mkgandhi.org/articles/half-naked-fakir.html.
2. See, for more about this campaign, 'Major Initiatives,' PMIndia, accessed on 26 January 2021, https://www.pmindia.gov.in/en/major_initiatives/swachh-bharat-abhiyan/.
3. Samudra Gupta Kashyap, Esha Roy, and Vandana Kalra, 'Off with Gandhi Statue by Legendary Sculptor,' 9 August 2017, https://indianexpress.com/article/india/assam-to-dismantle-47-year-old-distorted-gandhiji-statue-made-by-ram-kinkar-baij-4787837/.
4. This was one reason, among others, that compelled an art critic and theorist of culture such as Herbert Reed to exclaim, 'To hell with culture!' See Herbert Reed, *To Hell with Culture and Other Essays on Art and Society* (London: Routledge and Kegan Paul, 1963).
5. See Anand Coomaraswamy, *Art and Swadeshi* (Delhi: Munshiram Manoharlal Publishers, 2001).
6. There have been discussions on Raja Ravi Varma aplenty. For example, see Geeta Kapur, 'Ravi Varma: Representational Dilemmas of a Nineteenth Century Indian Painter,' *Journal of Arts and Ideas*, nos. 17–18, 1989; and Tapati Guha Thakurta, 'Westernization and Tradition in South Indian Painting in the Nineteenth Century: The Case of Raja Ravi Varma,' *Studies in History* 2, no. 2 (August 1986): 165–195.
7. See William Mazzarella, 'Branding The Mahatma: The Untimely Provocation of Gandhian Publicity,' *Cultural Anthropology* 25, no. 1 (2010): 1–39.

24

Lost and Found, Friends and Enemies, Buried in Ordinary Trousseau

An eminent Sri Lankan artist, curator and writer named Anoli Perera created innumerable works of art in a series titled 'Memory Keeper',[1] exhibited in Sri Lanka, India, Bangladesh and across the globe at various exhibition spaces in the so-called first world. The artwork retrieved the idea of lost and found by showcasing things that may be buried deep in our consciousness. The art installations in the series brought alive everything we may otherwise deem long dead. There were cotton balls with images underneath, tumbling down from cupboards, bedspread, cloth lines and the attics of existence. The series also had installations on papers, but the memory balls attracted greater attention since they were telling tales about secret treasures. The series summoned the beholder to walk back in time and see the vestiges of tomorrow stitched on the collars of today! Artists seem to have done this much-needed 'hindsight for foresight' far better than formal historians.

A significant experience from the faded memory of childhood is the experience of stumbling upon your mother's trousseau, the very private kind of trunk newly wed brides carry along. They neatly keep their stuff, some clothes, some cosmetics, some ornaments and many things of strange value, and when the bride becomes a mother, the trunk gradually becomes a less visited entity. It stays somewhere, quietly, with all those mementos of youth, beauty and bygone times. Such a box, trunk, suitcase or sometimes a special shelf in the cupboard is a magic box for the child who discovers it. Rummaging in this magic box, we can recall, we fished out things that we wondered about. I always remember a special-looking button my mother had saved for ages in her old, rusted trunk, which also had some of her old saris, a piece of ivory (a pale part of elephant tusk) and some lac bangles. I had many questions to ask my mother after I encountered the secrets buried in the magic box. To all my questions, my mother had layered answers, muffled in smiles and silence. It was like a growing boy flipping through the pages of his mother's life and inviting the woman to revisit her youth. Two lives begin to merge, two souls begin to unite and two bodies connected since conception return to a social unison.

There are such ordinary trousseaus tucked away in attics, cupboards and suitcases. They invite our otherwise busy selves, quietly, to a silent return to what we are—ordinary, emotive humans. Such magic boxes sometimes appear in the form of our old school bags, the satchels which were our best companions in our struggle in schooling. Once in a while, if we can manage the time and patiently look at them, we come across a piece of pencil or eraser that carries stories about our school friends, classmates and childhood enemies. A torn notebook may allow us to relive the haunting memory of an angry teacher who nearly tore the page in disapproval of what you had written on that page. Slow and silent reliving makes it possible to negotiate what was otherwise a bitter experience. In one of those bags, you find a steel ball pen. Many ghosts tumble out of the cupboard of memory. This was the pen you had stolen from your classmate's bag or you just stealthily kept it when you found it lying on the school assembly ground. You decided not to return it to the school office. Instead, you took pride in the fact that it became nature's gift to you. Why should you disown what nature or coincidence graciously gifted you? Then, you recall many classmates with whom you did not share very comfortable relations. Such unavoidable reveries of friendship and animosity waft out of the bags, almost like the aroma of stale food trapped in the threads of jute bags. No matter how many times and how nicely it was cleaned up, parathas, chapatis, sandwiches and even chocolates could still be smelt in the bag in which you carried your lunchbox. One such school bag reminds you of the days when you bunked school: when the schoolboy followed William Blake's poetic defiance of the regimentation of school and the school bag was a silent eyewitness, serving the role of a pillow on those afternoons when the boy decided to just stare at the sky lying on the grassy field a mile away from the school premises.

Lost does not always mean lost in the experience of ordinariness. In the experience of extraordinariness, maybe there is no chance of return. For ordinary stuff is only vaguely forgotten, temporarily, and then rediscovered afresh as though it was never past.[2] These veritable magic boxes offer such enormity. You come across a small suitcase of a brand that was very popular among the middle class some decades ago. It was the suitcase you were given to carry your clothes when you undertook your first journey alone from your home to some place. Your father added a long list of instructions, perhaps still lingering in the innards of the suitcase. You are reminded of those firm, resolute and sensible instructions. Perhaps, you never get rid of them, even though you have forgotten about that suitcase. The same instructions recur in various forms when you undertake a journey even now. It may be that the tone and tenor are different. Your wife or husband invariably sounds some of those instructions in slightly differently worded formulations. At times, you feel terribly at a loss. You do not know how to react to these never-ending instructions, reminders and words of caution showered upon you by your kith and kin, parents and spouses, friends and enemies and then growing kids.

In such suitcases of olden times, you discover small naphthalene balls, the phenyl *goli*, meant to protect the items in the boxes from insects. After many years, those balls may have been reduced to the size of lizard eggs or may have disappeared altogether. Maybe it is only what your eyes believe since you still smell them all around the magic box. They disclose your intolerance to certain sounds, sights, smells and tastes.[3] Such sensory testimonials may also bear the imprint of our social locations in a hierarchical society. Our caste, or intersections of caste, class-gender, etc. are buried in the sensory experiences in everyday life. They disclose the truth of your intolerance to things and humans. You instantly remember the boy who abused you and the way you had livid nights contemplating revenge that could never happen. You still, equally strongly, regret not having got back at that boy or that girl or that man and woman. They are quite a few. The memories of enemies return to us as comfortably as that of our friends. At times, enemies seem to be more powerful than friends, or is it always so! Though they both are now buried in the magic boxes and they both are lost forever, one weighs heavier than the other. The one who bullied you comes to your mind so effortlessly, to whom you wanted to scream, almost bursting your throat, 'Go to hell!' Then comes that schoolteacher who never appreciated all the efforts you made to please him or her. You nearly loved that teacher, spending hours strategising ways to impress them. Apart from such loved teachers, you also effortlessly recall the one you hated from the core of your heart, the one you always thought of pushing down the stairs. You still regret not doing something terrible, really terrible, to that teacher.

Then, what about your rivalling sibling? They are buried there too. They may have grown into men and women now, settled happily wherever they are. During the social and family get-togethers, you may be so cordial to each other that you do not show any sign of scars.[4] Deep or faint, many scars hide in the subterranean levels of the human psyche that manifest in our personalities, behaviours and practices. But there are also visible scars, which your growing kids can ask you about while intimately examining your body. 'Baba! What is this mark on your left hand?' 'Ma! Why is your left toe slightly twisted?' This is not a formal examination by a professional doctor or the police. This is a disarming query arising from a body mark that a winsomely curious child catches hold of. One scar is because you went tumbling down while playing *pakdam-pakdai* (catch and run) or *chhuwa-chhuwi* (tag). Another one is from that evening when you had a bad scuffle since you wanted to hold the new thing brought to the household. Yet another one recounts the bitter memory of your parent punishing you without meaning to hurt, and when they discovered your bruise, they were so guilt-ridden that they forgot everything wrong you did. So many such scars, taking you to the world of lost and found! Some of these scars also remind you of your tendency to experiment with your own body. There was an itch of some kind on which you applied your father's aftershave lotion, and it became a permanent mark on your skin. You perhaps did not mind these marks on your body and, hence, you have many of them. Just return to them and you can fathom the journey of your body through the signposts of ordinary experiences.

Thus you return to some people who did not belong to your list of clear-cut friends or enemies. You always had mixed feelings towards them. You were never sure whether you wanted to think ill of them or good. You thought you were indifferent to them as you never felt an explicit rush of love, hatred, anger or anything for them. They are the most faded things in the pale memory lane of experiences. At times they resurface in your life with a new lease of significance you never imagined. Some of those boys who you did not see properly during your school days turn out to be a rediscovery when you are a fully grown adult. Some of those girls who never belonged to your immediate circles are reincarnated into the most fascinating friends. Sometimes, you figure out that the one you ignored the most is indeed the most charming fellow. Such are the surprises that unfold due to everything buried in the magic box of ordinary experiences. Gems, or perhaps more priceless than the most precious, are these mementos, reveries, signs and symbols, in the scheme of ordinary semiotics. Such ordinary possessions create memory pathways that we tend to step aside or indulge once in a while for nostalgia. They exude an abounding volume of intangible feelings if we relish them in repose. There are, indeed, more meanings attached to them than we can anticipate. Hence, every now and then, when we revisit them, we rediscover something anew or we feel something novel about those things of the past. Various instances come our way. For example, the school photograph has always those potential surprises. We strain our eyes to notice in the old photographs some of those blurry faces standing in the last row, sheepishly looking in the direction of the camera and yet escaping the collective glare of the bunch of boys and girls. Similar dynamics of visuals surface for attention in the family albums. In addition to those visible in the photographs, a whole range of others such as photographer, studio, type of camera and roll, and others solicit attention. Such visuals curate an idea of sociability, of connections and flows, that remains at large due to our rush for the clearly visible. The invisible underneath the visible marks out the ordinary sensorium.[5]

    Furthermore, take out that dog-eared book from the shelf. It emits a distinct smell, more than the chemical compounds dissolved in the air as soon as the pages are flipped. You smell many intrigues in them, and on the first page, you do have an articulation of it. A word of affection, a signature with a date, a reason why this book was picked up—fresh memories unfold. Sometimes, in the pages of the book, you discover an old letter, a tired postcard on which your father had asked you to return home for your ailing mother! Or a letter that you had written for someone with such passion that it never got finished. That unfinished letter and our unfinished lives sing the songs of sweet melancholia in unison.[6] All such instances are about scars, and yet they are all about remembering and forgetting, lost and found. It is in such a book that we come across some sentences by the author of the book, so heavily underlined by us as readers that we become vicarious authors. The notes that we noted at the margin of the book may have left the book in tatters. But the whole of this book is a silent narration of how I felt, how I grew up and how I have become and unbecome.

None of these and many more such things are any different from a bride's secret trousseau. It contains not only material things but also a great deal of emotions, feelings, sentiments and such that are becoming exceedingly rare in the flurry of progress. Those things we fish out from our elder sibling's trousseau tell us the kind of truth to which we may not have liked to be an audience: how and why a mother suffered, how and why a sister manoeuvred, how and why a brother felt the pangs of going away. So many *how*s and *why*s dot the criss-crossing biographies of known and unknown individuals. This is something theoretically inclined scholars have discussed as criss-crossing ontologies, in which negotiations and contestations surface with equal ease. It means many *beings* come together in the totality of our sensorium. That friend and enemy, that teacher and electrician, that doctor and barber, that priest and tailor master—all dramatis personae in the theatre of ordinariness.

Notes

1. See, for more, 'Memory Keeper', Anoli Perera, accessed 26 January 2021, http://www.anoliperera.com/project/memory-keeper-2/.
2. It is worth thinking of Veena Das's seminal work on the experiences of victims of violence, whose speechlessness (or loss of speech) communicates and demands from an anthropologist what Das calls a descent to the ordinary. See Veena Das, *Textures of the Ordinary: Doing Anthropology After Wittgenstein* (Delhi: Orient Blackswan, 2020).
3. Elsewhere, in a theoretically sophisticated manner, Gopal Guru and Sundar Sarukkai lead us to curate a sensorium of the social in everyday life

framework, more precisely caste experiences, by emphasising smell, taste, touch and sight among others. See Gopal Guru and Sundar Sarukkai, *Experience, Caste and the Everyday Social* (Delhi: Oxford University Press, 2019).

4. For a fascinating psychoanalytical text along this line, see Sudhir Kakar, *The Inner World: A Psychoanalytical Study of Childhood and Society in India* (Delhi: Oxford University Press, 1978).

5. Many scholars have taken interest in reading visuals in South Asia, and despite the variations in methodology and research questions, the engagement with visuals thrives on such a premise that underlines the dynamic intricacies of the seen and the unseen in a visual testimony. An acclaimed sophisticated work is by Christopher Pinney, *Camera Indica: The Social Life of Indian Photographs* (Chicago: University of Chicago Press, 1997). Also see for a more recent work, Sasanka Perera, *The Fear of the Visual: Photography, Anthropology and Anxieties of Seeing* (Delhi: Orient Blackswan, 2019).

6. This is reminiscent of the anthropoetry by Rosaldo in which the death of a loved one becomes a perpetually unfolding experience, not only for a grieving individual but also for everyone who has an idea of it. An individuated melancholia in everyday life is truly a well-drawn process. I intend to emphasise the idea of 'unfinished lives' in such instances. See Renato Rosaldo, *The Day of Shelly's Death: The Poetry and Ethnography of Grief* (Durham, N.C.: Duke University Press, 2014). Besides, it is worth looking at another similar but differently framed work closer to home. See Avijit Pathak, *The Rhythm of Life and Death* (Delhi: Aakar Books, 2011).

25

Living and Dying, Medicine and Songs, and Folk Philosophy

An octogenarian woman had a six-year-old grandchild. She had lost her eyesight, and, whenever the grandchild visited her, she cupped his face in her hands, felt the curves of the cheekbones and forehead, kissed the cluster of hair and then declared his identity. That was a magical experience for the child, who never had to introduce himself to the visually impaired grandmother. One day, the grandmother died, almost as gently as a leaf falling from an upright tree. Her dead body was lying on the floor; she was as still as the leaf resting on a desolate part of the earth, ready to be buried under the mud flung over her by the wuthering winds. The grandchild took the hands of the dead woman in his hands, made the fingers of her hand run over his face and said, 'Sleep, Grandmother, see you later!' He went about playing his games with his friends afterwards while the elders of the household prepared for the cremation.

Such an ordinary idea of death and dying may appear bizarre in the light of the skyrocketing numbers of death in the time of the pandemic. The nature of death reveals the nature of a society; this is a fundamental idea we learn in some of the earliest, modern reasoning on death and dying. The burgeoning instances of suicides during the lockdown, dying due to absence of assistance in returning home from metros, and death in penury and helplessness reveal the unravelling of society. One gets a clear idea that the ordinariness of death and dying may be undergoing a massive transformation in the wake of these kinds of deaths around us in disturbing abundance. This is a challenge to think of an ordinary death, after living a life fully conscious of the end in the offing. Unfortunately, we have little on offer about death education, worse than what we have in the name of sex education in India.

Hence, it is likely that we are prospering as a society with little idea about the aesthetics of death and dying.

An ordinary engagement with death aids in developing a sense of a quality death since we locate it in our everyday life in spite of a due dread of death, the irredeemable disappearance of the corporeal existence. No deceased body comes back even though we have the aid of intelligent rationalisation or an ingenious cosmology coming from religious mythologies. We do not know anything for sure about what happens after death in spite of informed thinking and intelligent guessing. It is as sweet or sour as cyanide. The person who tastes it barely manages to write a letter 's' and dies, leaving intelligent guesswork to decipher the ambiguity. Documentation on the paranormal, the supernatural or black magic does not exhaust the meanings to such an extent that we could be comfortable with any conclusion. So, ordinarily, it is natural to have some fear but not necessarily fear psychosis that will not allow humans to creatively engage with death and seek for a quality experience. Hence, an aesthetic lightness about death and dying prevails in ordinary life too, if we care to ferret it out and fathom it with empathy and interest. I have known a Sri Lankan artist named Jagath Weerasinghe who created a series of artworks on death and dying in engagement with the imageries of cremation grounds on the bank of the river Ganga in Benares (Varanasi). Jagath once said that the viewers of his artworks usually ask him why he does not create art about the beautiful things of life! Usually, he smiles at such requests that are guided by an ignorant presupposition that death is morbidity to be avoided. There is no love for death, the morbidity, but there cannot be ignorance of an evocative and aesthetic phenomenon of dying. Jagath has also created artworks with riots of colour to depict the violence and genocide in the civil war tearing Sri Lanka apart. He also considered it a responsibility of aesthetes to present accounts of all kinds of death and dying.[1]

In villages, people crack all sorts of jokes about death, dying as well as the dead. There is little hesitation in doing so despite the equally admitted fact that it is an occurrence after which the dead do not physically return. Spiritually, they may return or may have never gone away from the midst of the surviving family members. After the cremation, the dead become venerable names to be uttered on specific occasions. But right before one dies, one may become the target of light ridicule. For example, an old man was lying on his deathbed awaiting his last breath for months. Everyone who called on him ended up asking, 'When are you really going to die?', and the dying man either shooed them away or sombrely said, 'Stupid fellow, is it up to me?' Such is the magic of mundanity that renders the whole set-up of living and dying into a naturally curated show of art and aesthetics. This is also loaded with pathos. I can recall the significant experience of a friend whose mother had passed away. I accompanied him to the cremation. Before cremation, the body of the deceased mother was cleaned up, wrapped in a new colourful sari, decked up with new bangles and vermillion and then she was taken to the banks of a river. My friend, the son of the deceased, had to fetch wood for the pyre from the nearby shop, which he was doing. I noticed that he picked up each log and carried it as gently as he could, as though it were a tender flower. Along with others, he placed the wood around the body lying on the funeral bed made of logs. He showed such tenderness and care in placing the wood that I could almost imagine my friend telling me, 'She is as important in her death as she was in her life'. As the deceased mother's body went up in flames and the crackling of bones and smell of burning flesh wafted in the air, I saw a rivulet flowing down my friend's cheek as quietly as the caring whisper of a loving mother in her son's ear.

A friend died a couple of years ago. He was a Christian Dalit, in typical official parlance. But throughout his life, he never wore his identity on his sleeve. Almost as though he were a liberated soul all his life, delivering immaculate lectures on the implicit violence in caste-creed identifications, a strange event unfolded upon his death. His burial was prepared in the Christian way. His dead body was in a black suit, lying in the coffin, when I saw him last. The rituals had begun, and I had a strange feeling that he would spring up from the coffin any moment and castigate everyone preparing to bury him as a Christian. The process added socio-religious significance to his death, and it was indeed not to impede the flow of emotions. We cried about the departure of our dear one, laughed recalling his acute sense of humour and offered a fistful of mud when his coffin was interred in the ground.

In the end, we all consoled each other for the quality of death that our friend eventually arrived at.

Quality of life seems to be a common concern. Quality of death is perhaps an anathema. Never to be heard and spoken about, death and dying are not glamorous selling items for industries. This may attract some disagreement since there is a whole lot of commerce behind the huge procession accompanying the dead body and the fanfare of cremation. One has heard of jazzed up versions of coffins, expert services for cremation and also the latest arrangement in Europe to generate consumable energy from the electrical cremation of dead bodies, known as dead heat. Dead bodies are subject to the same logic of exploitation as living bodies, so to say. Crematoriums have started installing turbines to convert the heat generated in the combustion of corpses into electricity to be sold to power grids. It is an advanced version of something one has heard, locally, across India. The ice slabs used to keep dead bodies from rotting is recycled as consumable ice in the market. Hence, there is an idea of 'quality of death' that guides the merchandise. That said, there is no talk about the quality of death as far as the experience of dying is concerned. Our experience is mostly about denying death its due respect by indulging in the consumption of products available in the market.

Avoiding, delaying and cheating any sign of death is a superhit business. A good line of cosmetic products is primarily to ensure that we can hide our age. This may range from hair dye to Botox, a toxin used to paralyse muscles so that skin does not wrinkle. This is still nothing if you take a note of the list of cosmetic surgeries and medical interventions to ensure vivacious youth when the downslide of age begins. Many self-help pocketbooks deemed bestsellers are available in the market. They have telling titles, such as *The Hot Young Widows Club*, *Younger Next Year (For Men and Women Separately)*, *The Seventeen Day Plan to Stop Ageing*, *365 Ways to Look and Feel Younger* and *Why We Age and Why We Don't Have To* and so on and so forth. Additionally, all kinds of packages are on sale that would medically ensure that you live long enough to follow your bucket list, as it were. Many ageing men and women now plan an extra innings of work life post retirement. They do not want to stop for the fear of losing out on the quality of life and inching closer to the sense of having aged. One wants to die in the full swing of work, almost as a workaholic. This goes against the ordinary scheme of life in which one enjoys studenthood, family life and then retirement. For a long time, we have heard of the fourfold division in the course of life that Hindus tend to practise, which even they seem to have forgotten about. There is, to begin with, *brahmacharya*, basically meaning the austere life of a student avoiding any indulgence other than learning. This is followed by *grihastha* (life of a householder with a family) and *vanaprastha* (when one begins to gradually detach from everything in order to start on another journey), ending with *sanyas* (total renunciation of this world). In some way or other, everyone lives along more or less a similar arrangement in life, or so we think since everyone fears ageing, decaying and dying. The traditional imagination prepared one to accept the end of life, and so did its secular versions in which retirement meant a repose in things which one had ignored during the heyday of activities.

Now, given the constraint to ordinary ways of living, such arrangements have succumbed to suspicion. Unwittingly, everyone seeks to be an Ashwathama, the son of the great archery teacher Dronacharya in the Mahabharata. Ashwathama had to forgo his source of strength, a gem on his forehead, and live a long life with a festering wound. He was born with a *mani* (gem) that made him immune to hunger, thirst and fatigue. Due to this power, he was called *Chiranjivi* (immortal), and he could not be killed or defeated by anyone. He and his father fought in the battle of the Mahabharata on the side of the Kauravas against the Pandavas. As legend has it, the Kauravas were defeated in the war. But immortal Ashwathama was seething in anger to avenge his father's death and sneakily entered the camps of the Pandavas in the dead of night to kill them. Mistakenly, he killed the five sons of the Pandavas instead. This led to a combat between Arjun and Ashwathama in which each attacked the other with a *brahmastra* (an extremely destructive weapon). The great sage Vyas interfered and asked them to withdraw their respective weapons on account of the devastation it would bring to the planet. Arjun obeyed, whereas, Ashwathama, instead of withdrawing, diverted the already unleashed brahmastra toward the pregnant Uttara's womb (wife of Abhimanyu, the son of Arjun). Ashwathama intended to end the lineage of the Pandavas by killing the foetus in the womb. Enraged by this, Krishna cursed and punished Ashwathama. In punishment, he had to surrender his immortality gem to Krishna and roam aimlessly in the forest for 3,000 years with a festering wound in his forehead. He cried for death, and it did not come to him.

The contemporary Ashwathama tendencies are only slightly different. There is plenty to generate a sense of everlasting youth, an illusion that the gem, the source of strength, is intact. Hence, everyone seeks to be at work and avoid retirement, and everyone is certainly against a journey towards another destination, that is, death. Presumably, dying like this would be less painful than dying with the sense that one was going to die. In this extraordinary scheme of dying, the religious practice of some Hindus retiring to *mukti bhawan*s (various shelters where folks await death) in Benares may appear foolish.[2] One wonders what individuals with the Ashwathama tendency would make of the Jain practice called *santhara* (voluntary fasting to death).[3] In those practices, there is a will to undertake the journey to death. There is a sense of ordinariness attached to the idea of death and dying. Therefore, there is a notion of quality of death. Whereas in so many services, consumable commodities, abounding around us, obsessively emphasise 'quality of life', as though life and death could be separated. One only works towards ensuring quality of life and hardly ever towards quality of death, as though life and death were divorced from each other. A bit of fear, and a lot of industrial intervention, has nearly destroyed our art of dying, let alone living. Too much class conditioning has rendered dying into a consumer's choice. Just like it is with weddings or birth or matchmaking, our experience of dying is another saleable item. Those who can afford it, die the way they want; and those who cannot are left at the mercy of fate.

On various occasions, when we read news reports of accidental deaths, we mourn our institutional failures, and certainly we are disturbed about the loss of life. Every now and then, we hear that a few dozen lives ended in an accidental fire that lapped up a disaster-prone building. A flyover crumbled, taking the lives of half a dozen children commuting in a school bus. A calamity caused the fateful deaths of poor folks who could not fend for their lives when they lived. Even worse, there are examples of genocide and pogroms, the state machinery inducing brutal death in ordinary lives. This gets more macabre as one goes on listing the news reports of accidental deaths. One gets upset for a while and then forgets about them until the next news report comes in. Death becomes banal with the loss of its ordinary aesthetics. The lustful approach to life, not necessarily love for life, has obscured our need to ensure a quality death. The State does not admit it, nor do various other agencies, that it is high time we shift our attention to 'how we die'. Then, probably, we would understand better how we live. Our death education is truly poor and value of life thickly obscured. Hence, we seldom think before causing deadly harm to fellow humans. Whataboutery and retrospective thinking about what we intended and what was the effect do not absolve us. Everyone who is at ease with or ignorant of the loss of the ordinary art of death and dying is a veritable serial killer, on a spree to see the compromised quality of death. It used to appear in newspapers almost every year that someone shot at a co-commuter in a road rage incident during a traffic halt in a mega city. Someone ran over an elderly pedestrian in a case of rash driving. Even more heinous, there are those saddening news reports of rape and murder about which we have almost reached tipping point. Do these instances of bad death not make us accomplices? The criminal cases of death, caused by crime, too remind us that we have been fairly ignorant about what kind of death we value. In short, we have compromised on the cultural imagination of death and dying.

We adopt that funny approach to death about which Yudhisthir warned in the Mahabharata when he was asked a question by Yaksha. He said that we always think of death in our neighbour's house. We forget that it comes to everyone, in one way or other. There is an inherent ordinariness to the idea of living and dying. It is by and large due to this ordinariness that living and dying are nearly conjoined twins. You separate one from the other and you end up distorting both. The ordinary folks did not pursue the unholy separation. They saw them both with one eye, a perspective in which the two could be seen together. They sang along with their cinema characters, mythological figures and even historical icons, and what they sang expressed their generous imagination of living and dying. At times, we feel far more blessed with the peppy lyrics that enthuse our surrounding. People sang after they saw half a dozen dreadful criminals singing with V. Shantaram, who directed as well as acted, and Sandhya in *Do Ankhen Barah Haath* (Two Eyes Twelve Hands, 1957), '*Ai malik tere bande hum*' (O lord and master, we are your devotees). They hummed along with Manna Dey as they saw the compassionate face of Balraj Sahni in *Seema* (1955, directed by Amiya Chakrabarty), '*Tu pyar ka sagar hai, teri ek bund ke pyase hum*' (Ocean of love that you are, we seek your compassion). They also revelled in a fairly frolicking song sung by Mukesh to the tune composed by Salil Chowdhury: '*Zindagi khwab hai, khwab me jhooth kya, aur bhala sach hai kya* (Life is a dream. What is a lie and what is the truth?). Picturised on Raj Kapoor, the character singing the song in the film is a middle-class alcoholic caricatured on a Bengali Bhodrolok, member of the elite class. This was *Jagte Raho* (Stay Alert, 1956), a rare production of Raj Kapoor's company, with Amit Maitra and Sombhu Mitra as directors, still considered a masterpiece.

Through these songs, they dealt with the complexity of existence, mediation of the divine and the inevitable nature of death. If they sang with the so-called romantic star Rajesh Khanna in Hrishikesh Mukherjee's film in the early 1970s, *Anand* (Bliss, 1971), '*Zindagi kaisi hai paheli hai, kabhi ye hansaye kabhi ye rulaye*' (Such is the puzzle of life, it makes you laugh and it makes you cry), they had no problem with the angry young man's enigmatic articulation too. The crooning of Manna Dey charged the lyrics of Yogesh and conjured a popular cultural imagination to music by Salil Chowdhury. Almost everyone knew that the *Babumoshai* doctor (Amitabh Bachchan) of the cancer patient Anand (Rajesh Khanna) is to learn a lesson about the inevitable end—the death of his patient-friend. The doctor is perturbed by the ease with which his friend, Anand, has accepted death as destiny. His aggression comes to an end with the end of the tale in which death is accepted with grace. As though Hrishikesh Mukherjee had more to say on this issue, there came another film, *Mili*, in 1975 in which the character of the doctor was replaced by an angry man in the making, essayed by the same actor, Amitabh Bachchan. The protagonist Mili (essayed by Jaya Bhaduri) is suffering from cancer, and the man is a cynical character intolerant to everything that seemed lively and exuberant. But then he could not stay immune to the enchantment of the vibrant Mili, with whom everyone sang, 'Maine kaha fulon se hanso to wo khilkhila ke hans diye' (When I persuaded the flowers to burst into a smile, the buds bloomed into endless joy). The lyrics were by Yogesh and the music was by Sachin Dev Burman, which came alive with the sonorous sound of Lata Mangeshkar. This was, however, to meet with an end; everything about enchanting life comes to die.

The dramatic additions became prominent with the success of the angry young man, Jay. He fiddled with the coin in Ramesh Sippy's cult drama *Sholay* (Embers, 1975). His coin always gave him the desired result intended to protect life. Jai died a fairly melodramatic death for the life of the joyous Veeru, his bum chum. We loved the coming together of living and dying in a violent tale of revenge. It became more fun a few years later when we sang with Amitabh Bachchan in Prakash Mehra's *Mukaddar ka Sikandar* (1978), lyrics by Anjaan and music by Kalyanji–Anandji, 'Rote huye aate hain sab hansta hua jo jayega, wo mukaddar ka sikandar janeman kahlayega' (Everyone comes crying but only the one who departs with a smile will be known by all as the conqueror of destiny). They sang with the angry young man despite the anguish of history, the frustration of politics and the dismay for social stratification. This was the ordinariness of engagement with the ideas of living and dying in the popular imagination. It shared a lineage with the traditions of saints, mendicants and folks from posterity. One can hear the implicit orchestra of the Baul singers of Bengal informing us about the union of life and death, mortal and immortal, mundane and divine. Many traditional performances, from *Jatra* to *Yaskhagana*, have done this for us since time immemorial. It showed up in the cinematic performances of the sadhu in cameo roles too. The actor Sudhir Dalvi was immortalised by doing the role of a famous saint in *Shirdi ke Sai Baba* (1977, directed by Ashok Bhushan) amidst the glamorous stars such as Manoj Kumar, Rajendra Kumar, Dharmendra, Hema Malini and so on, appearing in cameo roles in the film. The same actor, Dalvi, appeared as the beggar-like sadhu in *Apnapan*, along with his accompanist, a young girl, singing a soulful song in the film, 'Aadmi musafir hai, aata hain jaata hai, aate jaate raste me yaden chhod jata hai' (Humans are eternal travellers; in the flow of arrival and departure, they leave behind innumerable gems of memories). With music by Laxmikant–Pyarelal, these words of Anand Bakshi, sung by Mohammad Rafi and Lata Mangeshkar, became a marker in the soundscape of ordinary folks.

If this seems too folksy, one can remember the international production based on the novel of Herman Hesse, translated into a screenplay and directed by Conrad Rooks, named *Siddhartha* (1972) in English, with the Hindi cinema star Shashi Kapoor essaying the role of the wandering protagonist. Classical and classy from all possible angles, the film however narrated the becoming of a wandering sadhu, with a moment in his journey echoed with a Bengali song as the background score. The song was adapted from an old Bengali film directed by Mrinal Sen, *Neel Akasher Neechey* (Under the Blue Sky, 1959), sung mellifluously in both films by Hemanta Kumar Mukherji: '*O nodi re, ekti katha shudhai shudhu tomare, bolo kothay tomar desh, tomar nei ki cholar shesh*' (O river, may I ask you humbly, where do you belong, and where do you end). In *Siddhartha*, the song is punctuated by a dialogue between two wandering friends, one a sadhu and the other Siddhartha, the protagonist who is a boatman during the song sequence. As the song reaches its zenith, the sadhu friend arrives at the bank of the river, asking to be ferried across, to which Siddhartha asks, 'Where are you going, what are you seeking?'

The friend answers, 'I have been seeking for the right path all my life.'

Siddhartha sighs and says, 'Maybe you have looked for too much for too long, dear friend Govinda.'

The two friends hug each other, Govinda evidently accepting Siddhartha's wisdom.

Siddhartha continues the conversation, 'The trouble with goals is that one become obsessed with the goal. When you say you are seeking, it means there is something to find; but the real freedom is in the realisation that there are no goals. What happened yesterday is gone; what will happen tomorrow we never know. So we must live in the present, like the river ... I remember Buddha and all those who we have loved and who died before us, and I have come to recognise that we must forget searching.'

People were more inclined to work out a quality of death by imagining living and dying with the same cultural ease. This was not to entirely dismiss the intervention of a doctor, a hakim or a vaidya, and none of them exert a non-cultural power. The men of knowledge and technic were also men of culture. Executing knowledge, they enacted cultural scripts. They knew when to enter the scene and when to humbly bow out. If they did not, there was conflict. Industries have entered too far into the intimate experience of living and dying. All such intrusions make it worse to die ordinarily. Of course, a great deal of accidents and mishaps destroy the very simple logic of living and dying.

Notes

1. For more on the artists' remembrance of the civil war in Sri Lanka, including the works of artists at Theertha International Artists' Collective, Colombo, post 1990s, see this fabulous account in Sasanka Perera, *Violence and the Burden of Memory: Rememberance and Erasure in Sinhala Consciousness* (Delhi: Orient Blackswan, 2015).

2. Elsewhere, there is an interesting discussion on the sociability in a mukti bhawan (also called mumukshu bhawan; 'mumukshu' refers to someone aspiring to die at a sacred place and be liberated from the cycle of birth and death) in Varanasi in, Anakshi Pal, 'In Search of a Neighbourhood among the Kashivasis: An Ethnographic Account of an Āshram in Banaras', in Sadan Jha, Dev Nath Pathak, and Amiya Kumar Das, eds., *Neighbourhoods in Urban India: In Between Home and the City* (Delhi: Bloomsbury, 2020), 63–92. Besides, see for an interesting nuance on lives of the social in the context of Kashivasis in Ravi Nandan Singh, 'Many Lives of the Dead in Banaras: Towards an Anthropology of the Indefinite Social,' *Contributions to Indian Sociology* 50, no. 1 (2016): 27–51. A little over-canonised work on this is, of course, Jonathan P Parry, *Death in Banaras* (Cambridge: Cambridge University Press, 1994). My favorite narrative by far is an embodied account along this line in a 2016 film titled *Hotel Salvation*. See 'Hotel Salvation,' IMDB, accessed on 20 February 2021, https://www.imdb.com/title/tt5997928/.

3. The legality of Santhara was a bone of contention in 2015. See Shekhar Hattangadi, 'Santhara in the Eyes of the Legal,' *Hindu*, 15 August 2015, accessed on 26 January 2021, https://www.thehindu.com/opinion/op-ed/santhara-in-the-eyes-of-the-law/article7541803.ece.

Index

A

abuse-filled relations, 63
abuses, 62
academic orchestration, 126
Academy Award, 219
Acharya Chatursen, 181
Adi Parv, 207
adiyal ghoda, 52
aesthetic alterations, 220
aesthetic judgements phenomenon, 219
age-old
 cultural mechanism, 61
 institutions, 107
Agrawal, Purushottam, 139, 144n2
A History of God: From Abraham to the Present, 137n4
Ai malik tere bande hum', 238
All India Radio, 114
All That is Solid Melts into Air: The Experience of Modernity, 173n2
Amar Chitra Katha, 220
Ambedkar, B. R., 67, 188, 218
Ambedkar statues, 218
Anand, 180, 238
Ananda Coomaraswamy, 217
Anandmayi, 7
An Autobiography or the Story of My Experiments with Truth, 140, 144n2
Andha kanoon, 25
Anthropological Explorations in Gender: Intersecting Fields, 39n1
anti-Marxism, 93
anti-movement forces, 77
anti-relational abusive-offensive words., 61–62
anxiety-driven approaches, 54
Aparajito, 40
Apka Bunty, 51
Armstrong, Karen, 137n4
art and culture, 217

artha, 56
artistic imagination, 215
Aryaputra Samant, 5
Ashwathama, 235, 236
Attenborough, Richard, 219, 220
award-winning teachers, 111
Ayodhya, 154

B

Bachchan, Amitabh, 180, 238, 239
Bachchan, Harivansh Rai, 180
Bahuguna, Hemvati Nandan, 183
Baij's sculpture of Gandhi, 219
Bakshi, Anand, 19, 240
Bakshi, Byomkesh, 178
'banking education,' 209
battle of Mahabharata, 235
BBC, 114
'Best Teacher of the Year' awards, 111
Bhaduri, Jaya, 181
Bhagwad Gita, 45
Bhandari, Mannu, 51
Bharatiya Janata Party (BJP), 222
Bhattacharya, Siddhartha, 216, 222
Bhishma Parva, 209
Blake, William, 77, 225
blogs, 87
Bose, Nandalal, 216
brahmacharya, 235
brahma muhurta, 115
brahmastra, 235
'branded' service provider, 97
'Branding Gandhi,' 219
Buddha Dordenma, 221
Burman, Sachin Dev, 239
Butler, Judith, 94

C

calendar art (chromolithograph), 218
candlelight marches, 75

charkha, 216
Chattopadhyaya, Debiprasad, 14
Chiranjivi, 235
Chitralekha, 5, 6
Chopra, Yash, 181
Chowdhury, Salil, 238
Churchill, Winston, 223n1
Clean India Mission, 216
Coolie, 184
cosmetics industry, 86
counter-allegations, 96
country-wide cleanliness campaign, 216
cultural orientation, 61
cultural template, 60
cultural texts, 60
cuss words, 64

D

Dadasaheb Phalke Award, 184
Dalvi, Sudhir, 239
Darwin's theory, 46
Das, Anam, 204
debates and lectures, 128
Deewar, 181
Delhi Sultanate, 106
Derrida, Jacques, 94
Descartes, René, 125, 129n2, 166
desi sexologists, 87
Detectives India, 98
Devi, Mahasweta, 77
'Devi Aparadha Kshamapana Stotram', 149–150
devotion, 159
Dewari, 156
Dey, Manna, 238
Dharmendra, 239
Dharmputra, 7, 8, 181
Dharm-yuddh, 67
Diaries of Franz Kafka, 120n1
disaster-prone building, 236
Discipline and Punish: The Birth of the Prison, 110n2
diurnal revolution, 85
Do Ankhen Barah Haath, 238
Dube, Leela, 39n1
Dube, Saurabh, 27n1

Durga Saptsati, 149
Dutt, Nirupama, 98

E

Eck, Diana, 168, 173n2
economic liberalisation and digitalisation, 126
educational-institutional administrator, 119
educational policy and administration, 121
Escape from Freedom, 17n7
experts, 97
  agencies, 96
  service providers, 97
external agency, 86
'extraordinary tampering,' 92

F

Facebook, 12, 94, 118, 175
Faust, 167
flirtatious friends, 84
fluid artistic imagination, 218
folk cultures, 86
Foucault, M., 110n2
Franz Kafka's diary, 113
freedom, 105
Freire, Paulo, 107, 209
Freud, Sigmund, 52
Fromm, Erich, 12

G

Gandhi, Kanu, 219
Gandhi, Mahatma, 23, 144n2, 158, 161, 172, 189, 204, 215, 219
  pragmatic rationalism rules, 144
  pragmatic scheme, 141
Gandhi Mandap garden, 216
Ganga river, 232
ganikas, 58n3
Gems, 228
Ghai, Subhash, 64
Ghumakkadi, 13
Ghurye, G. S., 168
Gita, 15
Goddess of wisdom Athena, 122

Index 245

Godse, Nathuram, 215
Gond community, 155
Google, 87, 164
Google-aided map, 169
Gora, 6, 8
government-aided regulatory bodies, 122
Grierson, George, 194
grihastha, 235
gupt-rog, 87
Guru Purnima, 106
guru-shishya parampara, 106

H

Haridwar, 164
Heer–Ranjha, 98
heroism, 3
Hesse, Herman, 240
hierarchical society, 226
Hind Swaraj, 142
Hirani, Rajkumar, 174
historical icons
   Ambedkar, 177
   Azad, 177
   Gandhi, 177
   Kabir, 177
   Nanak, 177
   Nehru, 177
   Paramhamsa, 178
   Raidas, 177
   Surdas, 177
   Tagore, 177
   Vivekananda, 177
History of Western Philosophy, 129n2
Homo narrans, 21

I

iconographic sculptors, 217
Illich, Ivan, 79n1
India: A Sacred Geography, 173n2
Indian art, 216
Indian Express, 216
Indian Institute of Advanced Study (IIAS), 195
industrial cities
   Chaibasa, 198
   Dhanbad, 198
   Ranchi, 198
industrial intervention, 236
industry-induced imagination, 88
In Quest of the Ordinary: Lines of Skepticism and Romanticism, 16n2
Inquilaab, 184
in-service training programmes, 121
Instagram, 94, 175, 176

J

Jackson, Philip, 220
Jagannath temple, 157
Jagte Raho, 238
Jairam, Vani, 136
Jakhoo hill, 221
Jankavi, 67
Jassal, Smita, 69n1
Jayasi, Malik Muhammad, 40
Jha, Hari Mohan, 68
Jha, Sadan, 162n1
'joking relations,' 61
Juliet and Romeo, 191

K

Kabir (Poem), 65, 108
Kalighat painting, *pat-chitra*, 218
kama, 56
Kamasutra, 56
Kapoor, Raj, 238
Kapoor, Shashi, 240
Karl Popper's criticism, 57n1
Kauravas, 235
'*Kevatsamvad*', 160
Khan, Nusrat Fateh Ali, 161
Khanna, Rajesh, 238
Khattar Kaka, 68
Khilafat Movement, 144
Khuda Ke Liye, 161
Khusrow, Amir, 106
Kingsley, Ben, 220
kinship networks, 63
Krishnamurti, J., 104, 105
Kumar, Dilip, 64
Kumar, Manoj, 239
Kumar, Raaj, 64

Index

Kumar, Rajendra, 239
Kurosawa, Akira, 21

L

Lage Raho Munna Bhai, 190
Laxman, R. K., 67, 218
Laxmikant–Pyarelal, 240
left-liberal scholars, 215
Linguistic Survey of India, 194, 202
Lokayat, 14
longer-lasting pleasure, 86
Loose Talk, 196
Lutgendorf, Philip, 156n3

M

Machwe, Prabhakar, 23
Madame Tussauds, 220
Madhubani/Mithila painting, 218
Malini, Hema, 239
Mangeshkar, Lata, 19, 239, 240
marriage and commitment, 88
Marx, Karl, 129
Maryadapurushottam, 46
masterpiece sculptures, 220
matrimonial advertisements, 97
'Matrimonial Investigations':, 98
Mazzarella, William, 219
Mehra's, Prakash, 239
'Memory Keeper,' 224
mercurial emotions, 95
Mili, 181, 238
Mishra, Jayakant, 200
mlechha, 7
Mukaddar ka Sikandar, 239
Mukesh, 136, 238
Mukherjee, Hrishikesh, 180
Mukherji, Hemanta Kumar, 240
'My Heart Leaps Up,' 73

N

Narlikar, Jayant, 118
Nastik, 138n6
National Curriculum Framework for school education, 107
Natyashastra, 45
'needs and expectations' of family, 96

Nehru, Jawaharlal, 67
Nihalani, Govind, 77
'noble profession,' 115
non-cultural power, 241
Nyctanthes arbortristis, 149

O

ocean of adolescence, 92
Oedipus complex, 35
online media portals, 87
On Social Constraints and the Great Longing: An Essay on the Human Condition, 16n2
orthodox philosophies
 Mimamsa, 14
 Nyaya, 14
 Samkhya, 14
 Vedanta, 14
owl of Lakshmi, 124

P

Padmavat, 40
Paigham, 64
Paleolithic rock art, 218
Pandavas, 235
paradigm of psychoanalysis, 53
Paramhamsa, Ramakrishna, 54
Parti Parikatha, 23, 24
'passive appendages,' 167
Pather Panchali, 131
Patil, Pratibha, 177
patriarchal sociocultural values, 61
Perera, Anoli, 224
Performance Theory, 27n2
'philosophy of phenomenology,' 11
pinjarapoles, 142
poetic epic characters, 94
post-Independence India, 77
PowerPoint (PPT), 128
Pritam, Amrita, 100
process of formation, 73
process of worshipping, 150
public relation (PR) agencies, 174

Q

*qissa*s, 92

Index

'quality of life,' 236
Quran, 21

R

radio stations, 114
   All India Radio, 114
   BBC, 114
   Voice of America, 114
Rafi, Mohammad, 240
Raghuvamsam, 160
Rahim Khan-e-Khana, 48
Rajaji National forest, 169
Ramayana, 31, 102, 220
Ramcharitmanas, 135, 136, 160
*Ramkatha*s, 46
Ramlilas, 152
   Hanuman., 152
   Laxman, 152
   Ram, 152
   Sita, 152
rape culture, 85
Rashomon, 21
rational procedures, 55
Ray's, Satyajit, 131
regional-linguistic-cultural identification of, 97
regressive sociocultural values, 61
regulatory mechanism, 86
research reports, 122
Reverence, Resistance and the Politics of Seeing the Indian National Flag, 16n1
Rooks, Conrad, 240
roshandan, 85
Russell, Bertrand, 129n2
Ryle, Gilbert, 129n2

S

Saat Hindustani, 180
Sabarmati ashram, 158
Sabri, Amjad, 161
Sahni, Balraj, 238
sajda, 86
Sanju, 174
Sarania Hill, 216
Sarayu river, 221
Sardar Sarovar Dam, 221
Sassi–Punnu, 92
'*Satyam Shivam Sundaram*, 20
Saudagar, 64
scheme of aesthetic judgement, 219
scheme of dying, 236
Science as Vocation and *Politics as Vocation*, 109n1
scientific procedure, 96
Scott, James, 25
sculpture
   Ambedkar, Babasaheb, 218
   Baij's, 216
   Gandhi, 216
Seema, 238
Sen, Mrinal, 240
sex, 57
   education, 231
   programmes, 56, 57
sexual acts, 56
sexual intimacy, 51
Shaadi.com, 97
Shah, Hashim, 92
Shah, Waris, 92, 99
Shahenshah, 184
Shakespeare, 53, 189
Shankara, Adi, 199
Shantaram, V., 238
Shantiniketan, 216
sharirik samiksha, 113
Sharma, Kidar Nath, 5
Shirdi ke Sai Baba, 239
Shirin–Farhad, 92
Shiva temple, 164
Sholay, 183, 239
Siddhartha, 240
Singh, Bhagat, 174
Singh, Dara, 219
Smile, 74
'social,' 91
Sohni–Mahiwal, 92
spectacular accomplishments, 4
Spring Temple Buddha, 221
Sri Lankan artist, 224, 232
Sri Lankan Tamil art critic, 217
State-imposed rhetoric of unity, 219
Statue of Liberty, 221

Statue of Unity, 221
studio-based professionalism, 220
Subjects of Modernity: Time-Space, Disciplines, Margins, 16n2, 27n1
Subramanian, Ramesh, 192
subversive components, 78
superstitions, 52
Swachh Bharat Abhiyan, 216, 222
Swachh Bharat Mission, 216

T

Taare Zameen Par, 210
Tagore, Rabindranath, 113, 133, 137n1, 216
Teachers' Day, 106
techno-mediated imagination, 220
Textures of Ordinary: Anthropology After Wittgenstein, 162n2, 192n1
The Analyst and the Mystic: Psychoanalytic Reflections on Religion and Mysticism, 58n7
Theertha International Artists' Collective, 241n1
The Metamorphosis, 125
The Mother of 1084, 77
'The Rainbow', 73
The Religion of Man, 137n1
The Scientific Edge: The Indian Scientist from Vedic to Modern Times, 120n3
The Seventeen Day Plan to Stop Ageing, 234
The Shadow Lines, 24
The Sound of Music, 37
The Statue of Equality with the sculpture of Ambedkar, 221
thick-skinned bureaucrats, 119
Three Idiots, 210
Tilak, Bal Gangadhar, 23

turbulent time, 92
Twitter, 12, 175, 176

U

Upanishads, 15, 133
'Urban Naxals,' 72, 93

V

value education and sex education, 57
vanaprastha, 127, 235
varnashrama, 141
Vasant Panchami, 123
Ved Vyasa, 22
'vernacular cannibalism,' 196
Vidyapati Mahotsav, 199
visual art, 218
Vivekananda, Swami, 222
Voice of America, 114

W

Wangchuck, Jigme Singye, 221
365 Ways to Look and Feel Younger, 234
Weber, Max, 103, 109n1
Weerasinghe, Jagath, 232
Wilson, Brian, 74
Wolf, *The Beauty Myth*, 58n4
'wordings of the world,' 96

Y

Yadav, Mulayam Singh, 184

Z

Zanjeer, 181

About the Author

Dev Nath Pathak is a founding faculty member of the Department of Sociology at South Asian University, a university established by South Asian Association for Regional Co-operation (SAARC) in New Delhi, India. He writes about folklore, art, cinema, mediated communications, theories and philosophy. He co-edits the journal *Society and Culture in South Asia* and is on the editorial board of *Journal of Human Values*. A few of his recent publications include *Living and Dying: Meanings in Maithili Folklore* (2018), *Another South Asia!* (2017), *Culture and Politics in South Asia: Performative Communication* (2017), *Intersections of Contemporary Art, Anthropology and Art History in South Asia: Decoding Visual Worlds* (2019) and *Against the Nation: Thinking Like South Asians* (2019). He was a visiting scholar at Brown International Advanced Research Institutes at Brown University, United States of America; a Charles Wallace Fellow at Queen's University Belfast, Ireland; a visiting scholar at Indian Institute of Advanced Study in Shimla, India; and scholar-in-residence at Indian Institute of Management Calcutta, India. He is associated with Galp Lok, a YouTube-based public intellectual forum.